Existential/Dialectical Marital Therapy

Breaking the Secret Code
of Marriage

FRONTIERS IN COUPLES AND FAMILY THERAPY
A Brunner/Mazel Book Series

Series Editor: *Florence W. Kaslow, Ph.D.*

Existential/Dialectical Marital Therapy

Breaking the Secret Code of Marriage

Israel W. Charny, Ph.D.

*Former Organizer and First Director
of the Graduate Social Work and
Postgraduate Interdisciplinary Programs
in Family Therapy, Bob Shapell School
of Social Work, Tel Aviv University*

BRUNNER/MAZEL *Publishers* • NEW YORK

Library of Congress Cataloging-in-Publication Data
Charny, Israel W.
    Existential/dialectical marital therapy: breaking the secret code
of marriage / Israel W. Charny.
        p.   cm. — (Frontiers in couples and family therapy)
    Includes bibliographical references and index.
    ISBN 0-87630-636-9
    1. Marital psychotherapy.   2. Existential psychotherapy.
I. Title.   II. Series.
    [DNLM: 1. Existentialism.   2. Marital Therapy.   WM 55 C483e]
RC488.5.C462   1991
616.89'156—dc20
DNLM/DLC
for Library of Congress   91-43195
                                                                   CIP

Copyright © 1992 by Israel W. Charny

Published by
BRUNNER/MAZEL, INC.
19 Union Square West
New York, New York 10003

Manufactured in the United States of America
        10   9   8   7   6   5   4   3   2   1

To
JUDY

with deepest love,
and with thanks

for professional collaboration
in our work and on this book,

and

for the best years of my life

Contents

A Jewish Legend About Making Marriages

Once a Roman matron asked Rabbi Yossi Bar Halafta:
"How long did it take the Holy One, blessed be He, to create the world?"
He said to her: "Six days."
"And from then until now what has He been doing?"
"The Holy One, blessed be He, is occupied in making marriages."
"And is that His occupation?" the woman asked. "Even I can do that. I have many men slaves and women slaves and in one short hour I can marry them off."
"Though it may appear easy in your eyes," he said, "yet every marriage is as difficult for the Holy One, blessed be He, as the dividing of the Red Sea." Then Rabbi Yossi left her and went on his way.
What did the matron do? She took a thousand men slaves and a thousand women slaves, placed them in two rooms and said: "This one should wed that one, and this one should wed that one." In one night she married them all. The next day they came before her—one with a wounded head, one with a bruised eye, another with a fractured arm and one with a broken foot.
"What is the matter with you?" she asked.
Each one said, "I do not want the one you gave me."
Immediately the woman sent for Rabbi Yossi Bar Halafta and said to him: "Rabbi, your Torah is true, beautiful and praiseworthy."
"Indeed a suitable match may seem easy to make, yet God considers it as difficult a task as dividing the Red Sea," Rabbi Yossi acknowledged.

From the Talmudic Legends
(*Genesis Rabah* 68:4)

Existential/Dialectical Marital Therapy

Breaking the Secret Code of Marriage

1

Unraveling the Mystery of Marriage

An Existential/Dialectical Perspective

All my life—personal and professional—I have wondered about the mystery of the "psychological chemistry" that makes it possible for some relatively few couples to enjoy deeply being husband and wife to one another for many years. It is my sincere hope that this book will advance us in that search.

There is in marriage for some—all too few—husbands and wives a wondrous pleasure, warmth, friendship and sensual joy; for most couples, however, marriage entails progressive disappointment, succumbing to emptiness, and development of bitter anger. I hope this book will increase the possibilities of marital therapists helping couples to move towards marriages that are more alive and wondrous.

At its natural best, the marital experience is the deepest and most effective "psychotherapy" for both husband and wife. Inevitably, each is impelled through the drama of marriage to encounter all that he/she is and isn't, to see and experience one's own finest and worst qualities. Years ago, veteran psychoanalyst Martin Grotjahn (1960) described marriage as the most encompassing and intense transferential stage on which each mate plays out all the unfinished business and issues of emotional development from his or her childhood background. In marriage, each mate is the would-be therapist for the other. Those couples who are lucky enough to enjoy an intuitive skillfulness and kindness may be able to take this "therapy" through its natural course—including the periods of tension and risk that must be parts of the process—and will enjoy not only increasingly successful and rewarding marriages, but the pleasure that one feels from being and becoming more and more of oneself as the years go by. However, most couples discover bitterly that there are no competent "doctors in the house." Like psychotherapies that turn sour, these marriages fade into dull repetitiveness or turn into acrimonious battles.

Most people seek a *steady state* of happiness in their marriages. The point of view of this book is different, that happiness is a successful *processing* of a drama of constant contradictions between the strong and weak parts within each mate and for the couple together as they create a fascinating interacting mosaic which today we refer to as their *marital system*. The processing includes acknowledgment not only of manifest or obvious major weaknesses and shortcomings that are so clearly parts of all of us, but also of weaknesses and distortions of character that, surprisingly, are the shadows or accomplices of even our finer traits and achievements. Acknowledgment of these weaknesses carries with it an acceptance of or yielding to the fact that we will never be able to be all things and achieve wholeness or perfection. At the same time, it means taking responsibility for correcting our limitations to some extent, being responsible for their impact on others, and trying to make up for them by sharing more of our better qualities. Altogether, such an orientation sets off a way of life that is authentic, adventurous, and full of possibilities for becoming more and more of what we can be.

Another point of view of this book is that just as couples err in seeking a steady state of happiness, so do many professional marital therapists err in adopting a professional dogma that restricts the process of psychotherapy to a single mode of treatment arising from the persuasion of the therapist or the "school" to which the therapist belongs. Thus, notwithstanding my emphasis on the marital system, I shall also emphasize that psychotherapy for marital problems involves addressing individual character problems as well as couple interaction, for people remain individuals in their marriages as well as creating a couple system. There are many ways of achieving therapeutic penetration and change; thus, one can work through varying combinations of couple, individual, family, and intergenerational sessions (as well as other modalities, such as group therapy, that are not dealt with in this book).

I believe that marital therapists need to be much more aware of the choices they make in settling on a given method or style of treatment. Both in marriage and in the practice of marital therapy, as in all life, people are at work making *choices* that determine in large part the outcome of events. In many cases, the choices people make in their marriages are not made consciously, as when the husband "chooses" to be so busy at his work that he has little time for empathic closeness with his wife. Unconscious though it is, a choice has been made that plays a large role in determining subsequent life events.

Marital therapists also make a great many choices in the ways they conduct therapy. Some cultivate the illusion that they are "simply" using a given
method of helping couples talk out their feelings, as if this were not a choice
and as if such a method could only help and never hurt anyone. However,
even a choice not to choose between different methods of treatment is also
a choice with definite consequences that may not always be desirable. Thus,
when a therapist elects to have a couple talk out their differences, without
the therapist intervening, about whether or not to get divorced, the predictable result can be that the stronger personality of the two mates, who is
exerting intense pressure for a divorce, wins out. Had the therapist taken
a more active role based on a choice of attempting to stop the divorce, the
outcome might have been different. Whether or not to take such a stand
needs to be thought about and the therapist then needs to stand responsibly
behind whichever choice is taken.

EXISTENTIAL AND DIALECTICAL APPROACHES

This book is based on the application of two central streams of theoretical
concepts: an existential orientation and a dialectical approach.

The only two observations of the human experience I know of that will
never be challenged by any learned colleague are that *man and woman are
alive* and that *man and woman are headed towards death*. These two immutable
facts of life and death define the basic existential givens and the core dialectic that shape and color every individual's existence as we are all buffeted
between the miracle of being magnificently alive and the dread truth that
we are actually dying all the time. Existential/dialectical therapy is a way
of *processing* the imponderables and mysteries that struggle within each of
us in an effort to come up with qualities of growth, development, strength,
and depth for living through the forever complex and unfathomable contradictions and limitations within each of us and in every relationship that
really matters.

Again and again, we see people who renounce the thrust of their basic
desire for life or who embrace death too avidly and literally succumb to
death.

A woman told her therapist openly that she wished her ulcer were,
in fact, a cancer. In the months of therapy that followed, she poured
out fantasies of reunion with her dead mother and adamantly declined
the therapist's efforts to help her contain her death wishes. Two years
later she was dead of a malignant cancer.

We also see that people who embrace life too strongly—that is, insist on living without weakness, hurt, shortcomings, grief or fright—also set themselves up for a possible collapse of their robust selves. The same is true of people who undertake too much responsibility for others at great cost to their personal selves until their burdens of obligation and effort become too great. This is also the case with good people who propose to live within a rigid framework of high ideals and deny any angry, destructive feelings in themselves until they are faced with threats of an explosion of pent-up destructiveness.

> To all accounts, the former military hero and now successful executive was a powerful, winning man. His wife and children looked up to him and followed his lead in almost all matters. He set very high ideals for himself and others. One day he found himself ill with a relatively minor and basically quite treatable illness. However, in his mind of perfections and absolutes, the illness ominously foretold decline, dependency on others, shame of weakness, and ultimate death. These he could not bear. He killed himself.

Traditionally, psychotherapists offer their services most to those who renounce or cannot organize their strengths and instead fall into and/or embrace willingly their weaknesses and failings. (I have called these *Disorders of Incompetence* and contrasted these disorders with forms of embracing life too strongly, which I called *Disorders of Pseudocompetence* [Charny, 1986a].) The point of view of existential/dialectical therapy is that we need be concerned no less with those who overvalue life, power, activities, responsibility, and goodness at the expense of the naturally weak and limited sides of their beings. Overly strong and "successful" people are a high-risk group, often headed for sudden and serious, even cataclysmic, breakdowns because they have not integrated the two real sides of the dialectic of life and death and its derivatives of strength and weakness.

An Existential Approach to Marriage

An existential approach to individual life experience and to couple relationships refers to an appreciation that *all individual human experiences and all relationships are bound to be visited by sorrow, pain, serious dilemmas, weaknesses, and shortcomings.*

Every individual—including the most competent and winning person—is, inevitably, an amalgam of significant strengths and no less significant weaknesses. The management of these weaknesses is, clearly, a challenging task; even with the best intentions and finest efforts, many of these shortcomings, lacks, and downright failings of a person cannot be overcome.

Now join two mates together in marriage and the marital system they create is an intriguing patterning that includes both mates' strengths and weaknesses, each a human drama in its own right. Now both people also touch, influence, and impact upon one another to create a *shared field of experience* which also can be described in terms of both strengths and weaknesses. The strengths and weaknesses seen in the couple as they operate in their specific union are not necessarily the same that would be seen in either of them in other relationships. For example, a normally sexual man and a normally sexual woman in their particular togetherness can generate an impoverished and dysfunctional sexuality; conversely, two people with weak sexual development can touch one another deeply and bring into being a lovely sexual essence. Insofar as a couple *together* does not succeed in generating competent and satisfying functions in one or more key areas of marital experience, they are faced with "problems." Existential theory posits unambiguously that *all* couples will be faced with such significant problems (Charny, 1980b).

This is not where the difficulties end. Thinking from the additional conceptual leverage of a dialectical approach (which will be introduced shortly), we arrive at a further existential given—that a person's and a couple's outstanding strengths also bring on distinct, if more unexpected, problems. A person's strengths tend to become too much of a focus of his/her personality and life at the expense of other vital functions, including distracting a person from paying needed attention to weaknesses. Thus, a mother who is outstanding as a parent is likely, in response to the simple laws of reinforcement, to become overly involved in mothering at the expense of the other sides of her personality. One common outcome is that she neglects her attractiveness as a wife. Or a couple who together are unusually capable in their management of their family home and economic affairs may be too involved in these tasks to be sufficiently responsive parents to their children.

Moreover, excessive involvement in one's successful or strongest talents also tends to become consuming and exaggerated to a point where a distinct shift in the quality and meaning of the experience takes place. What was once an admired area of achievement can turn into an unattractive, damaging behavior and character style. A quantitative "too much of a good thing" at some point will change qualitatively into something different than it was at its best and often takes on meanings of a bid for power over the other person(s). Thus, a style of warm interpersonal relating that turns into an "institution" of unending togetherness and involvement with another person becomes invasive, strangling, and oppressive. Fascination with, devotion to, and great success in one's vocation can become workaholism, prestigeaholism, and a clearcut threat to a mate's and family's needs to live with their successful worker as a real person and family member, and not only in his/her work role and success.

A Dialectical Approach to Interplays of Strengths and Weaknesses in Marriage

A dialectical approach posits that a creative tension is set in motion in the apposition of strengths and weaknesses in each individual and between the two mates. This dialectical tension challenges and invites the individual and couple to reorganize themselves in a series of new syntheses that are intended to maximize the accessibility of the strengths and minimize the disruption and damages brought on by weaknesses (but not necessarily to get rid of them entirely since they, too, are parts of us).

This dialectical process continues indefinitely throughout life, moving, hopefully, to successively higher levels of integration in each mate and in their experience together as a couple. At no point are weaknesses conquered forever; in fact, to the extent that an individual or a couple perceive themselves as having overcome all their weaknesses, the dialectical approach implies that a new form of breakdown then becomes more probable.

The dialectical principle leads us to a new appreciation of weaknesses not only as existentially inevitable, but also as productive of a welcome partnership of appositions of strengths and weaknesses that set in motion creative processes of growth. When the dialectical process is suppressed or avoided, such as by sameness and doing everything "correctly," there is a failure to grow that therapists have come to see in couples and families who suffer from pseudomutuality, enmeshment, and lack of self-differentiation, as well as from eruptions of acting out, violences, and illnesses if and when the pressure of the suppressed dialectical process breaks out.

In addition to the assumption that each individual and couple have different strengths and weaknesses, the dialectical approach also assumes that there is a basic tension of contradictions *within* any specific area of human experience. Thus, there is no such thing as total competence in communication in a marital relationship or total competence in parenting; there can only be relative competence in the context of a many-sided pattern of functioning which will always include some tendencies toward, and a need to deal with, weaker and more undesirable aspects of oneself. The surprising implication is that an unvarying letter-perfect performance in any human experience area is, by definition, "too good to be true," or an invitation to problems *because* it sets too high a standard. Thus, we see poor parenting when parents neglect or reject a child, but we also see poor parenting when parents overdo their caretaking role, devoting all of themselves to parenting at the expense of not developing their own personality and investment in other roles, or when parents present themselves as totally loving without any anger at the child (Winnicott, 1965).

One of the decided advantages of the dialectical principle is that it identifies too-good performances as well as those which are more obviously poor or nonfunctional. *Although outright incompetence and neglect of a personality function will be picked up by virtually any scheme of observation, one of the strong points of a dialectical viewpoint is that it also picks up excessive investment, commitment, or perfectionism.*

A dialectical conception of human experience calls attention to the inherent possibility of overdoing any type of experience to the point where the quality of an initially lovely experience will be transformed by sheer excess to something less attractive. There are many problems in marriage that result not only from personal weakness in an important area of functioning, but also from overdoing what one is best at, whether working too hard at making a living, talking too much about feelings, or having too much great sex. Thus, to love one's mate should mean to honor, cherish, appreciate, care for, and more; it should not mean to neglect, disrespect, or abuse one's mate. However, it also should not mean to care so much that in the name of love one takes over possession of the other or does everything in the world for him or her, creating an obligation to be indebted.

Similarly, to be sexually attractive and competent should mean being alive, sensual, attractive, pleasureful, and skillful; it does not mean being sexually driven and overdemanding, unable to differentiate between the legitimacy and desirability of various sexual outlets, or splitting off sexual pleasure from genuine regard in a caring relationship.

In addition to the fact that "too much" changes the quality of what one is doing for the worse, being too involved and invested in what one does best generally also means not paying enough attention to one's poor functions and weaknesses, so that there is less energy available to correct, or at least to acknowledge, them.

The dialectical viewpoint sets as an ideal that people and couples work at being as "all around" effective as they can, which means reducing excessive weaknesses as much as they can, acknowledging and dealing responsibly with weaknesses they cannot change, and toning down overinvestment in any single role or area of experience.

Wile (1979, 1981) refers to couples developing not only their own observing egos or ability to monitor themselves, but also a "relationship ego" or an "observing couple ego." Couples who are "big enough" to handle weaknesses that cannot be fully corrected will help one another with their respective areas of weak functioning—and accept help from one another appreciatively. Each mate will stand by in the other's area of weakness. For example, a less than effective parent will nonetheless participate with a more able spouse in disciplining the children, as well as try to compensate for weakness by a greater giving and graciousness in a stronger area of competence. Up to a point, couples can absorb a certain amount of weakness and even profit considerably from the humanity, humility, challenges, and humor that their limitations evoke.

CHOOSING OUR GOALS AND WHAT WE WILL DO ABOUT THEM

A key tool for shaping our own destiny is our ability to choose what we shall seek in our lives within the degrees of freedom available to us. Equally important is our choice of how we will go about attempting to achieve these goals.

Most couples are genuinely interested in living well with one another when they set out in their marriages. They want a genuine friendship and romance with their chosen mate. However, they are not aware that they must choose over and over again the extent to which they will work at developing their marriages, as well as the nature and extent of their commitment to their mate. Other couples do choose more clearly what they want to be, but their choice is to attempt to live so correctly and without risk that they will never again have to face another choice—which is impossible. These are what we have come to know from Wynne (Wynne et. al., 1958) as *pseudomutual* relationships.

> Both of them had seen plenty of marital distress in their parents and had long since vowed to themselves that in their marriage they would never be angry or unreasonable. Their efforts to please one another and fit in with one another turned into a style of accommodation and disregarding of self in a forever-false cheeriness. As the years went by, they were convinced they had achieved a marriage made in heaven. They had no idea why one after another of their children failed to thrive. Some of the children suffered intense learning problems and one was evidently mentally disturbed. The therapist claimed that all of these problems grew from the fact that the family home was seemingly too happy and thus did not leave room for the children to learn how to cope with stress and to develop as individuals.

In the practice of marital therapy, therapists also have many choices to make as to how much to support a given marriage. Presumably, all therapists intend to help couples to be emotionally healthier and happier, but in some situations it will be healthier for the marriages to come to an end. The therapist who comes to this conclusion will steer the therapy process towards this outcome. In other instances the judgment will be that it is healthier for couples to overcome their difficulties and remain married. When therapists choose not to choose, they are in effect choosing to allow the momentum of wherever the greater power lies in the current couple system to play itself out.

This way of working has the advantage of not involving the stranger-therapist in tampering with the destiny of the patients. There is something to be argued for the fact that people who come to a professional should be the ones to choose their own fate. On the other hand, people do come to professionals to get help to stop destructive processes from taking their toll. When the therapist elects *not* to take a stand against the oncoming rampages of a deteriorative process, he or she is not offering medicine or help to people who have knocked at the door precisely because they sense or know that they are in trouble.

I believe there is no such thing as *not* taking a position. Therefore, the professionally sound goal is for therapists to be aware of choosing the goals they will work for, as well as the means they will employ to reach these goals. Responsibility to our clients and patients lies in such awareness, along with an increasing ability to discipline our choices as we learn more about what helps and doesn't help.

Existential/dialectical therapy teaches us that although our destinies are determined by forces that are beyond us, there is also a continuous process of choice-making within the constraints imposed on us by life. The act of choosing and the courage exercised in making our choices enrich and fortify our personalities. The resulting benefit sometimes is so great that it may even compensate us for what were really bad choices. On the other hand, not choosing one's direction characteristically leads to a constriction of the human personality and spirit and creates a kind of weak personality even if the result is ostensibly a good one that offers security.

When one views the marital process in this light, the implication is that husbands and wives face daily choices about how to deal with the tensions and problems in their relationships with one another. Not to do anything about problems is a form of gaining ostensible certainty, but it has a price tag of stagnation and non-growth, along with a kind of "aging" of the personality and the marriage. On the other hand, the effort to deal with issues and make choices can set off considerable anxiety and tensions of possible failure. Yet couples who are not afraid of such tensions end up enjoying greater vitality, self-respect, and appreciation of one another than do couples who are afraid to face up to tensions and challenges.

A question should be raised regarding simple, hardworking couples who live a very steady routine that is acceptable to both of them. Such couples often appear not to need to maintain an ongoing process of struggle and conflict with each other, and through the combination of their hard work and stability appear to reap the good life many others fail to achieve. I think this "solid marital style" should be respected and appreciated, but I still believe that an absence of *process* (dialectical sequences of tension and resolution) will weaken the individuals and the couple. As a result, they will lack resources for coping with certain kinds of stress and also miss out on certain thrusts of energy, talent, and pleasure for themselves.

EXISTENTIAL/DIALECTICAL PSYCHOTHERAPY

Existential/dialectical therapy is based on the polarities of strengths and weaknesses in the human condition of each person that are inherent in all human relationships such as *closeness* and *distance, love* and *hate.*

The helping process in existential/dialectical therapy in itself is also based on a polarity between *helping and supporting* people and *confronting and tearing down* existing structures. The traditional shibboleth of psychotherapy as an offering of total acceptance and understanding is not acceptable in this point of view. In fact, existential/dialectical therapy by its nature is not restricted to any single prescription of therapeutic technique that builds any single mode of experience. Just as life is seen as a complex, unfolding process of profound contradictions beginning with the facts of life and death, so therapies are based on a selection and integration of a variety of growth-inducing processes. The expectation is that a responsible professional will think hard about the techniques he/she selects for the particular couple in therapy (see Salin, 1985, and Schwartz & Pessotta, 1985; also the fascinating methods of dialectical analysis adopted in the *Encyclopedia of World Problems and Human Potential*, 1986).

Existential/dialectical therapy is not a fairy tale of successes and living happily ever after. It is not a glib solution to all problems that is easily taught or learned. It is much more difficult to learn for professionals who seek highly structured interventions and prescriptions. However, I believe that existential/dialectical therapy is a serious and basically systematic method of problem-solving that has a potential for shedding greater light precisely on the more elusive and absurd complexity and caprices of human beings.

Treating the Interplay of Strengths and Weaknesses

Existential/dialectical therapy confronts the individual with the interplay between his/her strengths and weaknesses and how one processes them in a dynamic system of continuing growth. If one fails to harness the interplay, one lives in some fixed, rigid mode.

For optimal psychological well-being, each of us needs to pay attention to at least four major processes with regard to our strengths and weaknesses:

1. Working at fulfilling our known or evident potential.
2. Developing an ability to acknowledge and take responsibility for our major weaknesses.
3. Developing an openness to discover and take responsibility also for our more hidden weaknesses.
4. Undertaking courageously to press for development of still undiscovered and unfulfilled potentials hidden within us.

Broadly speaking, there are four types of distortions or disturbances of these processes.

1. People who are not successful because they do not take a chance and instead take the easy way of avoiding challenge and giving up.
2. People who are so very "strong" and successful that seemingly they get away with not paying attention to any of their weaknesses.
3. People who deny and flee any sign of weakness or incompetence. At the first sight of problems, they redouble their efforts to do everything the "right" way.
4. People who "elect" roles of losers, incompetents, mentally ill, social deviants, and so on in order to "win" at life, ironically by being chronically weak.

An existential/dialectical model is based on the belief that each person's weaknesses are important not only as problems to be removed or minimized, but as *necessary and desirable statements of the challenge of incompleteness that is an important part of our human experience*. Our weaknesses enhance our strengths. If despite our weaknesses we achieve good things, we have good reason to value our achievements that much more. The fact of our weaknesses challenges us to find new ways to overcome and correct or at least balance out what we do poorly. Surprisingly, we could say that existential/dialectical thinking actually encourages a certain degree of emotional problems rather than encouraging people to feel competent, adequate, and secure in all respects (which is the great American dream).

Most people get stuck with the rigidification of one position or another in major areas of their functioning. They are in trouble because:

1. Being *too much* of any emotional quality without its contradiction also

being present means going too far out on a limb that will be under a great strain.

> He is a thoroughly outgoing, cheerful personality and does not need anyone to take care of him. The result is that when he is tired or ill, he doesn't know how to be taken care of and won't let anyone get near him. If ever he faces what appears to him an "insoluble problem," he will be in serious trouble, because he has no one to whom he can turn.

* * * * * *

> He is an overly dependent person who functions well when he is given direction and support. When he needs to be independent, he doesn't know how to take care of himself. When the day comes that his parents pass away, he will not know how to go on.

2. However positive any experience is to begin with, when unduly emphasized, it tends to become more and more extreme and turns into a runaway force in the direction of its very opposite quality.

> She loves her children so much that she doesn't realize that she has become dependent on their receiving her love. Whenever a child takes steps towards separating from her, she becomes enraged. Since she cannot admit to her anger at the child, she turns it into a coverup of feeling ill and needing the child to cater to her.

3. Whatever a position, when it is rigid and unchanging, people suffer a loss of flexibility that in itself creates a major source of strain.

> He knows himself as an entirely devoted husband. Whatever his wife needs, he does twice as much. He has always been careful to balance his involvement in his work with the emotional needs of the family, so he doesn't understand at all why his wife considers him insensitive and involved only with himself. "I've never failed her or any of the children." The fact that he is in love with always being right and commendable is completely beyond his ken, and he does not understand his wife's rebellion against this superior position he has carved out for himself.

In traditional language, we are for success and against weakness, but in the language of dialectics we are for *both* success and weakness. They complement one another and balance, fulfill, enhance, and ensure the potency of the person (Assagioli, 1973, 1975).

For me, the most fascinating aspect of dialectical thinking is the paradox that when strength or weakness are taken to their extreme, without the balancing of their counterpart, each turns into a replica of its denied opposite. Thus, an overpursuit of success eats up a person's personality and creates an impoverished life style; the inability to shift from areas of success to deal with weaknesses and lacks of skill unwittingly turns a successful person into a handicapped one.

> A very successful business executive who owned a major industrial concern was asked by his 10-year-old son, a poor student with a serious learning disability, if he could bring his class to show them the company offices and manufacturing plant. The boy was just beginning to show a response to family therapy and beginning to make an effort in school, all of which followed very clearly the father's having begun to take more of an interest in him. The father agreed to his son's request, but scheduled the day of the class visit for a time when he would be away on one of his many business trips! In response to the incredulity of the therapist, the father explained that he had no idea that his presence was so important to his son.

Strange as it sounds, the same principle of an extreme turning into its counterpart is also true of a weakness pushed to its absurdity. Thus, people who insist on announcing their incompetence turn secretly into extremely powerful persons who control others through their weakness. The chronic weakness and ineptness seem beyond their control, yet they secretly generate power to dominate and harass others.

> He said it openly in the last family therapy session: "You want to cure me. I'll show you who is in charge. I'll have a breakdown when I want to—don't worry, just enough to show you that I am in charge." Four days later he was behaving strangely and was hospitalized as "schizophrenic."

In both cases, the exaggeration of one emotional pole sets off the opposite quality as a runaway extremist force. Where healthy persons build and renew themselves through accepting and balancing contradictory aspects of their personalities, people who are *only* a certain way become literally one-sided, inflexible, and addicted to their single way of being. Their very insistence on one direction catapults them without their knowing into its mirror image. Compare the following:

He is so devoted to his intellectual research that as a personality he is plain dumb. He can't ever relax into being a regular guy.

* * * * * *

He is a serious person in his scholarship, but he takes time off to laugh and enjoy people.

An existential/dialectical treatment approach is designed to lead those being coun-
seled toward other sides of themselves that have been neglected, avoided, or denied,
whether these be potentials for successful mastery and self-expression that have not
been brought to the fore or truths of their limits, weaknesses, and failings. The
approach aims at releasing a natural energy that is generated by an authentic
interplay of strengths and weaknesses.

For our logical "Western minds," probably the most difficult concept to
grasp is that every manifest quality of strength or weakness of a person
necessarily should be seen as linked to a corresponding opposite trait. For
example, a successful high achiever will carry within him a complementary
quality that is aimed, as it were, at non-achievement, such as a denied wish
to be passive or a nasty indifference to the very essence of achievement save
for the success itself. These secret shadows (a wonderful Jungian word for
the hidden, opposite sides of our known qualities) ultimately become time
bombs that threaten the continued possibilities of achievement.

So too with manifest weakness. Thus, in dialectical thinking, unattractive
selfishness is presumed to be backed up by an undeveloped potential for
an opposite quality of caring and unselfish commitment. Knowing this
gives therapists a conception of the possibilities of change. It is, of course,
clinically important to know that often it is already too late for such changes
to be effected, but theoretically the potential for the opposite side of being
still is there inside the person.

Much of our penchant for gossiping about others is provoked by our looking to ferret out the non-authentic and weak sides of people that lie hidden
beyond their achievements. People especially like to look at the great and
near-great not only to see their greatness, but to seek out their secret weaknesses which we sense are present in them as they are in all of us.

He is a craftsman par excellence in his work, the kind of international
business genius they study about at Harvard business seminars. But
for all that he is able to move many people to great heights of achievement, he is without any influence on his wife and children who long
ago grew tired of his unavailability to them.

The dialectical framing of opposite and contrasting processes is a story both of hope and despair in the human condition. It says that every achievement of the human spirit is inevitably anchored by counterpoints of inner weakness that cast their shadows of non-meaning and threaten a person's effective functioning. It is also a story of hope because it links serious and troublemaking weaknesses to latent potentials for overcoming them and tapping undeveloped beauty and creativity.

The drama of each person's continuous personality development sets off tension and anxiety, creates challenge, and ultimately releases powerful energy for becoming more of ourselves. Failure to process our ongoing contradictions, to struggle with them, accept them, and actually enjoy the process leads to a loss of energy and vitality.

The victims of non-processing are both the ostensibly strong and too successful and those who are weak and failing. They are people frozen with the pomposity of success and ignorant of the corruptions that lie behind their achievements and character traits; and they are a variety of inadequate personalities, pseudo-personalities, dropouts, marginal people, and underachievers who never really fought to be the more that is in them.

Here is a psychological framework for seeing a whole familiar cast of characters: the smug and the crippled; the great and the inadequate; the pretentious and the helpless; the winners who don't dare ever lose and the losers who cannot stand winning; great professionals who are poor human beings in their personal lives and simple human beings who are in touch with a true greatness of their humanity. An existential/dialectical approach to therapy gives us a useful way of seeing and understanding many of the unending contradictions in the human drama.

2

The Unique Interplay of Strengths and Weaknesses in the Couple's Marital System

Existential/dialectical marital therapy is based on the mystery, challenge, risk, and tension of the possibilities of growth and joy in marriage versus the sadly common conditions of emotional stagnation, boredom, bitter disappointment, and misery that characterize so many marriages.

My conception of therapy is that we must accept the tensions of being caught in a life-to-death process of contradictions that never end. At the same time, we are not only called on to accept our weaknesses and our mates' weaknesses, but also to confront them and seek to change them.

This kind of thinking opens up a more complex and authentic picture of couples than one gets from looking through rose-colored glasses which hold to absolute contrasts between mature versus immature, good versus bad, or healthy versus sick and sees therapy as an attempt to suppress all the negative and weaker elements so as to replace them only with healthy, good and mature sides of people's personalities. I also find it a more vital way of thinking about marriage than the notion of accepting a spouse as he or she is and never trying to make any changes in either party.

How many people know how to live with an honest self-accounting of their strengths and weaknesses? Many of us are taught a false modesty and do not know how to acknowledge our strongest qualities nor how to use and enjoy our talents. Many bright, capable people work far below their real level and many attractive and charming people opt for long-term sexual and emotional celibacy. Others of us who were taught to be aware of our strengths nonetheless may transform our finest qualities into facades of conventionality, a kind of I-am-a-conventionally-successful-person-in-the-world posture whose purpose is to neutralize deep personal pleasures and peak experiences that we might have "sinfully" enjoyed if given a freer use of ourselves.

On the other side of the ledger, if and when a person makes it appear to himself or to others that he has no weaknesses, that in itself constitutes a weakness of hubris. Such hubris in turn is likely to lead to overstriving and overdoing, which turn once genuinely fine skills and qualities into unattractive, even monstrous, qualities. When no weakness is acknowledged, there is no energy or impetus to lead a person to be responsible for growth. Insofar as a weakness could have been corrected to some extent, as many can be, that person's spouse will have an added resentment that the mate didn't even try to reduce the problem. Thus, a poor parent can still help in parenting through a kind of standing by and "pitching in" alongside the more skillful parent. In fact, many weaknesses can even be elevated into qualities of one's personality for which one is appreciated, as when one tries to do one's best with one's shortcomings and make up for them.

There are also ways of compensating for one's weaknesses by giving much more of oneself in other areas of experience and functioning, as if one is saying: "Sorry that I can't be more of a help with the children, but let me arrange for a good family vacation for all of us, and you will all know how much I appreciate our family." Obviously, if one denies from the outset any weaknesses in oneself, there is no reason to try to develop any compensations or alternative ways of giving of oneself to one's mate and marriage.

I think of myself and all of us as engaged throughout our lifetimes in a never-ending play between strong/adequate and weak/inadequate parts of ourselves. Our overall goal is to achieve a basic self-respect and pleasure in ourselves, but not to be carried away by narcissism and not to be cut off from humility and realistic acknowledgement of how much is missing and unbalanced in us.

As couples, we constitute fascinating shared systems of strengths and weaknesses. Each of us, in effect, is saying to one another: "I must live with you as you struggle with yourself throughout your life to love yourself and to encompass your incompleteness." In the best of circumstances, we have an opportunity to see and learn from our mate how he/she succeeds at this difficult process. In the worst cases, we are witnesses and are affected by the failure of our mate.

Readers who are interested in a clinical-research method for analyzing marital interaction according to the existential/dialectical framework will find it in an article in *Family Process* (Charny, 1986c). Each spouse is scored for his/her functioning in five basic areas of marriage (family management, companionship, relationship, attraction and sexuality, and parenting) in accordance with five values (competence, commitment, respect, control, closeness).

Together the husband's and wife's scores yield a picture of their interaction: both effective, one ineffective and the other effective (a complementary pattern), or both ineffective. Ineffectiveness is scored either as *minus scores*, meaning poor quality functioning or too little investment of self, or as *plus scores*, which represent overcompetence or overinvestment.*

The story of what happens to two people who are variously gifted and variously limited is intriguing for its possibilities. Every couple joined together in their union soon discover that in some major areas of experience they are not sufficiently talented to meet the needs of everyday life. Sometimes, neither mate has the ability to make friends comfortably. In other instances, mates may find that even though they are both quite capable sexual performers, they are pressed into serious sexual tensions by underlying personality needs of competitiveness and efforts to best one another for the position of "top dog."

In other instances, one mate will be competent in an area of functioning such as earning money where the other may be handicapped. They begin by hoping that the competent one will compensate for the other. This kind of *complementarity* is common in young, new couples, and is even considered to be an important aspect of normal attraction and mate selection. But as I shall develop at greater length later, it is at the very least questionable that couples can sustain such major differences indefinitely, especially if they get locked into a relationship pattern of adequacy-inadequacy.

> He does much of the child-rearing while she is forging ahead in her career and bringing in a great deal of money for them. They like it this way. He is more nurturing and caring, while she is more practical and oriented to doing things in the world. Together they make a fine combination. As a modern couple, they are satisfied with their arrangement, but only time will tell whether they can continue to respect each other in this arrangement.

The meeting up of mates in their different strengths and weaknesses cre-

---

* Several dissertations at the Bob Shapell School of Social Work at Tel Aviv University have applied this clinical rating tool. Machlin (1988) and Asianeli (in press) demonstrated high reliabilities of ratings. Kirschner (1988) has created a quantitative method for scoring the profile. Specific subject studies in connection with the use of the profile include a study of the usefulness of the model for therapists evaluating a marital therapy case (Arnon, 1984), adjustment of couples following the husband's suffering a stroke (Machlin, 1988), treatment of mid-life crises (Kirschner, 1988), a study of marital difficulties of couples where one is the child of a Holocaust survivor (Erel, 1990), and development of a paper-and-pencil questionnaire based on the clinical rating tool (Asianeli, 1988).

ates a series of what are, in effect, "political challenges." Many couples succumb to one or another form of inequality and create a system where one of them is the competent one/hero/leader and the other is a devoted admirer/ puppy dog. Other couples create marriages that can survive only so long as they are *both* stars who do everything right; there is no room for forgiving and loving one another in any weakness. Then there are other marriages where couples evade the issues of growth by locking into an agreed mutual plan for neither of them to be competent or strong (Charny, 1987). These three patterns will be discussed later in Chapter 5.

THE TENSIONS OF HIDDEN WEAKNESSES

The picture becomes more complex when we realize that whatever we are not attaches itself as a shadow to what we are, thereby also transforming the heroic in us into problematic aspects of our personality (Assagioli, 1973, 1975). The shadows and, often, nemeses of our best qualities are, by definition, their opposites and contradictions. These shadow sides of our finest qualities lurk beside and behind our good traits. Although these shadows were not necessarily major parts of our personalities at first, the more we succeed and live with the good parts of ourselves, the more we also have to meet up with our shadows and arrive at some policy positions about them.

> A proud, independent, self-made man denies ever needing to receive anything for himself from others. Without knowing it, his demands for others to confirm his toughness and lack of need for them make him progressively more dependent on their loyalty and devotion to him.

It is a standard observation of married life, though I disagree that this has to be the case, that most couples get "turned off" after a certain number of years. The explanation generally given is that couples become accustomed to one another and there is no longer any mystery or marvel. Also, they discover the unattractive qualities in their mate that they were blinded to earlier when they were "in love." The hidden qualities we are describing here as necessarily attached to whatever we are good at are large factors in the falling out of love that most couples suffer. As one gets to know the "real character" of one's mate, our spouses turn out to be in a number of ways the opposite of what he/she appeared to be at first meeting (Whitehouse, 1981). (One can hear many a spouse telling a friend or lover, "I finally got to know what he/she is really like".)

Carl Whitaker (Whitaker & Bumberry, 1988) observed thus:

> I believe we select partners we are psychologically matched with. It's not really a random process at all. I don't believe we end up married to a particular person by mistake. The excuse of "temporary insanity" doesn't fit with my experience. Of course, there typically is massive collusion in this process, whereby we mutually agree to be a certain way with each other as part of the sales effort. His temper somehow doesn't show until after the ceremony. Her perfectionism is viewed as neatness until it's turned on him during the honeymoon. But to say that they were completely unaware, to infer that they truly didn't realize what they were getting into, is ridiculous.
>
> While on the surface it appears that we select someone who will meet all of our needs and make us whole, the real relationship lies deeper. Paradoxically, the more clearly our selection seems to meet our surface needs, the more profound will be the struggle to really become a healthy couple. It often seems that by virtue of our marriage selection, we are faced with the opportunity to struggle with some of our most terrifying fears. Marrying a spouse because his strength makes you feel secure eventually comes around to your needing to challenge and defeat his strength in order to be a person. As you defeat his strength, he must then face the fears and uncertainties it masked. Selecting a wife because she's so thoughtful and attentive to your needs ends up in the dilemma of being bored by her lack of individuality. The twists are endless, with tremendous variations and diversity of style. (p. 135)

Even people who are able to be relatively fair about acknowledging their *overt* shortcomings may resist strongly acknowledging their *hidden* or covert weaknesses. We observe many people who are blind to their destructive use of talents and qualities for which they are otherwise admired.

A mature personality senses these shadow truths. Thus:

"I know that I am demanding appreciation from my children." Or, *"I sense that I am getting too interested in being admired for my writing and that it is getting in the way of my creativity for its own sake."*

A person who tunes into these saboteur/aliens within himself and is able to acknowledge their presence may be able to cultivate a measure of conscious self-discipline to hold these deteriorative parts of himself in check. To achieve this kind of strength, one needs to be bravely humble enough to recognize the nastiness inside of ourselves—which is not a pleasant or easy task. However, people who need to be invulnerable, always competent, and sure of themselves will not be in a position to watch for their hidden weaknesses which, by definition, will then become more powerful.

THE TENSIONS OF UNDEVELOPED POTENTIAL

The dark sides of our minds include not only our hidden limitations but also what we have not made of ourselves, that which we may be able to become, and, sadly, that which we could have been but did not and may never develop in ourselves. These undeveloped potentials exert no less powerful forces in our feelings about ourselves, even though ostensibly these are aspects of ourselves which do not yet exist.

In my experience, there is a cry of deep pain, mourning, and also of rage whenever we leave meaningful potential talent within us undeveloped. I have been impressed in my clinical work at the profound suffering that grows from not becoming what we really wanted to be or could have been. Such suffering often is responsible for greater despair and breakdown than the hurt and suffering that grow from our actual failures. The idea that we did not try, that we were, in effect, so deeply disloyal to ourselves that we did not risk developing, can tear deeply at the inner spirit. It also is a powerful trigger of pent-up aggression, for the very energies that we could have used to become more of ourselves seem to protest our failure to call on them.

There is, after all, a huge undeveloped potential in all of us. One needs to learn to "listen" to the sounds and calls of these talents from within. Even in areas where we are truly inadequate, there is a potential for growing, at least to move beyond the dismal incompetence we may show at the start of the game.

> He really does not know the first thing about how to talk to his wife, but if he makes an effort—even by forcing himself at first—he can learn to listen better and then even to share with her something about his ideas and feelings.

It should certainly be noted that unusually high degrees of anxiety can be set off when one *does* allow oneself to be aware of one's unused potential, and especially when one makes the decision to try to develop the unused parts of oneself. This observation is connected with Rollo May's (1977) definition of anxiety years ago as the fear of not being able to develop one's fuller potential. As we approach the shadows of our unclaimed talent, we become frightened and anxious that we will not be capable of harnessing our gifts and we need to be able to muster a degree of tolerance for our anxiety if we are ever to fulfill our talent. Many people fall back at this point. They are too afraid of the experience of anxiety to persist.

Those who undertake the struggle can reap very rich rewards, indeed, beginning with a growing pride in their courage, let alone the joys of the skills and mastery they achieve. To be truly alive as a person is to grow, expand, and discover new parts of ourselves. When we do, we become filled with a warming confidence as well as a joy and pleasure about ourselves, so that in addition to our own greater happiness we become that much more alive, attractive persons to our mates. Of course, success is not guaranteed and the risk of trying to develop is that one may fail—even badly—and be so hurt that one becomes "smaller" and more restricted in one's personality than before. There is no easy answer to the question, "Is it better to love and lose than never to love at all?" However, it is a question that each person must choose to answer in many areas of life.

THE DEVELOPMENT OF THE COUPLE SYSTEM

Two people living with one another and sharing their lives is a drama of a fascinating field of forces.

Given that each of us is organized so complexly, then two people living together create even greater complexity. The marital process is infinitely complicated as it includes couples living alongside of each other, both with their apparent and hidden strengths and weaknesses, both with their undeveloped potentials. The many combinations of all these create a field of pattern or *system* that is unique for each marriage.

We begin to see something of the fascinating mosaic or system of strengths and weaknesses that is unique to each *couple*. I venture to suggest that when we look at the interplays and interactions between two people sharing the complexities of their innermost selves, we are into a "mathematics" that has never been written, and into a "physics" of attraction and repulsion between positive and negative qualities that we sense but actually know very little about to this day.

One could begin simply by *adding* up a chain of the strengths available to the couple in their jointness: He is so smart *and* she is so vivacious and pretty; he is so friendly to people *and* she is so efficient.

Similarly, one can put together the chain of weaknesses of a couple: He is overly involved in sexual prowess *and* she is undeveloped intellectually; he doesn't like to spend time sharing experiences with her *and* she isn't very interested in parenting.

Just "adding up" the different strengths and weaknesses of each of the two spouses will begin to produce a pattern picture which already has some flavor of a highly idiomatic "fingerprint" or unique picture of a specific couple. In effect, the "printout" of shared assets and debits summarizes a series of subjects with which they, as a team, are going to have to struggle as they apportion roles and develop policies for how to relate to each other's best and worst qualities.

On the surface, the necessity of dividing roles sounds easy enough. If, in fact, the couple were originally drawn to one another on the basis of some significant complementarities, which means that he is strong where she is weak, and she is strong where he is weak, the situation might be thought of as ideal. Such complementary attraction seems to be an important aspect of initial mate attraction and selection. However, we know today that although tradeoffs and protection of one another are very useful and perhaps even ideal starting points for couples, over the long run they can produce very negative outcomes if there is no change and growth into new, more equal patterns. As we shall see more fully later, there are complementary relationships which seem satisfactory to a couple even for a long time, but the inherent inequality in them is likely to set off chains of negative consequences.

> He is a fiery, independent person so unlike his compliant, accommodating wife who always lets him take the lead, and he falls head over heels in love with a woman who is a volatile "Carmen" type. His wife feels totally betrayed when she finds out about his affair and the fact that he wants to leave her and marry his "Carmen." She is shocked because all these years he hadn't complained and had seemed only too pleased by her continuous admiration of him. She had no idea that he did not respect her for being a rubber stamp to him.

Note that resentment can issue from the side of the more adequate one, as in the above illustration, or from the side of the less adequate one. The inadequate spouse may not even know that s/he is resentful, and yet unconsciously can go to great lengths to retaliate for being kept as an inadequate and junior partner. One way is for the weak person to take over in another area of marriage and put the "superior" mate in his/her place. We often see this when wives who feel themselves on a lower status retaliate by taking over children and taking them away from their fathers. Other times, the process of retaliation by the weak one is completed through their going to a further extreme of weakness, such as turning into a chronically dependent, invalid personality.

It is an extraordinarily complicated matter to decide how to relate to one's spouse's strengths and weaknesses. Should I always be considerate? Shall I say to my beloved that I accept him/her as is, no questions and no complaints? That, after all, has been the time-honored advice of many marriage counselors and well-wishers. However, the deceit in such unquestioning acceptance, as well as the lack of stimulation, is often not appreciated by one's partner. But how can one know how far to go at any given time in conveying criticism and calling attention to obvious and hidden problems? If one encourages one's spouse to develop new parts of the self, will the encouragement be appreciated as well-intentioned and loving, or will it be so threatening and anxiety-provoking that it will be treated as an attack and bring on retaliation?

For couples who insist on being only winners and only competent and successful (which we have noted as the western ideal for marriage), any juxtaposition of strength and weakness raises an unbearable level of tension. There are many couples who are unable to tolerate any kind of failure (Framo, 1976, 1981, 1982). They pretend to have no shortcomings and they appear outstanding to others who may envy them. When failure finally forces itself into their experience as a couple, they are humiliated and disheartened. One or both of them is likely to blame the other for the "disaster."

> "You are so busy with your office and being a doctor. You leave me with the children all day long and I simply can't cope with them. It's your fault that I am screaming all the time."

Such couples often break up because they cannot bear the shame of being unsuccessful in any important area. Their breakup is difficult for people around them to understand since their overall record seemed better than that of many other couples who lived with much worse shortcomings.

Other couples are not as upset by limitations as they are panicked by the emergence of a strong talent or strength in either of them that may change the balance between them. Success is an enemy; if my mate moves up to a new class which I can't reach, I'll be left behind:

> "My husband left his company and opened an independent consulting office. I was against his making the move on the grounds that we needed the financial security of his job with the big corporation. Now he's doing very well and in a way I'm proud of him, but instead of feeling good, I'm getting more and more nervous and don't understand why. I'm very afraid that we are going to be driven apart by his success."

Healthy couples will see and appreciate each other's strengths and weaknesses as parts of the drama of existence and they will welcome the opportunity to encounter both talent and weakness within their shared experience. They will try not to blame one another for weakness or resent the emergence of new talent. When anxiety mounts and they find themselves attacking and blaming the other, they will try to correct themselves and to respond constructively to the criticisms of their spouse.

> After they moved into their large, lovely new home, he moved his practice there too. The first day, as she saw him going about comfortably, receiving his numerous patients, she felt terrible. She told him how inadequate he made her feel. She couldn't help but be somewhat abusive in the way she spoke. His reply was very firm and, surprisingly, relieved her: "I enjoy my work. I want you to feel good enough about yourself that you are not jealous of me."

Unfortunately, anxiety is such an uncomfortable experience and the majority of people have not learned to value it as a signal and catalyst for growth. They fear it and seek to flee it at any cost. Thus, so many couples seize upon pseudosolutions to their tensions and anxieties.

Probably the most common pseudosolution is for a couple to organize along the lines of the strength of one of them at the expense of the other's weakness. It is a heady temptation to take over the position of the one who is wise/competent/potent/worldly/or what have you at the expense of the other less competent, if not lowly one. On the other side, there are also temptations for people to be passive/dependent/hero-worshipping, even if it costs them a measure of their dignity. The combination appeals to many couples and is often welcomed as ideal. Both styles of relating are understandable and seductive. At one time or another, we should all have experienced surges of feeling good and superior in the presence of someone who is doing poorly, as well as the relief of being able to depend on somebody who is so masterful that we can give our full admiration. It takes a readiness to risk anxiety not to succumb to either of these patterns. However, many couples are seduced by the comforts of being locked into a steady-state of strong/weak. The growth process that depends on the tension of contradictions between what we are and what we could be is then brought to a screeching halt. Although these marriages can appear to satisfy the needs of both parties, we know that they are intrinsically at risk because they are based on inequality.

Wholesome couples successfully avoid the dangers of this polarity. They do not agree to either of them moving into either of the two positions. Intuitively, these couples know that any arrangement that freezes one of them into a dependent, second-class position will damage both their personalities and their marriage.

The Couple Develops a System for Relating to Their Hidden Qualities

As if all the above were not sufficient, each couple also has to deal with the extraordinarily difficult issues of their hidden and unknown strengths and weaknesses. To be reminded by one's spouse of one's known and obvious weaknesses can be problem enough, but to be reminded of one's unacknowledged, disguised weaknesses can be even more threatening. These, after all, are the shameful aspects of our character, the shadows that we have the greatest trouble in recognizing and admitting in ourselves.

Insofar as we do not face up to unattractive parts in ourselves, it is likely that we are going to discover the same or similar problems in our mate which we will then criticize and attack. This is a common way of our human state; whatever we dislike and disown in ourselves, we are likely to project onto another person, and who is more available as the object of our projections than our marital partner? One of the oldest rules of thumb in marital therapy is that if you trace back from a spouse's main complaint about the other, most likely you will find waiting in the complainer, hidden from his or her consciousness, the same or an equivalent problem. (The classic presentation on marital projections will be found in Dicks [1967], which I have for many years considered the single most important book for marital therapists.) The complaint against the mate often is as much a response to being terrorized and frightened by one's *own* weakness as it is a legitimate complaint about one's spouse.

The reminders of our own hidden weaknesses are there each time we see weaknesses in our mate. When the issue concerns an *obvious* weakness in our spouse, we are not likely to realize how much of our upset may be the fact that this obvious weakness is a reminder of our own unknown weaknesses, so that we are not only upset at our spouse but with ourselves. An even greater irritation often follows our discovery of a *hidden* weakness in our spouse. At first flush, it seems as if our protest justifiably is coming from our having exposed some corruption and unreliability in the other, but often the discovery of the other's hidden weakness triggers other voices we do not want to hear from inside our own hiding places.

> She is a beautiful and apparently cheerful woman, but inside she is really depressed and bitter. Since her childhood and now in her marriage, she feels alone, but she insists on keeping her head up and not giving in to dependency. Her husband prides himself on being a strong man, but he has been on the edge of developing hypertension. Whenever he speaks of feeling ill, she turns against him sarcastically. He is obviously making himself sick, she insists disparagingly. She has absolutely no sympathy for him. In a way

she is right about him—he doesn't like to admit to himself that he is sick at heart about not feeling loved by her, and that these feelings are helping make him sick. But she is also furious at his reflection of her own denied dependency needs, as well as her guilt that she is not taking care of him.

Similar processes are triggered by the unrecognized and undeveloped creative energy and talent in our spouse, which may also trigger unconscious anxiety about whatever unused potential in ourselves we are not doing enough about. As noted earlier, many people are more frightened about being faced with their potential talent than they are with meeting up with their weaknesses. I have seen people virtually go psychotic in the face of compliments and invitations to apply their talents, while the same people would even welcome being criticized and beaten down. Spouses whose talents are threatened by the spouse are often driven to ridicule and insult their mate in defensive ways, most likely in messages that are aimed at cutting down the other's talent or energy.

> "Do you really have to go off to your choir again? You may be another Mozart, but you aren't going to have a home to come back to if you keep going out all the time."

In contrast, here is a brief example of a couple where his use of his talent *used* to drive his wife mad with upset until she found a way to channel the upset towards her own further development, which he was glad to support.

> She used to get enormously upset every time he took a business trip and more than once went off to act out sexually in retaliation. He loved his business world and she hated his business achievements with a vengeance. While there was little question that he really overdid his travelling, it also was clear that she could not bear to be alone. Being alone set off in her a deep panic of being abandoned. After a particularly bad time she realized that she was going to break down unless she did something more constructive. She decided that she was going to open a boutique and go into her own business. He was delighted at her decision and took every opportunity to help her develop this new venture. Once she succeeded in her business, she stopped being upset and resentful about his travelling, and even became somewhat more effective in holding him back from his excessive travels.

The manifest strength of one spouse may be a clue or hint of the hidden potential waiting in the other. Thus, the implication will be that the long-

admiring wife who sees her brilliant attorney husband on the stage of success while she operates far behind the scenes as a retiring, shy woman at
home may be harboring inside herself a community leader who might be
no less successful than her acknowledgedly brilliant husband. (There have
been a good number of prominent cases like this in public life, as a matter
of fact.) I can hardly guarantee that such springs of talent are going to be
discovered in every person. But it is a lovely idea to anticipate the possibility
that the evident talent of one spouse is the best "divining-rod" clue that
similar treasures of self-expressiveness, albeit in different contents and
styles, may await in the other.

One of the most interesting yields of this way of thinking is the series
of clues it gives us for understanding many instances of marital distress
in terms of projective accusations of one's spouse. A reliable rule of thumb
in working with couples is that whenever a spouse is bitterly angry at the
other, consider the possibility that the accusation, even if right, is pointing
the way towards a corresponding problem in the accuser, whether it is the
same or a direct opposite and thereby as if the same.

Developing a Couple Policy in Response to Strengths and Weaknesses

Each partner in marriage is, in effect, required to formulate and execute
three policy positions. The first refers to each individual's relationship to
his/her own package of strengths and weaknesses; the second involves each
spouse's approach towards the other's strengths and weaknesses; the third
involves each spouse's way of responding to the other's policy towards him/
her regarding his/her strengths and weaknesses. Every one of these subjects is complex and inherently invites serious errors and pitfalls.

The seemingly well-intended position that is culturally reinforced in western society that a spouse must "always" respect and stand by the mate
without intruding, without being critical, and without making any
attempts to change him or her really means being a rubber stamp for the
continuation of one's spouse's weaknesses.

I have already referred to the temptation to identify weaknesses in one's
spouse in order to take advantage of them—sadly, a common human trait.
There can be a thrill and a false sense of mastery and security in feeling
superior to one's spouse; "rubbing in" a spouse's weaknesses can excite "top
dog" or superior-seeking inclinations in every one of us. Even ostensible
protests of a spouse's weakness can actually be ways of blaming and degrad-
ing one's mate, in effect telling him/her that we appreciate being given a
basis for being superior and would he/she please continue to be weak. (One
often sees "psychologically sophisticated" couples who ostensibly know
that they need to encourage one another to face up to problems, but their

metalanguage or the style of the "encouragement" is enough to kill the other.)

Similarly, with respect to a spouse's undeveloped talents, one can ignore the issue and accept the fact that one's husband/wife is growing stale in spirit as a person who does not take on new tasks and challenges; out of "kindness," one then does everything to suppress the emergence of any new power in the mate. Or one can tease out through criticism, ridicule, and accusation one's mate's unused potential and underline their awaiting talent, while conveying in the metalanguage that it feels good to be connected to a failure and please continue not being the stronger person you could be.

The concept of *projective identification* is a very useful one here. It refers to the influence one person has in inducing another to behave or respond in a given way. The recipient is "forced" to respond to the dynamics of the projector. Without realizing it, the recipient absorbs the energy-style and unconscious pressures of the projector and responds as "expected." Thus, some people force others to reject them, others get people to serve them, others exhaust the other person with their insincerity, and so on. In the marital process, each mate necessarily brings an "emotional dowry" or characteristic style to bear on the other and can't help but attempt to reproduce the kinds of influences—good and bad—he/she is accustomed to having. Cashdan has emphasized correctly that:

> Replaying pathological object relations scenarios of one's early years constitutes an attempt to revise the bad endings of early childhood. People who resort to projective identification as a means of structuring their relationships desperately yearn for a "good ending."
>
> In the marital drama, if one experiences one's spouse's policy as overly controlling, or dependent, or seductive-sexualizing, or sacrificial-obligatory, one has to "fight back," in as constructive but as vigorous ways as possible, the goal being to refuse to play the role one is being assigned—for the combination of one's own sake and one's mate's sake. (Cashdan, 1988, p. 100)

The desired position is for a mate to appreciate and care for the other, but not to hesitate to criticize constructively the other's weakness or failure to develop and to defend these criticisms. A spouse who genuinely cares about the other's development *for the sake of the other* is freer to respond with anger at the other's weakness or failure to develop his/her potential. So long as the basic thrust of such criticism and anger is rooted in authentic feeling for the other, it is likely to be helpful. To be critical and angry on the basis of one's own needs is also justified, but the limits of such criticism and demands *for oneself* are much more severe than when one is genuinely interested in helping *the other* to grow.

Each of us must also develop a policy towards our mate's policy towards our strengths and weaknesses.

One of the most common problems in marital therapy is what to do in response to an insulting mate. To be passive is obviously wrong, but, paradoxically, to fight back too strongly can also confirm one's being insulted. If I react to every insult with huge rage and powerful retaliations, my policy confirms the fact that I am vulnerable to these insults. Moreover, if I really succeed in beating the insulter down to a pulp where he/she will not be heard from again, I may create a situation where I will no longer have any criticism and challenge, including the healthy criticism and challenge I need. You see this in many marriages where too much conflict is resolved by the creation of an angry silent détente and a virtual end to genuine interest in one another and any possibility of stimulating interaction.

The requirements of sound policy towards one's mate's policy must not only be towards the obvious or stated position of the spouse but towards the inner meanings of their position. It is important to fight back against overly nice gestures and too-good intentions of one's mate that can be damaging precisely because they do not stimulate growth. Where a spouse is always accepting and understanding, one is left without the vitality of genuine feedback and criticism. It is easy to fall into a collusive relationship of accepting such well-intentioned behavior, let alone that one can fall for manipulative pseudogoodness, as well as pseudonormal or pseudomutual relationships that over time are so damaging to everyone's emotional vitality.

In healthy marriages, it is often necessary to be angry and fight (Bach & Wyden, 1969; Charny, 1972b; Wile, 1988). How does one do so without being insulting? If one must insist on strong differences, how does one do so without triggering threats and fears of separation and loss in the relationship? The ideal is hard to come by. It requires thoughtfulness, discipline, and an ability to bear the tensions of a dramatic process that will need time to be played out.

The interplays of manifest and latent strengths and weaknesses in two spouses who have come together in their unique partnership of marriage are fascinating combinations of

> the coming together of parts that complete and fulfill one another—
> the romantic marital dream
>
> *and*

the coming together of differences that clash and polarize with one another—the nightmare reality of marriage at its common worst!

The admittedly small percentage of couples who do achieve a degree of integration of the complex dialectic process appreciate and respect one another's beauty, but they also seek to challenge one another—even painfully—to grow further, to stand up to their secret weaknesses and unwelcome qualities, and to address their unused potential. They are authentic in their irritations and anger at one another as well as in their genuine respect and love for one another. They really want the best for themselves and for their spouse.

Wholesome couples are challenged by the interplays of strength and weakness within their own selves and between them, and by the opportunities to experience intimately the dramas at work in their spouses that correspond to the dramas within them. With human ups and downs, they enjoy the combination of being sources of both challenges and assistance to the other. The juxtapositions of their strengths and weaknesses are tapped as triggers for growth and not as threats that must be met with defensive responses of inadequacy or superiority.

Couples who miss the mystery of mutual growth are more likely to get locked into rigid positions of anger, accusation, blaming, and attempts to undermine one another. Life together may become a serious threat. If one mate then tries to break out into greater authenticity, the effort is likely to be met with competitiveness, remonstration, and attack.

For those couples who are not threatened by the drama of one another and together find a way to translate their marital interaction into opportunities for mutual growth, marriage represents the best "medicine" and therapy in the world. Over the years, one sees both mates getting stronger. They look well, and one can see that they are obviously enjoying their lives as individuals and in their marriage to one another.

3

Marrying Our Potential Helper/Rescuer Versus Our Torturer/Destroyer

Marriage as Effective Psychotherapy

Each marrying partner marries his/her potential helper/rescuer or potential torturer/destroyer. It depends. Even when a couple did not select one another by falling in love and asking and agreeing to marry one another, the same two-sided potential is built into their being husband and wife. For in their essence, each man and woman is a complementary force or process that can complete what is so sorely lacking in the other.

By supporting *and* challenging one another in a basic context of love and respect, couples can generate a wonderful merger for growth. However, if the union of the complementaries fails to achieve and maintain a basic balance between the two, one side may emerge as the superior and the other as the inferior, and the two together will constitute and unleash a destructive process of control and submission, smugness and self-abasement, triumph and revenge. Alternatively, husband and wife may both be "the same kind," and create a marriage of two stars or gods on the Olympus who will be in danger of exhausting themselves or burning themselves out because they will have left no room for byplays between strengths and weaknesses. Other couples may both be so nice, accommodating, and cooperative that they will bore themselves and age into premature greyness.

At its best and finest, the union of two mates and the completion of one by the other are intended to bring each person closer to wholeness and release a basic generativity. Being together provides a wonderful presence and protection through which each can be so much more of what s/he can become but cannot become so long as s/he is alone.

Just as maleness and femaleness meet, so do other differences; in each

32

Alternative 1 of many

He is a powerful, excitingly masculine person, she a pretty and vivacious feminine person. Alone, he is driven by macho and disquiet; and she alone, would melt into ineptness, forcelessness, and nonbeing. Yet, together, he is tender and she is strong, he pretty and she vigorous, a tribute to the wholeness in each of them that lay waiting, and the merging of the two of them that completes them as they could not do alone.

Alternative 2 of many

He is a powerful, excitingly masculine person, she a pretty and vivacious feminine person. Alone, he is driven by macho and disquiet; and she alone, melts into ineptness, forcelessness, and nonbeing. Together, he is brutal and insulting and exploitative of her femininity and weakness, while she displays her femininity as weakness and dependency. Together, they mock that which is exaggerated in each of them.

case, the possibilities are for "better or worse." The examples are as endless as the many qualities of our personalities: one is so finely intelligent, the other is so dearly caring; one is marvelously sociable, the other is sensitively genuine; one is a top-notch disciplinarian of children, the other a master of language and music who charms children's imaginations and minds. Each, alone, could become too much of what he/she is best at and become a kind of caricature of special skill taken too far: intelligence can then become unforgiving, cold logic, deep caring can be turned to possessive hovering, and so forth. Together they can become better versions of what they really are as well as a lovely couple. Or the "together" of a couple can make them vicious antagonists and competitors. The skills of one can be committed to confirming that the other is the lesser of the other; the rumbling lesser of the other can set off repeated waves of upset and anger in the confident one as reminders of the weaknesses that lurk in him/her too. At its worst and most destructive, the union of a couple who fail to complete one another is a dread reminder to both of their missing wholeness. Being together turns into an accusation and humiliation for not being more of what each could have become and now cannot because their being together is so insulting to their spirits.

It is fascinating that the same person often acts very differently in a different marriage! With one mate s/he will be involved in a power struggle "unto death"; remarried to another person, s/he will develop a positive cooperative style and ability to process tensions and differences for the benefit of both of them. The second marriage still involves many tensions and pulls towards the ugly personality possibilities that await that same person, but somehow, in this marriage and in the specific couple system it generates, s/he is able to put off the threats of the deteriorative sides of his/her personality, grow, and help the other to grow. The crucial question is, why

His strength really *does* frighten her. She feels weak next to him and there is a part of her that wishes he were less than he is, so that she could be more. Yet he does not use his strength against her and he really wants her to grow to be as much of herself as she can; she does not turn her fright of his strength into sabotage, espionage, or attacks on him, because she is also so proud and respectful of what he is.	*Her strength* really *does* frighten him. He feels weak next to her and there is a part of him that wishes she were less than she is, so that he could be more. Yet she does not use her strength against him and she really wants him to grow to be as much of himself as he can; he does not turn his fright of her strength into sabotage, espionage, or attacks on her, because he is also so proud and respectful of what she is.
His weakness really *does* upset her. She wishes he would be so much more, and that she could respect him and depend on him. However, she tells him her criticism fairly and straightforwardly, encouraging him to grow to be more than he is, while conveying her appreciation of the other fine qualities he has. He, in turn, strains to take in the value of her criticism, appreciates it, and acknowledges his weakness, and makes plans to stretch and grow as much as he can.	*Her weakness* really *does* upset him. He wishes she would be so much more, and that he could respect her and depend on her. However, he tells her his criticism fairly and straightforwardly, encouraging her to grow to be more than she is, while conveying his appreciation of the other fine qualities she has; she, in turn, strains to take in the value of his criticism, in fact appreciates it, and acknowledges her weakness, and makes plans to stretch and grow as much as she can.

and how do some couples manage to process and turn their differences into a sharing that becomes a synthesis and re-creation of both of them?

The difference between growth and destruction seems to me to lie in a *commitment to grow,* in each mate and as a couple. This commitment, in turn, seems to be fed by an inner decision not to allow oneself to be drawn towards one's potential destructiveness (a version of which awaits inside all of us). It is accompanied by a basic readiness to acknowledge one's own weaknesses without being defensive and without projecting on to and blaming the other.

There are many couples who are committed to grow, yet they are relatively rare in the context of millions and millions of couples. They create lovely partnerships, where both are simultaneously strong and weak, right and wrong, male and female, mature and childish, and all manner of other perplexingly beautiful combinations. Each yields to the need for one another and for being needed, the pleasure of giving and receiving; each endures the annoyances and threats of the other and yet feels safety and joy in being one another's best friend.

Such couples are not only at ease. They are happy. They are alive. Not that they do not suffer a great deal of sadness and upset. They get in trouble, each in his/her own self, as well as the two together as a couple, but they learn that their troubles are signals for renewed growth and even learn to appreciate trouble as an opportunity to learn, to help and be helped. These couples create marriages that are generative, self-correcting sequences of checks and balances—democratic systems at their best. The story of such marriages is a love story of equals.

MARITAL PROJECTIONS: A POWERFUL AND DECISIVE PROCESS

> And he shall take the two goats, and set them before the Lord . . . and Aaron shall cast lots upon the two goats; one lot for the Lord, and the other for Azazel. The goat, on which the lot fell for Azazel, shall be set alive before the Lord, to make atonement over him, to send him away for Azazel into the wilderness . . . And Aaron shall lay both his hands upon the head of the live goat, and confess over him all the iniquities of the children of Israel, and all the transgressions, even all the sins; and he shall put them upon the head of the goat, and shall send him away by the hand of an appointed man into the wilderness. And the goat shall bear upon him all the iniquities unto a land which is cut off; and he shall let go the goat in the wilderness. (Leviticus, 16)

Technically speaking, there are several meanings to projection, but all involve attributing to another person some quality that actually resides in or pertains to one's own self. The particular type of projection in which we are interested here—probably it is also the most important type of projection, certainly the most virulent—involves projecting on to another individual qualities inside of us which we cannot bear recognizing in ourselves.

"You're mean and cruel," says an irate spouse who cannot bear his/her own cruelty. "You're trying to push me around," claims an embittered spouse who cannot acknowledge his/her own bossiness. Often projecting one's denied negative quality is sufficient to reduce tension. But all too often the projection sets in motion a further sequence in the person doing the projecting; once the negative quality is attributed to another, there follows a quasi-judicial kind of sentencing of the other in his/her badness to such and such sanctions, punishment, banishment, and worse.

No black-and-white words and definitions can really capture the tremendous power of the projection mechanism as it regularly grips all of us

blindly and demonically. We seek to remove the tension or threat of expo-
sure of our hidden negative qualities by attributing that same quality to
another person or to an entire race or nation. It staggers the imagination
just how much bloodshed in this world is accounted for by this mechanism.
Wherever one people has set out to rid the world of another in stark genocidal extermination, it is this mechanism of projection that has been a central, satanic driving force (Charny, 1982).

There are powerful natural processes underlying the projection strategy
of thinking. Much of what we seek to project has its origin in negative attitudes towards us by parents which we incorporate within our own images
of ourselves and then want to get out of our insides. Different types of psychotherapy have provided helpful ways of thinking about these internalized
ideas. In psychoanalytic psychotherapy, we are privileged to witness truly
exciting moments when a person succeeds in "casting out" the "devils" of
such parental images and attitudes towards them as a bad person. Often,
these feelings constituted an alien, one might say "tumor-like" mass, which
blocked the ability to experience oneself as fully alive. In Transactional
Analysis (TA), these bad attitudes towards ourselves from the past are
defined as the "Parent" talking to us, and we try to learn how to be guided
more by our real "Adult" self than by this "Parent." So long as we do not
find a way to remove these bad attitudes towards ourselves, they remain
a dangerous alien force inside of us. Often, these are the attitudes we try
to project from ourselves on to others. Gestalt therapies have provided
important techniques for addressing these parts of oneself in order to bring
about change.

Few if any human beings are so emotionally strong as to escape using
projection to a considerable extent. James Russell Lowell has said: "Truth
is said to be at the bottom of a well, for the very reason, perhaps, that whoever looks down, in search of her sees his own image at the bottom."

The powerful projection mechanism plays a major role in marital problems as it creates a sequence of tensions between husband and wife. There
is much to be said for all of us being challenged by serious tensions and
even major crises to impel us to deal with our worst weaknesses. The natural clash of projections of husband and wife is guaranteed to face both
mates with what is lacking and problematic in each of them. *It can be much
more serious when there is no struggle over projections in the marriage and the mate
is seen as all-perfect.*

British psychiatrist Henry Dicks notes in his excellent study, *Marital
Tensions* (1967): "Idealization prevents the treatment of the partner as a safe,
real person, and thus hinders the continuation of growth into a full mutual
commitment because the 'other half' of the ambivalence is not offered for
reality testing—one is, oneself, acting a false part. The less secure the rela-

tionship, the more does it have to rely on various defensive devices—e.g., the absence of aggression, or even sexuality from it" (page 43).

It is all incredibly humorous, if you know how to enjoy "gallows humor" or appreciate existential absurdities. It is also, realistically, a prescription for tragic hurt and failure for those who end up trapped in marital despair by the complexity of such dynamics.

There is another intriguing and instructive similarity to the violences of larger groups—racial, ethnic, religious, and national. Even when a group is committed to the worst genocidal destruction of another people, in virtually all instances the destroyers defend their behaviors as *self-defense*. Much as we may not like to face it, in most cases the destroyers really believe their victims were out to destroy them. Sometimes, the threat is seen leveled at the symbolic survival of one's people, hence we must destroy the heathens who do not believe in our god. Other times it is a people's racial existence that is considered under attack—the other race or color will contaminate our genetic survival. Or the threat may be political and/or economic, hence the aristocrats must be wiped out or they will destroy our revolution for liberty. Often, the threat is experienced on the level of a physical danger— they will kill us unless we get them first—which is always a convincing basis for striking the first blow. In all these examples, the claim of self-defense is consciously sincere, but it is an unconscious protective device which conceals our own primitivity.

Family therapist pioneer, psychiatrist Don Jackson told an eerie old European tale of a detective posing as a lodger in a boarding house where a number of mysterious suicides had occurred (Jackson, 1972, p. 79). He notices across the courtyard from his window an old woman who is weaving. As he becomes entranced by her elaborate movements, he begins to mimic them. Then, with slow horror it becomes apparent to him that it is she who is following his movements, not he who is following hers. As the cause and effect become inextricably tangled, he throws himself out the window at the spinner.

Jackson (1969) gave several clinical examples of the balancing mechanism within a marriage and how the symptoms of one spouse may convey not only that spouse's problem but also the potential or latent disturbance of the other:

1. A young woman undergoing psychotherapy for recurrent depressions began to manifest increased self-assurance. Her husband, who initially was eager that she become less of a burden to him, called the psychiatrist rather frequently and generally alluded to her "worsening" condition. The therapist had not made an appraisal of the husband; when the extent of the husband's alarm became clear, he had become too antag-

onistic to enter therapy. He became more and more uneasy, finally calling the therapist one evening, fearful that his wife would commit suicide. The next morning he shot himself to death.

2. A husband urged his wife to enter psychotherapy because of her frigidity. After several months of therapy, she felt less sexually inhibited, whereupon the husband became impotent.

3. A young woman with anorexia nervosa was persuaded by her husband to enter psychotherapy. Following a period of intense, rather dangerous acting out, she began to relate more intimately to her husband. The husband's initial pleasure was marred by his developing a duodenal ulcer.

It is unfortunately very common to hear people saying that they tried everything they could to save their marriage, but it didn't work because the other spouse was so unreachable. We now know enough to question whether, optimally, the divorcing party ever met up with the part of his/her own self that was in the spouse.

The "simplest" way to find the painful truth about oneself before leaving a marriage is to really listen to one's spouse. Amidst all the garbage, abuse, and unfairness of an overly-angry, even persecuting, spouse, there generally lies much of the truth. One must discipline oneself to concentrate on extracting this inner truth from the spouse's angry messages rather than to get caught up in the outer barrage of insults and incitements to rage. Givon (1974) writes: "The ability to listen to one another, in other words to be in conscious contact, indicates a strengthening of the ego through the weakening of dependence on unconscious factors. On an unconscious level, when one person listens to the other he also comes face to face with that suppressed part of himself that has been projected on the other" (pp. 8–9).

Sometimes when one succeeds in seeing oneself in the unbelievable mirror that is the spouse at his/her unbearable worst, something very poignant can take root that is a compound of humility and sympathy, both for one's difficult mate and for oneself.

> "Here I've been angry at a quality in you which is in me! I've never been able to lick mine, but I wanted you to lick yours. For the first time, I think I understand how you have been trapped. I think now that I may be able to help you move out of your trap because I've gotten a sense of my problem which I intend to overcome."

In any case, even in marriages which have broken down and cannot be restored, it is wise to encounter the parts of oneself that have been represented in one's mate.

SEEING YOURSELF IN YOUR "SPOUSE MIRROR"

Mirror, mirror on the wall,
Who is the meanest and ugliest of them all?
No doubt at all, your unbearable spouse,
But mark well, you too live in the same house!

At its core, the marital process is stunning in its complexity, despite the fact that many of us chose marriage believing that it was largely a "simple" matter of marrying a lovely other person with whom we would share major interests along with a deep attraction to one another.

Most of us seem to share with our spouse a basically similar inner level of emotional strength and weakness, but we seem to reach our similar "sum total" by different routes. In the existential/dialectical theory we describe, we posit that some of our spouse's strengths are generally where we ourselves are at our weakest. We are, therefore, naturally envious. Similarly, some of our strengths complement our mate's weakest areas of behavior; now it is his/her turn to be envious. To top it all off, hidden within our very key strengths there generally lurk very opposite inner qualities and hidden within our worst weaknesses there lie untapped potential talents and sensitivities. The same is true of our mate. Each one's manifest strengths and weaknesses are also reminders of the other's hidden weaknesses and untapped potentials.

The resulting interplays are little short of fascinating, and too often bewildering.

Example A

HE: I've always been an intellectual playboy. I know I'm smart, but I've never really gotten myself down to work. You're just marvelous. The way you do your course papers at the university is great. I just wish I had the same skill.

SHE: His compliment is like my getting another A in school, and I get plenty of them. Nobody seems to respond to my real inner feelings that I am so obsessed with getting A's that I don't really enjoy my success. What bothers me most is that a lot of the time, I don't really feel like I'm learning. Once in a while, I do get a glimpse of what learning really is, and how different it is from competing for grades. I wonder if I'll ever really get to be a genuine learner.

The unconscious marital process. He is bright but he has rebelled against using his brightness in protest against being expected to perform for others. Since he never licked the real underlying problem of feeling obligated to perform for others, he has made himself look like a "Who-Cares Playboy," but part of him really would like to be a more serious student. Predictably, he will get jealously angry of her ability to learn, but once he also realizes how shallow she is, he will get more upset and critical because she has the same weakness he fights off in himself, namely the belief that one has to work for others. She, in turn, can be expected to get furious at him for his apparent shallowness and indifference to it all. In part, she secretly admires him because at least he isn't doing the performing for others that she hates in herself, but at the same time she is angry at his superficiality, which is just like hers despite her outer effectiveness. Good enough material for at least a few fights.

Example B

HE: complains bitterly that he can't touch her. She's a cold fish. She throws him off whenever he wants to be affectionate or sexual. Sometimes they get to the sex, but even then there are all sorts of touchings that he is not allowed. He is really furious. He threatens that he wants out.
SHE: doesn't trust him. Oh, he says he wants to be affectionate and is eager for wine and song and nice feelings for one another. But then it feels to her that he's insisting that she perform for him. She's also furious at how much of the time he's never around. He's so involved in his business that you'd think that was his whole world. When he is home, he often makes a few ceremonial advances, and then retreats into anger at her for being so untouchable.

The unconscious marital process. Each is afraid to ask to be loved. He looks the better of the two, but the truth is he is delighted that she is unavailable. He blames it all on her, but he too really is unavailable. He hides in his work. If and when she allows herself to be somewhat available, he takes her as if "it" is due him, but not as an expression and opportunity for loving. She hates him because he doesn't help her release her blocked loving. He hates her for being an iceberg, without seeing that he exploits her fears of loving and closeness to cover his own. It is a rich script for intense marital problems and an especially easy one to read the wrong way by defining the wife's obvious frozenness as the issue rather than the shared problem that both are afraid to ask for love.

Example C

SHE: loves the children very much. She is a devoted mother who is almost always cheerful with the children. She shows an interest in each of them and encourages each child to do his best. Strangely, though, the children don't do that well. They have all sorts of troubles. One of them is very ornery and negative. Another is a sweet pussycat, but seems to need too much attention and reassurance; he stays home a lot and doesn't do well with friends. The children have had many allergies. Another child is on the edge of a relatively serious eating disorder.

HE: hates the way she babies the children and keeps them under her apron. Also how under the guise of encouraging the children, she seems to be telling them what to do over and over again. He is a hit-and-run father of sorts. When he is good, he is very good, but when he is bad, he is very bad. He likes the children, but doesn't seem to love them in a sustained way; at least, he can never hang in there for too long. He is always finding something else to do to get away. If he does hang in there, it takes about 20 minutes at most before there is a fight between him and one of the children or maybe with the whole bunch together as he rants and raves and yells his "Do this" and "Don't do that" pronouncements. She is furious at his seeming not to care for the children, and furious at his storm trooper ways.

The unconscious marital process. On the surface, one spouse looks like a good parent and the other like a very poor parent. The truth is that both want to be good—they both care for the children, but both have a bad defect: Each believes that children are supposed to function for grownups more than for themselves. She does it by a superb "con job." She inveigles her way into the children by charming them and telling them to eat for her, do their homework for her, be nice for her, and all the rest. He does it by blowing up in a demandingness that screams his exasperation that the children aren't being great kids for him. Since he can't stand his own pushiness any more than the children can, his best defense is then to lose interest in the children and get away from them. He has never tried to help his wife with how much she tries to live off the children, and she has never really tried to help him with his styles of brutalization and abandonment. Both parents have the same underlying hang-up, which they hate in each other.

Our spouse often is a looking glass in which we are privileged to see the worst in ourselves marvelously disguised in an outer form that is opposite to our style, so we can pretend not to recognize ourselves. We rail, rant, scream, and protest the more because it is the hidden quality of ourselves within the other that we despise so much. We also wish our spouse could cure us of our weakness, and we are furious when that doesn't happen.

It really stunned me when I came to the realization that I have never seen a single aggrieved spouse who has not sincerely felt victimized by the aggression and destructiveness of the mate. It is an amusing, even poignant, conclusion to reach. It is even more deeply instructive to realize that every spouse experiences his/her own hate and angry acts as arising entirely in response to the Other's attack and, thus, essentially justified as self-defense.

MARRIAGE AS EFFECTIVE "THERAPY"

The most real "marital therapy" takes place in marriage itself. Most often, unfortunately, the therapy fails, but in those cases where it is successful, the results are impressive.

If and when a marriage as a process works well, the marital experience is one of the best therapies in the world because, in the context of a secure and loving home, each mate is privy to a continuous, authentic encounter with his/her most mature and positive qualities as well as with the most immature and negative qualities. In a genuinely successful marriage, just as in effective marital therapy with a professional, there is continuous feedback from one's mate. The feedback is at once respectful and critical, rendered in love and acceptance, yet unafraid to penetrate and hurt with truth. In the context of a relaxed and safe emotional home, the marital process offers repeated opportunities for each partner to see how his/her personality style and actions are impacting on and shaping the marital and family environment, mood, and development.

The basic contexts of the "therapy" in providing a comforting and secure home are celebrated in lay observations and in folklore through the centuries. For the male, to marry is to settle down, to have a wife who will take care of him, to enjoy pride in his marriage and then in his family, and pleasure and confirmation of his value and worthwhileness through all that he succeeds in bringing home and providing for his wife and children. For the female, traditionally, marriage is an end to the possible dangers of never being chosen to be a wife, the safety of being provided for by a protector-husband and head of the family, an opportunity to be confirmed in her attractiveness, to become a child-bearer, and to prove her capability as a homemaker and her womanly wisdom as her husband and children thrive in her nurturing presence. Even when we redefine these classical metaphors in modern representations of man and woman choosing one another and being chosen more equally, and giving and receiving in the relationship far more as peers, the basic promise remains that marriage, to both sexes, is an opportunity to take care of and be taken care of lovingly. One is protected and confirmed in one's essential talents and worthwhileness. Can one ever ask for more from any therapy with a professional?

Notwithstanding the intense battering that the marital institution has sustained in recent decades from the evident facts that, in all Western societies, the majority of marriages fail bitterly, no ethnic or other collective folklore has ceased to attribute to marriage a wonderful potential for healing, stabilizing, and freeing mates to new security and growth. Although it is now known that most people do not achieve this potential, and there are huge numbers of people who are understandably genuinely afraid to marry because of the obvious possibilities of misery as well as painful consequences of separation and divorce, the mystique of hope and promise that marriage may be the most wondrous experience of one's life still prevails for most people.

If we accept as an existential premise that *every* man and woman will bring to marriage an enactment of his/her ongoing process as it pulls between attractive, capable qualities and various weaknesses of poor character and unattractiveness, the intensely intimate contact between any two mates will necessarily thrust on each a confrontation-invitation to see themselves as they really are and to work at new growth. What more can one ask of any therapy with a professional?

Regrettably, most married people are "resistant" to the possible "therapy" of their marital experience. Most couples try to transform their marriages into some kind of a certainty of a conventional style of expected roles and obligations performed as required in their particular culture. They then become disappointed and resentful, if not actually bitter, at their mate's failure to perform as expected. In effect, most people seek to suppress and banish the *natural therapeutic process* that is inherent in the drama of marriage by turning marriage into a scripted play that is to be performed over and over again.

Those who, for whatever reason, are blessed with the intuition and talent to create their marriage as an authentic growth process are, first and foremost, *real friends*. They like, respect, and appreciate each other, and are delighted to rely on one another as partners, playmates, and trustworthy confidants. They come to value and rely on one another as someone who can be counted on in a crisis and be reliably present in everyday life to process their experiences with one another.

Robert and Jeanette Lauer (1986) studied 351 couples who had been married a minimum of 15 years, 300 of whom indicated that both spouses were happy with their marriages. They wanted to know how these couples explained their success and what factors they regarded as most important in their experience. People explained their long-term satisfying marriages mainly in terms of four key aspects:

> Having a spouse who is one's best friend and whom one likes as a person; commitment to marriage and to the spouse; consensus on fundamentals; and shared humor. (p. 183)

As noted earlier, many years ago Grotjahn (1960) promoted the concept that the marital arena is the single most powerful transference stage for adults, surpassing the power of the vaunted transference state that is cultivated in a successful psychoanalysis. What he meant was that in the marital interaction each spouse necessarily projected onto the other his/her own unfinished business of emotional neediness, upset, and rage brought from childhood homes. Thus, the helpful and maturing corrective experiences of a good marriage could help each grow out of the neurotic childhood pattern. Meanwhile, in the clinical practice of psychoanalysis over the years, cumulative experience led to the conclusion that the all-important transference state could be induced in a treatable form only in a minority of patients (Chessick, 1971; Wolman, 1972). In comparison, in marriage the induction of the "transference state" follows intrinsically from the couple joining together in marriage, but the "trick" then is to "treat" the condition successfully through a wholesome marital process. Obviously, this is not easy.

The "transference" in marriage is no picnic. All too soon, even genuinely happy, loving couples find out that a special "transferential hell" also awaits them in marriage. Even reasonable exercise of goodwill will not be enough to hold back the grim shadows of ancient issues breaking out from behind the "masks" of the genuine maturity and integrity both mates attempt to live by.

Her father had walked out on her mother and, of course, on her, too, when she was a little girl. The years that followed were an agony of trying to comfort an inconsolable, childish mother. She grew up a "psychological orphan" who brought herself up. Like many children who are prematurely charged with responsibility, she tried with all her heart to be a very good girl, with no exceptions and no compromises with sadness or mediocrity.

Now a charming young adult woman, she marries a young man who is her counterpart as a self-made man, outstandingly successful as a student and young professional. The marriage is a dream marriage, including their wonderful sexual/loving passion for one another. They consider themselves so lucky—theirs is the best marriage they know. Moreover, in marrying and setting up a home and then having a baby, each experiences a surge of new kinds of pride about no longer being a child and especially about "finally having a home."

Yet before four years have passed, their marriage is in a shambles. He is out of the home at her request after she discovers that he is having an affair—one in which he is very much in love with his girlfriend. From her point of view, he had left her. It sounded so familiar deep down in her and almost as if she had always known she wouldn't be able to have her own stable family. She responded with all the force of virtue and absoluteness that she knew how to muster when faced with an emergency. Even when he wanted to convey that he had given up the girlfriend and was genuinely remorseful over the serious mistake he had made, she wouldn't agree to hear him out. Wrong is wrong and right is right—the forever-orphan in her knew only how to think in clear-cut terms and to make absolute decisions.

It is inevitable: Each mate "discovers" in the partner the familiar traces and replays of whatever kind of threats to which they were most vulnerable in childhood. If the behaviors aren't really there, the mate nonetheless seizes on those strands of statements and actions that can somehow be connected with his/her own historical nemesis, and mentally blows these up bigger and bigger until they are truly familiar photographs of the past. Through the powerful mechanisms of projective identification, mates seduce and draw one another to act and respond in the very ways they fear, but unconsciously want to happen again (Cashdan, 1988). With worse luck, some of the same qualities of personality and character actually are prominent in one's chosen partner, for after all one of the fascinating pieces in the puzzle of marital selection is how often people pick as their lifelong partners *either* reincarnations of their original nemeses, *or* their exact opposites—which, in dialectical terms, also leads you back to the same starting point.

Worse yet, so many of the original nemeses come dressed in happy and good-looking clothing: Mother, who was overprotective and invasive of her child's personality, was a lively, loving personality. The damage she did by not giving her child room to breathe could hardly be seen for what it was, so how in the world can one fault that child's choice as a young adult to marry a so-loving and charming mate who, of course, turns out to be invasive, controlling, and dictatorial to the point of abusiveness? "I never bargained for such a mean person," says the again-wounded mate as the marriage is revealed in its grotesque nightmarish replay of childhood, but of course the truth is that somewhere inside there is a part that knew very well that one was selecting a mate who would repeat the trauma of the past.

What Grotjahn and Cashdan have speculated is that such unerring repetitions of the past are basically *intelligent* efforts to create the conditions for completion of the unfinished growing up in damaged or undeveloped areas of one's personality where there is work to be done. It is potentially a very sound idea to call back the skeletons, ghosts, and limitations of one's spirit and development through the person of somebody whom one also appreciates, respects and loves. However, as noted earlier, the problem too often is that the couple as a team do not qualify as sufficiently knowledgeable and mature "therapists" who can guide the natural healing process past the Scylla and Charybdis that can sink their marital ships.

Many students of marriage have described the disappointments and trag-

edies of how couples trigger the worst in each other by getting lost in a spi-
raling, escalating process where each hurt, insult, and failure triggers further legitimate acts of "self-defense" by the aggrieved mate, which in turn
constitute more confirmations for the first mate of the abuse and injustice
he/she is convinced exist.

It is a remarkable idea that, basically, couples head into creating these
troubles not simply because they are sick or immature, but because they
are attempting to exercise *a natural wisdom* of bringing up the areas in their
development that most need attention in the hopes that their chosen partner
and their marital partnership will help them.

When marriage counselors propose to couples that they should think
good thoughts, do good things, hold their tongues, compromise liberally,
express caring and loving feelings and never be immature, unknowingly
they may be giving advice to couples that they should not attempt to do
their own "marital therapy." If couples do avoid their therapy, they will be
spared the painful escalating tensions just described, but the odds are that
they will have another kind of serious problem in their marriage—feelings
of boredom, lack of passion, mistrust of the authenticity of their mate, and,
as they move into middle-age, greater fears of deterioration in both their
personal and marital vitality.

Creative couples generate a fascinating dialogue and theater in which the
puzzle and mystery of becoming much more of a person than either was
earlier are played out. Couples who are able to be their own effective "therapists" are blessed. They really are friends with one another so that even
the powerful dynamics that various aspects of the marital experience set
off do not shake or change this basic fact. Their commitment, loyalty to one
another, liking and appreciation, and wanting a good life for one another
are not coerced by pious or other well-meaning but ingenuous resolutions,
nor are they conditional even in the face of the natural passions and strange
emotions that are inevitably set off in the "treatment."

Successful "therapists" possess an intuitive skill and wisdom for
assigning troubled emotions and experiences such as jealousy and anger
to a zone of personal ambivalent feelings, which they bear as part of the
human experience without being rattled in their basic love and caring. They
also realize that they must submit distressing emotions and issues to a genuine dialogue with one another. In the process of dialoguing, these couples
discover still another experience of authenticity and intimacy which brings
them closer together.

Successful "marital therapists" are not afraid of losing one another and,
therefore, can take risks in their dialogue and in the depths of their emotional experience. Whether the lack of fear of losing one another derives
from the good luck of a basic emotional security prior to marriage or is a

tribute to the sound friendship and loyalty that have been created in the marriage, the "marital therapy" is not hampered, consciously or unconsciously, by a fear of addressing difficult issues and painful truths. These couples persevere over the long haul in approaching issues which are not easily or immediately amenable to treatment, including longstanding secrets and defects in each one's personality and character. Guided by love, respect, and courage, these "marital therapists" believe in the necessity as well as possibility of their mates' changing. Like all good therapists, they know that redefinition and real change of a major system is a process that is not arrived at in a single illumination or hysterical experience, but grows out of a sequence of encounters with a difficult side of oneself. They are patient and tactful and leave enough time between "sessions" even as they stay rooted on the long-range target.

Do Creative Couples Challenge "Untouchable Issues"?

One of the important tenets of popular marital folklore is that one should not marry a person in order to try to change him/her. How, if at all, can one reconcile this adage with the basic thrust of this presentation of "marital therapy" by a couple themselves where there certainly is serious work going on to encourage and even demand major changes in one's spouse?

The popular advice not to try to change one's mate seems to me true in all those situations where one falls in love with a person whose basic lifestyle is very deviant or seriously problematic, such as an alcoholic or convict, many-times married person, an obviously cold and rejecting personality, and so on. The undertaking of "therapy" of such a mate is a Don Quixote-like mission that is self-deluding. Marriage and the intention to change such a partner often disguise a hidden need in the would-be rescuer to be on the receiving end of the "punishment" that most certainly will be meted out to him/her. The kind of mutual help we are talking about here as a natural "marital therapy" does not involve an effort to rescue the other from major pathology or a pattern of chronic failure.

Even so, many individuals who love and respect one another also discover before long that the spouse's life-script harbors a not-nice secret and/or a certain kind of depressive or tragic possibility for which he/she is not asking any help, and the question is whether the "marital therapist"—each mate—should be so intrepid and so ambitious as to undertake to penetrate these zones in which the mate does not ask for help, and often is dead set on refusing help.

In a sense, every person has a core of personal and/or moral weakness and limitation which he/she doesn't intend to touch, if only on the basis of not being able to conceive that this part could ever be changed. This core weakness becomes so familiar to a person that it feels like an inextricable part of his/her identity and organization; in addition, many of the weaknesses and problems people harbor also produce huge payoffs of certain pleasures, which they don't want to give up.

The natural therapy of fortunate couples who transform their lives into an optimistic process of continuous growth requires each mate to challenge the other not only when there is an issue of being personally offended or victimized, but also when one sees and feels one's spouse surrendering to or locking into a character weakness.

The motivation for these challenges on one level is one's love for one's dearest friend, hence a spontaneous desire and hope that one's friend can grow and become stronger. On another level, the motivation derives from a kind of natural esthetic responses to the mate's attitudes and behavior, which are experienced as basically unappealing and unattractive. Because the couple are authentic with one another, the mate who has this reaction says so. On a third level, the power for the critical confronting response also comes from the mate's feeling that his/her interests will be neglected or damaged so long as this aspect of the spouse's personality prevails.

The mate's challenge of a deeply-held aspect of personality obviously will be met with anxiety and resistance, for that is the nature of human beings when we are confronted about habitual aspects of our personality. However, with relatively wholesome couples, the resistances will not be expressed so adamantly, nor will they become a basis for retaliatory insults, projections, and character attacks. The door is left open for repeated observations and interactions around those recurring weaknesses, and a lovely "dance" develops between the couple where each becomes aware that there is an opportunity to become so much healthier and stronger a person if one submits oneself to the process of challenge and feedback that is available from one's spouse.

What is so lovely in this dance is that both husband and wife lead and are led. It is, like other aspects of a basically egalitarian relationship and like the most beautiful lovemaking, a sharing of leadership and yielding, an enjoyment of helping one another and in turn being taught and helped, where both mates play both roles alternately and reciprocally.

However, "marital therapy" is no more a totally romantic or blessedly enriching experience than any other serious psychotherapy. There are peaks of despair and crisis, resistances, and escapes from the issues, all of which have to be negotiated and survived in good humor, especially when one spouse has to draw the line about the other's weakness because it is affecting their security beyond a point that they can tolerate. After sufficient periods of "therapy," creative long-term couples learn to trust the process and enjoy it—much as individuals who learn not to be afraid of being anxious as a signal of unfolding growth in them.

If one records only the words that a couple say to one another, it will often be impossible to differentiate those who are succeeding in creating a genuine dialogue that includes strong criticism and confrontation within a context of basic love and positive intentions from those who are telling each other off and, under the guise of mental health values of growth and authenticity, are carrying on a war to establish superiority over the other. When a couple are wholesome, there is a gentleness in even the toughest marital communications; there is a sensitive gauging of one's mate's ability to hear and tolerate the tension of confrontation at the time and a readiness to let go and wait for a better time and place to continue the process; there are subtle reminders of one's abiding respect and love; real pain is felt for the spouse at their most difficult moments and is conveyed poignantly, though without abandoning the basic position of criticism; if revenge and nastiness well up, they are quickly put aside as not befitting the intrinsic quality of the relationship; the prevailing message is one of expectation of growth in one's partner so that life can be enjoyed even more.

Unfortunately, even though most couples do not intend to be bad to one another, we know that the majority run out of energy, will, and spirit to process aspects of their own and one another's personalities authentically. Prevailing cultural conceptions that marriages should be based on compromise, graciousness, and constructivity do not help, of course, but the problem goes beyond cultural input. Many people sense well enough in their hearts that there is great power in straightforwardness and speaking genuinely, but they still walk away from authentic engagement of their spouse. Their comments and associations often point in the direction of fears of being left alone. They are afraid to lose their mate if they "stir up too much trouble," so they take the course of "courtesy" and denial of their real feelings. Others are afraid to undertake a process that could involve grave hurt and disappointment to the other until growth is achieved. How many people are willing to tell an overly fat person that he/she is fat, let alone unattractive, or grotesque? Thus do most "marital therapies" performed by couples themselves fail, and thus do most marriages succumb at best to mediocrity and dull routineness.

THE NATURAL INTERGENERATIONAL THERAPY OF SPOUSES BY ONE ANOTHER

An intriguing and especially complex aspect of real authenticity between couples is that sooner or later each spouse will be doing battle with the continuation in the mate of the worst traits of the mate's parents. This seems to be another one of those phenomena that we have sensed subliminally, but have not identified.

Couples naturally come to understand how their spouses are continuing in various ways some of the worst traits of their parents, especially those traits they may have been most concerned about when they once vowed "never to be like them." What a spouse does with this crucial information is most important: To accuse and humiliate one's mate with the comparison is obviously abusive; on the other hand, never to share this information with one's mate is to deny a vital piece of feedback.

Many disturbed couples often have very destructive fights built around "you're just like your mother or father" themes. The obvious implication of such scenes would seem to be that couples should refrain from such invidious comparisons with one's spouse's parents. Powerful information should not be used for undisciplined spouse warfare. Understanding the unhappy similarity of one's mate to the defects of a parent, including the very traits he/she vowed consciously never to adopt, is very powerful medicine indeed, which should be administered thoughtfully and appropriately.

Some people undertake a self-therapy of reversing "totally" an especially undesirable aspect of a parent's personality, but then the radical escape from everything that is reminiscent of the parent may lead to a dialectical extreme that in itself unconsciously forces them back towards the hidden opposite they are fleeing and which lurks behind their new extreme (the hate that is in too much love or the jealousy that is in too much generosity). To deny any continuation of the familiar parental trait in oneself has to be a lie which relegates that aspect of one's personality to the shadows of concealment from where it will operate as a true saboteur. The man who was brutalized by an overwhelmingly tyrannical father and who has sworn that he will be a loving, non-authoritarian companion to his sons can be totally unaware that in the egalitarian, respectful style he has adopted with his children he can be hiding ruthless demands for loyalty to and appreciation of himself. The woman who was humiliated and spurned by her bitter mother may not recognize in the selfless charm she shows toward her husband the powerful retaliatory hatred she releases if he does not respond to her in the way she wants.

Like it or not, there have to come points where each one of us lives out aspects of a style of being annoying, hurting, and obnoxious to our mate that we learned only too well from our parent(s). There then develops a most important choice on the part of our spouse: whether on the one hand to let us continue our behavior as if it weren't noticed, accept the bad behavior in the name of goodness or marital peace, and simply surrender to it weakly, or on the other hand to express dislike of the behavior, criticize the spouse for it, block use of the behavior, threaten to impose sanctions against its continuation, or respond in other conflict-producing ways.

Each such decision is an important moment in the life of a couple. These are test moments of the authenticity of the marriage relationship. An overt peace of sorts may be gained by accommodating or surrendering to one's mate, but a larger price is being paid that includes the inner realization of both parties that they do not tackle issues honestly and cannot rely on one another to deal with complicated, troubling matters. What is at stake is whether or not one is going to get the kind of genuine feedback which is necessary for one's further personality growth and to complete a further stage of separating from one's parent(s) and family of origin.

The confrontation of the annoying and hurtful parent-continuing style cannot be simply criticism or challenge of one's mate, but in effect *becomes a kind of showdown with the parent(s) of that mate*. And one must always remember the rule that deep down, inside all of us, there are invisible emotional loyalties even to one's most hated parent(s) and a resentment of anyone who dares to say bad things about *my* mother or father (Boszormenyi-Nagy & Spark, 1973; see also Framo's works referred to earlier). Thus, the moment of choice as to whether to clarify and confront one's spouse's parent-continuing style is a test of courage to stand up both to our spouse and, in a way, to his/her parent(s)—a combination of people already outnumbering us.

I have become more and more convinced that this process is a little-known drama on behalf of both the mental health of one's spouse and the genuineness of one's marriage. Couples who do not risk the process but play it safe by allowing the parent-continuing behaviors may save the peace but lose an essence of personal and marital growth. Couples who confront the issues badly, by responding in too-powerful outrage at the injustices and unfairnesses done them, who are insulting, bitter, and vengeful, create nightmares of hatred and divorce. On the other hand, couples who engage one another firmly but respectfully and convey that their power is committed both to helping each other to be stronger and happier and to making their marriage together better are likely to build mutual respect and appreciation, while they enhance their marriage.

Case Example

> He was a lovely guy, generous, sincere, and loving of her, but he had a terrible, lifelong habit of not following through on his promises. Whether in big matters of money, trips, or arrangements, or in hundreds of small matters of the fabric of life together, he was always "forgetting" to complete an expected and even promised behavior.

In this way, he was the image of his mother who had managed to keep him constantly distraught as a child. How many promises there had been which turned into frustrating teases! She seemed to be entirely devoted to him, yet there were so many discrepancies in her behavior that he was thoroughly confused and upset.

His wife had tried many times to bring up this issue of his disappointing her and, many times when he failed to complete a task or promise to her, she responded with appropriate insistence that he stand behind his word. He would then get things done, but somehow nothing seemed to make a dent in the underlying pattern which he kept repeating again and again. Although she tried to hold him to his responsibilities, she somehow never went all the way. She didn't get powerfully and decisively angry, nor did she face him with how similar he was to his own mother.

Slowly but surely, the position he held in the invisible politics of the marriage and the family became that of a lesser person, a seemingly attractive and respected husband and father, but one who was really disliked and belittled for his inability to be a man of his word. In the secret truths of the messages that are passed between the hearts of people in families, he became more and more an object of anger and disdain. For all that the marriage looked good, they both looked increasingly tired and distraught.

Although neither of them had any conscious idea of the connections between his behavior at home and in his work life, there, too, there were repeated instances of people becoming angry at him. Despite his evident talents and much work success, the advancement that he sought in his work was denied him because he disappointed people in many small ways of being late in completing jobs, failing to return calls and letters, and so on. His basic problem remained unresolved both at home and at work.

Case Example

He remembered the moment well—both the moment of the decision in him to tell her "as it is" what was going on and then a kind of thud that he felt as he sensed that his remarks had penetrated and she had opened herself to taking them in.

The fight had been triggered when they were riding in a cab together. She suggested that they get off at an earlier destination than they had originally ordered the driver to reach; he agreed and told the driver to stop. Then, after the driver had clicked off the meter, she began to ruminate questioningly whether or not to proceed to their original destination after all. At that he snapped at her angrily. They left the cab and began to argue about the scene, she feeling insulted at his critical attitude and tying it to his perfectionism and superiority—traits she couldn't stand in him, while he was angry at her last-minute indecisiveness and lack of consideration for the confusion she created for others.

He knew she was right when she spoke of his making himself superior to her and to others, being impatient with errors and imperfection. He also knew she was right when she reminded him that he was similar in these respects to the father he had hated for just these qualities. He was aware how grateful he was to her for pointing out these qualities at other times and how he sensed that he was improving slowly but surely. With regard to the immediate fight, he told himself that although his anger under the circumstances was natural, the issue of her confusion-making was not only annoying to him but an important issue for her development. He told her that he knew only too well that her mother had driven her crazy with a constant changing of her mind as if it were her royal right to order whatever she would imperiously want. He told her he knew it had been difficult for her as a little girl to keep her own mind and think and study for school.

They were lying in bed hours later getting ready to go to sleep, all the more aware of the rumbling anger that still persisted between them. She had fought back against his insistence that she was repeating her mother's confusion-making. Now in bed she reviewed her anger at him. She was adamant that she disliked his manner when he became angry and she found him basically displeasing and unappealing when he erupted at her. There was an edge of threat in her voice that implied that if he were not careful he could lose his place as her beloved. This was a bad moment for him, but it was then that he felt an inner resolution that he had to stand up to her threat. He said to her that he was very hurt by her translating her anger at him into a basic dislike of him, and also angry at her threat of leaving him, but no matter what, he would not allow her to upset his mind with confusion and would not agree to her belittling herself in this way. As he spoke, he sensed her yielding to him with appreciation and respect. They lay beside each other silently for a while, and then she reached out and sought his waiting hands.

Couples who are willing to take the risk of unbalancing one another and the stability of their marriage for purposes of helping one another to grow are undertaking a painful and hazardous journey. But it often proves the road to a creative and more deeply enjoyable marriage.

4

What Is a Successful Marriage?

Alternative Models by Which to Marry and Be Tested

What in the world do we wish for modern couples once we know that it is relatively unlikely that they will live "happily ever after" in marriage?

The existential/dialectical view tells us in advance that every couple will suffer many disappointments and encounters with their incompleteness, find themselves unable to handle a variety of situations, and encounter problems also in some of the very areas in which they actually will function best but in which they will fall prey to hubris and overdoing. Under these circumstances, how can one believe that marriage is worthwhile? Contemporary cynics say that there is nothing worthwhile in marriage, that by its nature it is a corrupt institution, that couples are doomed to fail, and that those who pretend to succeed are, in fact, living stodgy lives of compliance and surrender to one another at the expense of each one's individuality and freedom. Alvarez (1983) has written ironically about successful marriages thus:

> We have reached the point where a good marriage seems as unusual, almost scandalous in some devious way, as a divorce did a generation or two ago. We wonder what the lucky couple are hiding or denying or missing out on, and what they are secretly doing about this aberration in their lives. Do they have religion? Lovers? Booze? Dope? Cancer? The possibility that they might enjoy each other's company, make each other laugh occasionally and be friends as well as lovers seems too remote to contemplate. Easier to assume that they are suffering from some obscure, undiagnosed sickness which has made them fatally dependent on each other. (p. 23)

54

From our existentialist/dialectical point of view, the idea of successful marriage is one which is characterized by the following:

1. Successful marriage is a *process* rather than a fixed state of achievement. A good deal of thoughtful effort is put into the process. The successful couple does not live in a guaranteed "happily-ever-after" state, but enjoys striving for improvement.
2. The successful couple deals authentically and constructively with their strengths and weaknesses; they
   a. help each other in areas of weakness;
   b. teach each other and help one another to learn how to improve in these respects;
   c. enjoy each other's strengths and achievements;
   d. offer honest, uncompromising, but respectful criticism;
   e. help each other to stretch and risk towards new, as yet undeveloped potential.
3. The successful couple are genuinely close friends—in fact, best friends who enjoy being with one another and sharing their lives. They appreciate one another as basically decent, reliable, and attractive people.
4. The successful marriage is a marriage of equals. Of course, each partner is very different from the other. In various functions one mate is clearly superior to the other, and in various ethnic traditions one of the two will be assigned greater importance in certain areas. But, overall and intrinsically, both spouses are basically equal to one another. They contribute to the marriage in equal value and give and take constructively to and from one another.
5. The successful marriage is vital and alive. Being together is experienced as interesting, stimulating, and enlivening—not as boring, tiring, or depleting.
6. Successful couples are not afraid of conflicts and even seek them. Conflicts become opportunities to speak with one another and to learn and develop both as individuals and as a couple.

I have purposely not said that a successful marriage is one in which the couple "love each other." Abraham Maslow, the founder of humanistic psychology, wrote in his journal (1981): "If I were to lecture on marriage, I'd stress at the very beginning tolerance, acceptance, and giving up the hope for justice and fairness and *quid pro quo*. I'd talk at length about individual differences, changeable and unchangeable, and our tendency to get irritated, offended, and threatened by these differences from ourselves. Then I'd stress compassion as a necessity—love is too difficult to expect (p.1154)."

Clinical experience tells us of any number of couples who do feel strong love for each other, but whose marriages then turn into failures.

> They loved each other very much. There was an air of excitement about them that was both sensual and loving. They shared beautifully their mutual world of art. However, he arranged it, with her agreement, that from the beginning he was Number One. She allowed her personality to blend with and support him faultlessly. Little did they know that their love, which was genuine, would deteriorate under the impact of his hubris and her self-abnegation. As their marriage deteriorated, all he knew was that she had ceased to excite him and that another woman, a new convert to the cult of his idolaters, did excite him. So it became time to change wives.

Enduring feelings of authenticity, friendship, equality, vitality, plus the ability to handle conflicts, prove more important to a successful marriage than the excitement of love as such. However, having said that, I add the hope that along with the above qualities there also be deep love—that wondrous excitement of man and woman for one another that is at once sexual and soulful, that can make life as a couple a jeweled delight.

MANAGING AND GROWING WITH CONFLICT

The "happy" qualities listed above won't raise any eyebrows, but not all readers will be familiar with the point of view that friction, irritability, disagreement, anger, and even eruptions of hurting and maddening one another are aspects of successful marriage (Charny, 1972b).

I think of the hope that a marriage be made and kept in a lifelong heaven as a suppressive model of marriage that demands that mates be loyal regardless of whether they really feel close and communicate with one another. The suppressive model is based on marriage fulfilling stable sociological roles of providing a home and a haven for the couple and their children as a family unit in a community, but it does not concern itself with the quality of the experiential process between the couple. It has to be acknowledged that being devoted and responsible family persons can make not only for stable marriages, but also for attractive and satisfied people, especially in traditional culture contexts. But I believe that overall, the "live-happily-ever-after" model tends to spawn a kind of tiredness, boredom, flattening of experience, and failure to grow intellectually and spiritually. It is a way of being in the world that denies a range of experiences of ambivalence, perplexity, anxiety, difficulties in coping, risk, challenge, and so on that I understand to be inevitable, and hence desirable, in all human experience, and therefore also in marriage.

An existential/dialectical conception of human beings leads us to expect in every one of us periodic bursts of ambivalences. I believe there is a symphonic mix of a broad range of emotions in our inner consciousness at all times. Except for peak trancelike moments of loving, such as in wonderful consummations of love/sex when ambivalences characteristically are pushed way to the background of a powerful anthem of total fusion with one's love object, there is in the human mind most of the time an inner stream of discomforting feelings of difference, tension, not-the-same-as-me-ness, and periodic bad thoughts and bad wishes.

A scientifically sound picture of marriage needs to be firmly based on the knowledge that all human beings, knowingly or unknowingly, experience deep anxiety as a constant refrain in life. Mature as we may be, still our anxiety leads us to nervous, irritable, contentious, and blaming responses to our intimates. The fact that these unfair and ugly responses on our part draw responsive criticism and anger at us is good, for otherwise we would be cut off from the feedback which we all need to help us correct difficult and unfair parts of ourselves.

There are also other reasons why conflict between couples is inevitable and natural. People vary in their needs. For all that a couple love each other deeply, at any given moment our respective needs to be close will vary, our needs to communicate intimately with one another will not be in "synch," and our interests, motivations and activity needs will vary and even conflict.

Normal couples need to process their tensions, beginning with their intrapsychic experiences of differences and the ultimate fact that no two people can fuse and become one. Then there are differences in their phasing and cycling of various emotions and needs and the unfolding of different priorities and imperatives in the life of each person. A married couple who love and respect one another will experience tension about these issues, but will transform their tension into signals for negotiating, clarifying, helping one another with each other's priorities, and finding joint solutions. In the process they will enjoy a whole new series of pleasures at being able to resolve conflict together, thus adding still another basis for satisfaction, love, and pride in the quality of the marriage.

It is a privilege to be able to work out differences and conflicts in an atmosphere of basic respect and commitment. Successful couples often report that they particularly appreciate that they can count on one another to be fair and not vindictive, nasty, or power-seeking when it comes to fights. Still, the fights of successful couples *are* upsetting. They are not happy occasions as they are portrayed either in wholesome families on television or in over-intellectualized psychology texts where the references to talking out problems constructively often imply that there will be no pain if one goes about talking in the correct way. A spectre of possible loss descends on the healthiest couples when they have their fights. There is a terrible feeling of fear that the wondrous feeling of being in love is gone and that this is what the future holds. However, for successful couples, these bad moments also become springboards for again seeking out one another and for efforts to understand each other's needs and emotions in order to find a common ground that will be satisfying to both. Over a long period of time, the positive experience that even big fights bring a couple together become a basis for still deeper pride, security, and increased caring for one another. It is a remarkable achievement, after all, to be able to turn warring swords into peaceful ploughshares.

Fights

Marital therapist Daniel Wile (1979, 1981, 1988) recommends that couples be helped in therapy to develop an ability to talk together about their troubled interactions. He clearly supports the value of arguments rather than attempts to suppress them, but the crucial point in his judgment is that the couple learn to have arguments which *make sense*. Wile prefers straight talk to any kind of "reframing" or stretching of truth to make problems reappear in a positive light.

Wile also wants to help couples become "expert" in observing their basic styles of interaction, such as a demanding-withdrawing dance where one mate characteristically is the one who demands responsiveness or closeness and the other is the one who flees into silence, distance, and unresponsiveness which irritates the first even more. Just as in psychoanalysis we learned about the very important capacity of people to develop an "observing ego," or an ability to stand by to see and monitor themselves even in the course of highly emotional behaviors, Wile seeks to help couples in therapy develop a "relationship ego" or "observing-couple ego."

Couples who achieve their "successful marriages" by neutralizing and removing irritability, conflict, and pain miss out on deeper revalidations of each other's fairness and reliability. In addition, family therapy has shown us that couples who are *conflict-avoidant* become—depending on the degree to which they force themselves to be totally in line with one another—prone to dangerous degrees of *unseparatedness, enmeshment,* and *pseudomutuality.* We know today that these styles of relationship frequently lead to a variety of disturbances, many of them quite serious. Thus, marriages without conflict are frequently a context in which children go on to suffer serious learning disturbances, failure to thrive emotionally, and even psychotic conditions (Wynne, et al., 1958; Dicks, 1967, Minuchin, 1974).

Adults in such situations frequently go on to suffer psychosomatic diseases that betray the bottling up of emotions for which they have no other outlets because they organize their conscious lives always to be positive and without dysphoria or anger (Alexander, 1950; Deutsch & Murphy, 1955; Dicks, 1967; Achterberg & Lawlis, 1978; McDougall, 1984; Miller, 1989; Gottman, 1991). There are even divorces that take place in the context of such a pattern that are remarkable for the similarity in their way of developing. Typically, after many years of a total conflict-avoidance marriage, one of the mates suddenly announces his intention to divorce. The other spouse is stunned, to say the least. Personally, I have never seen or heard of any such case where a marital therapist has helped to reverse the decision. When one considers these problems that derive from the avoidance of conflict, it would seem apparent that therapists need to promote a conception of marriage in which there is a flow of experiences of emotional separateness and disagreement between the couple. An existential/dialectical frame of reference gives us a way of differentiating forced and phony "successful marriages" from those which are based on genuine friendship, respect, and love.

DIFFERENT KINDS OF SUCCESSFUL MARRIAGES

We need a conceptualization of some kind of continuum of successful marriages to guide us in our clinical work. Consider, for example, many couples who do have considerable respect and appreciation for one another, but do not feel love-excitement with one another. Although they do not feel passion or even a joy of intimacy, these couples deal with one another's strong and weak points basically fairly and their marriages are good for them in a quiet way. Neither plays the role of buffoon, incompetent, or unequal, nor is one the expert in residence or superior one. They are equals and each is appreciated for his/her contribution to the relationship along with being subject to honest criticism and feedback for qualities and actions which are unwelcome to the mate. Although they are not blessed with passion and love, it is clear that a great many genuinely satisfying qualities are present; such marriages deserve to be respected as quite successful.

Similarly, there are traditional marriages which are based on a straightforward division of roles, not necessarily with that much respect for one another's personality or emotional presence as there is for the structural position each occupies. Satisfaction is gained from the successful performance of clear-cut roles, relying on one another to handle assigned responsibilities and sharing in the fruits of stable marriage and family life. Such traditional marital structures also have to be considered successful.

For better and for worse, most modern, educated couples seek much more in their marriages—in many cases because they saw the restrictions that traditional marriages imposed and the degrees of bitterness, as well as a lifelessness and dull routine in so many of their elders who "had to stay together." These moderns believe something more is possible. They want marriages that are not ritualized shells of automatic devotion that are maintained by conflict avoidance. They seek intimate, genuine processing of emotions.

Nonetheless, even in the context of modern society, there is a range of decidedly different models or ways of organizing marriages that are alternately pleasing and displeasing to people, depending on their backgrounds, life histories, and psychological development.

To understand a marriage and its success or failure is to understand the inner meanings of the marriage for the couple; to understand these inner meanings is to know what each has wanted all along. For, like in many other areas in life, people have entirely different notions of what they want from marriage and their dreams of what they want and hope for define the value they assign to the reality of their marriage. Some marital partners are grateful for a stable home; the quiet and routine in that home make them feel safe and secure. Others seek in marriage a profound emotional and spiritual relationship; they want to share intimately with the spouse their passage through life and they evaluate their marriage on that basis. Other marital partners want fun—a happy schedule of socializing, theater, vacations, and so on. Note that whatever is especially pleasureful and reassuring for one person in the above examples can easily represent a *serious* threat to the emotional security of a partner who wants one of the other goals!

There is no way to treat a couple without appreciating the enormous power of the metaphors—templates/images/myths/psycho-architectural drawings—which people carry within them for how they feel their marriage needs to be in order for them to feel good and complete. One of the major sources of these metaphors is the culturally sanctioned model that people grow up with in their group of origin—religious, ethnic, socioeconomic, community, and so forth. Another major determinant is the imprinting of the marital model one saw in childhood, whether the result is a positive wish to copy what mother and father had or a desire for a marital style that is directly opposite to what one's parents' style was.

I suggest that for the most part we can assign people's metaphors, or the models they marry by, to a continuum that is built around three models of marriage which I shall call (1) Traditional, (2) Conservative-Contemporary, and (3) Modern-Utopian.

FIGURE 1
THREE MODELS OF MARRIAGE

TRADITIONAL MARRIAGES	CONSERVATIVE-CONTEMPORARY MARRIAGES	MODERN-UTOPIAN MARRIAGES
emphasize fulfillment of responsibility and loyalty to family and community.	emphasize relationships and the quality of experience, but remain anchored in tradition.	are intended to provide constant and considerable qualities of pleasure, gratification and freedom from tension.

Traditional Marriages

Traditional marriages in most cultures emphasize fulfillment of the fundamental sociological family-maintaining functions—that is, the husband and wife pledge to be lifelong partners to one another who will maintain a home for themselves and their children. Responsibility, loyalty, integrity are the prime values. They will support each other economically and can be counted on to take care of each other in good and bad times. Although there are vast differences between cultures as to the style of relationship and communication that is mandated, in virtually all cases it is understood that courtesy is expected, along with fulfillment of the basic marital fealty.

Generally, there is relatively little emphasis on the quality of relationship. Communication is seen as a way of affirming respect ritualistically for one another to enable and facilitate the completion of tasks together. Sensuality and sexuality are relatively underemphasized, often to the extent of being treated as somewhat taboo and for the most part subsumed under the overriding commitment to procreation as the purpose of the sexual function— although some traditional cultures parenthetically "wink" at some pleasure as well. Separation and divorce are generally not to be heard of for they are the ultimate violations of the contract of a traditional marriage. Divorce means not only a betrayal of one's mate and children but a betrayal of the extended family and the community. In effect, divorce threatens the continuity of the traditional reference group and this continuity is one of the prime purposes of marriage in traditional groups which do not wish to lose their sons and daughters and weaken the "race" or group.

Conservative-Contemporary Marriages

Conservative-contemporary marriages represent a movement from the traditional model towards something more alive, exciting, and fulfilling of other dimensions of experience. If traditional marriages were arranged, conservative-contemporary marriages are acts of choice. If traditional marriages were based on practicality and suitability, the conservative-contemporary marriage is based on attraction and love. A new dimension is identified and sought—the quality of experience in being together. The intention of husband and wife is to be companions, friends, and lovers over and above fulfilling the basic sociological functions of building a shelter and bringing children into the world. There emerges a new emphasis on communication of experience between the mates. Couples seek to share more of their inner worlds with one another. Many couples who develop this style of experience learn that even sharing bad news and troubling experiences makes for intimacy and new depths of pleasure in being married.

The emphasis on quality of experience also is translated into a romantic interest in staying in love and, if possible, deepening that love over the years or at least preserving the broad outline of the original quality of feeling attracted to one another as persons and as man and woman. To fall out of love, become bored with one another, or "turned off" and indifferent are feared as the ultimate failure of the conservative-contemporary marriage, although many of these marriages also remain somewhat anchored in the traditional model value of staying married "forever" and couples may decide to stay married even after they realize they are failing to achieve intimacy.

In these marriages, sensuality and sexuality are generally valued considerably; there is an emphasis on the artfulness of lovemaking and on lifelong joys of erotic pleasure. However, eroticism is generally linked to the effort to build a close relationship and love of one another as people. Attitudes towards separation and divorce are far more flexible. Social shame as well as personal shame and blame over divorce are lessened and, if necessary, divorces are accepted as positive solutions to marriages that failed to meet the desired standards and goals. However, couples are expected to be duly circumspect about the decision to divorce, to seek help before making and ratifying such a decision, and to know that divorce does represent a failure or at least a non-success to themselves, their children, families, and to some extent also in their traditional community or social reference groups.

Modern-Utopian Marriages

Modern-utopian marriages are the breakaways in their respective cultures from the ancient traditions and the magic and respect that the latter still hold for most people in the culture. These marriages seek new utopian forms. They may be cast in entirely new molds in order to define sharply and totally the break from the past—such as communal living, or free love, as opposed to lifelong commitment and loyalty of a man and woman to one another. Many types of modern-utopian marriages also continue the framework of a couple who have certain commitments to one another but add to that framework utopian modes such as multiple relationships with others, open marriages, group sex, mate swapping, or, interestingly enough, platonic marriages which renounce sexuality, marital arrangements where the couple live far away from each other most of the time and meet with varying frequency, or marriages which renounce the goal of having children—probably the most traditional of all marital institutions. In various ways, a decisive rupture is made with the past whose metaphors, values, ideals are at best politely mocked, at worst castigated as reactionary and stupid.

The common thread running through different utopian arrangements is that they are intended to provide immediate, constant, and considerable quantities of pleasure, gratification, and freedom from all types of tension. A basic hedonism lies at the philosophical center of these forms; their implication is, most often explicitly, that if for any reason the marriage does not produce steady pleasures and unquestioned security from tension, it must be ended.

Modern-utopian marriages are for the most part antisacramental, and the commitment of marital partners is generally subject to the understanding that if a trouble-free way of life is not achieved, the marriage is to be terminated. The attitude towards separation and divorce is generally a relaxed one. In many modern-utopian marriages, there is almost an implicit understanding that most marriages will be ended after a certain number of years, and the search for utopian pleasure and relaxation will be moved on to a new place and person.

Commitment, Intimacy, and Passion as Three Types of Love

There is another very useful way of thinking about the models by which people marry—that is, to define the nature of the loving that these people bring to their marriages. Sternberg (1988) proposes that there are three kinds of love: *commitment, intimacy, and passion.* He portrays the three kinds of love as the three sides of a triangle. Complete love includes all of these, but there are endless numbers of people who are organized around only one or two of the three components of love.

Commitment, which is also seen as the cognitive side of the triangle, is the decision in the short term and the long term to love and maintain the love. The classic, basic love of a parent for a child is a model of an unconditional level of commitment. In marriage, commitment often builds over time and then levels off; depending on the marital partners, commitment that was high can fall back to zero. Intimacy, which is the emotional aspect of the love triangle, involves sharing, closeness, communication and support. Sternberg sees intimacy increasing steadily at first, then at a slower rate, until it eventually levels off. Passion, which is the motivational side of the triangle, is the physiological arousal and intense desire to make love. According to Sternberg, intense passion develops very quickly but also levels off rapidly. Sternberg compares passion to an addiction that can be induced rapidly, but once habituation sets in the arousal is reduced.

Sternberg gives us a useful way of describing different styles people bring to their love relationships by characterizing a series of triangles based on the presence or absence of the three components of love. There is, for example, a triangle in which there is no commitment, passion, or intimacy, thereby constituting a situation of non-love. There is a triangle of passion and intimacy but not commitment, or a situation of "romantic love." There is a triangle of intimacy without passion and without commitment; this is a triangle of "liking." A triangle of commitment and passion, but not intimacy, is characterized as a triangle of "fatuous love." Passion alone makes for "infatuation love." Commitment and intimacy but not passion makes for "compassionate love." Commitment with nothing else makes for "empty love." Finally, the ideal, all three components integrated with one another, makes for "consummate love."

Sternberg also reports some empirical research on the relationship between how people really feel about their mate, how they wish to feel or believe they would feel about an ideal mate, how they would want an ideal mate to feel about them, and how one mate thinks the other mate feels about him or her. In general, the closer the real, ideal, and perceived are to one another, the more satisfying is the marital relationship. In other words, the more the dream and the reality of one's feelings towards one's spouse and the experience of that spouse match one another, the happier the marriage.

The models presented earlier are intended to express sociopsychological patterns of thought and feeling about marriage which people adopt, generally in an unknowing process arising from their relationship to their original family and to societal tradition, which then constitute their articles of faith and expectation in their personal psychology of marriage. Sternberg's concepts do not refer to cultural patterns, but to the intrapsychic components of experiences of love and non-love. Thus, a man who is committed to a conservative-contemporary marital model which does call for a relatively ideal or consummate conception of love that includes commitment, passion, and intimacy, and nonetheless finds himself not feeling committed to his wife and not sufficiently excited about her, may terminate the marriage and go looking for a more consummate partner.

MARRYING WITHIN THE SAME MODEL AND ACROSS MODELS

Marital therapists need to identify the model-values of any given couple and evaluate the marriage in that perspective. Not surprisingly, most marital therapists, like most mental health professionals, tend to identify with the conservative-contemporary model of marriage, setting up a certain degree of prejudice against the traditional and modern-utopian models. This is not to say that marital therapists cannot argue cogently that marriages which are based on intimate communication, sensuality, and love are likely to be more fulfilling and supportive of growth and a better basis for bringing up children. But first of all we have an obligation to evaluate any ongoing marriage in the context of the expectations that the spouses themselves bring to their marital experience. Nugent and Constantine (1988) studied 103 couples in marital therapy; of 38 cases where both mates were identified with the same paradigm, 92 percent were judged treatment successes; in the others, where mates differed in their paradigms, only 60 percent were considered successes.

Evaluating marriages against their contextual values is not so simple. For one thing, there are countless instances where people marry "outside of their group" and choose a partner from another model-value group. In most cases, a greater weight tends to be assigned to the more traditional view of marriage, so that if a conservative-contemporary person marries a traditional person, the expectation is that, first of all, the traditional values will have to be satisfied—enduring loyalty, emphasis on ethnic identity-affiliation, etc. Only then can some of the new-model values such as communication, pleasure, and sensuality be added to the mix, but only so long as they do not cancel out the traditional model of the one mate. If a modern-utopian person marries a conservative-contemporary person, the latter's values will have to be satisfied first of all. In practice, all "mixed marriages" imply from the outset a potential for conflict and a greater vulnerability to divorce. Sometimes, when the distance and contrast between the two models is especially great, there is a sense from the very beginning of the marriage that the couple are undertaking an impossible mission that is doomed to failure.

There are times when one of the mates discovers *after* being married that the spouse is not really a true subscriber to the same metaphor-model. Fairly dramatic examples of this powerful dilemma are situations where sometime after the marriage one mate reveals that he or she is homosexual, thereby precipitating a major crisis that often ends in divorce. There are all manner of variations on the theme, each more or less severe depending on the intensity or inviolability of the values held by the "betrayed" mate. In one case, a very religious spouse comes to learn that the mate is not as religious as was assumed. In another instance, a traditionally oriented person may "discover" that s/he has married someone who is going to insist on much greater sensuality and openness to pleasure than was expected. Another time, a husband or wife who is solidly in the ranks of a conservative-contemporary model and believes in commitment and continuity may have to face demands by the mate for an open marriage. Any and all of these discoveries that the mate has a different marital model sets off a major crisis process.

> She had little question that what she wanted in marriage was to be in love with her nice-person husband, bring up wholesome children, and enjoy being a full-time homemaker. When she discovered that her husband was unable to work consistently and would not be able to support her and their family, her disappointment was a bitter one— not simply because she had to go to work to keep food on the table, but because her ideal of a marriage where her husband would be the gainful breadwinner was shattered.
>
> * * * * * *
>
> Though he was a modern-day businessman and college graduate, he nonetheless saw himself in his marriage coming home as the honored head of the family who would enjoy respect, appreciation, and various wifely services. Not that he expected his wife to conduct herself as an insignificant personality or to "know her place" as his subordinate. She was a college-educated woman of the world and he expected her to be a full partner to conversation and activities, but at the same time to be devoted to him in his relatively traditional role of Husband-Father-Man of the Family. When he discovered that she had much more a mind of her own and experiential needs that contradicted some of his values, he was upset not only because he had to deal with these needs, but because her separateness contradicted his basic psychological ideology.

CHANGED MARITAL MODELS IN A FUTURE SHOCK WORLD

For many couples, the problem is not that they marry out of their model class to begin with, but that one or both later change their mind about key aspects of their marriage and lose contact with one another. In our age of "future shock" (Toffler, 1971) permeating rapidly into every sphere of society, there are powerful forces of social change at work which can lead to drastic transformations of people's original metaphors of marriage. Thus, many times in our day and age, couples who start out with compatible marital concepts end up with at least one of them changing his/her ideas about marriage so much that it becomes a major barrier to their being able to continue to live together.

Our mental health culture also represents one of the new-era impacts which are bringing about radical revisions of existing traditions. In a way, without our realizing it, many of us are missionaries for the conservative-contemporary model. The mental health movement has certainly played a huge role in promoting the desirability and even emotional necessity of communication and relationship between couples, as well as of attractiveness and sexuality.

Many couples have gone on to divorce after *one* mate went for individual therapy. In therapy, the patient would undergo profound experiential and, often, value changes. Insofar as the other mate would be left out in the dark, and especially if the mate were by nature unable to "catch up," the "taste" would go out of the marriage. I think that our psychological culture has seduced many people into divorcing, and not always to their best interests. I for one am distinctly uncomfortable when I hear a "convert" to our ranks speaking with adamant conviction about having learned in therapy about the importance of communication and feelings, explaining that this is why he/she has to leave the husband/wife who refuses to see the light.

For many years, we would see cases of couples who got out of cultural/experience step with one another when the husband would change in the course of his business or professional life while the wife remained where she was or even "shrank," so to speak, because she was at home in the roles of housewife and mother to young children. "I-put-him-through-medical-school" type divorces are common to this day, but with a new ironic twist that now many women are employed in increasingly sophisticated posts and it is the woman who may leave the man after he had put her "through medical school." Today, it is more and more common to find the momentum for divorce coming from a woman who sees her new world beckoning; for her it is her husband who has stayed behind in a restricted range of functioning. Willi (1984) reported a study in Germany of 639 divorced women, 75 percent of whom had been the marital partner who had taken the major initiative for the divorce. In retrospect, 44 percent were very satisfied with their lives, 11 percent felt their divorce was a tragedy, and 45 percent fell in between.

The Political Process in Marriage: Choosing Whether to Change With or Without One's Mate

Of course, the processes of change are not only or simply a function of stimuli pouring in on people. They are also a function of the choices that each mate makes about whether or not to change by himself/herself without the spouse. Moreover, these choices are, in turn, a function of another choice by the *second* spouse who is seeing and feeling the call of change in the mate and in effect decides whether or not to insist on staying together as a couple—either by insisting on keeping up with the changes in the spouse's life or by calling on the spouse's loyalty to their mutual tradition and continuity as a couple and not agreeing to their changing.

Even powerful cultural stimuli and experiences are mediated through a decision-making agency in the ego of each person. Say a man falls head over heels for a beautiful woman of another nationality/religion. It is much more than infatuation; she totally excites his imagination and senses, they work together every day, and he really sees what a wonderful person she is. Without doubt he *could* fall deeply in love with her and project onto her his idealized object-hopes and fantasies of the happiest life together. Nevertheless, he still has an inner choice to make whether or not to do so. People who are resolutely loyal to their original ethnic/religious identifications will not allow themselves to fall in love even when they are genuinely drawn to such feelings. Many of those who find themselves in such circumstances report that their awareness of the importance of not marrying "out of the fold" stops their falling in love.

Couples who "open" the boundaries of their marital relationship to a separating process of major changes that puts them out of tune with one another are choosing, albeit unwittingly and unconsciously, to endanger their marriage. The more powerful the external context or environment and its danger of pulling the husband or wife into a different world away from the marriage, the more there is a need for intuitive wisdom and active efforts to keep the shared marital experience at the center of both partners' lives.

I recommend, for example, that mates visit each other's places of work regularly and participate with them in some of the holiday or other social functions that are part of their work world in order to stay in touch with their experiences and relationships there. I certainly recommend drawing one's mate into a great deal of conversation about his/her work world and the other people in it. It is also important to stay in touch with the everyday interests, hobbies, extracurricular pleasures, and cultural and spiritual experiences of one's spouse—even if these are not "interesting" to the mate, a negative position that in my experience is a very dangerous one to adopt. One needs to ask a great many questions, develop a degree of genuine interest and appreciation for the spouse's activity, and try to understand how and why it is so meaningful.

In many instances, couples unconsciously choose to go their separate ways by exposing themselves to the powerful winds of cultural change because they have reached a point of serious dissatisfaction with one another in their marriage. Changing one's life style means, in effect, going out to "shop" for a new life, including quite possibly a new partner.

> There was no doubt that she was out to find a new husband. Although she and her husband were to all intents and appearances a happy, devoted couple with their several children and a lovely way of life, she was bitter about his subtle way of being superior to her and insulting her. She embarked on the search by throwing herself into a series of wonderfully tempting relationships. Not only was she going to feel good in these dalliances and, in some instances, sexual affairs, she was actually interviewing to see which man would be willing to take her away. If you asked her about this at the time, she would have sincerely denied that she was doing anything other than having some fun. At this stage, she consciously claimed even to herself that she was satisfied with her marriage and that keeping her marriage was very important to her.

Sometimes people exploit the world of change and future shock in order to satisfy their need to bludgeon their mate. One can hang on the pegs of cultural and ideological changes ostensible justification for what is, intrinsically, disloyalty and hostility.

> The two of them had met in a cult and married in an orgy of conviction that they were living the one, true life, high on drugs and intense spiritual experiences. It is hard to say that they loved each other; rather they loved the state in which they were in together—a pseudoperpetual high. Sometime later, he underwent a conversion experience to a fundamentalist religious sect and she went along with him. At this point she welcomed the change. It took them both out of the drug culture of which she had tired and brought them into a family-respecting world in which the children that had been born to them in the meantime would have a much better chance. So they stayed together in the move from the first sect to the second. Again, it is hard to say that they came to love each other at this time in their lives, but they did love the safety they now gained in a fundamentalist world which offered answers to everything and removed the risks of the drug culture and its erratic people and tragic outcomes.

However, after some years, he pulled still another change and announced that he was leaving the fundamentalist group, its theology, and way of life. In the meantime, the whole family had been thoroughly immersed in this fundamentalist way of life. The children were fully identified members of the sect and the mother was a proud lady of the community who had committed herself totally to the sect's belief system and prescribed way of life. She as well as the children were caught with brutal surprise by his announcement. What it really meant was that he did not want her, nor in this case the children as well.

In his case, it also meant that he was the kind of person who could not love in a loyal way, nor could he make a genuine identification with any group. He was prepared to move about from one culture to another to satisfy his desire to taste different kinds of experiences no matter what the costs were to the people who were ostensibly the closest to him.

Resisting Fads and Radical Change

In any age of powerful social change, it is that much more important to realize that each of us has within us a power to remain ourselves and not jump, twist, and turn at every spin of the societal roulette wheel. The current fad is always glittering and promises instant gratification. However, there is a valuable quality in maintaining a basic rootedness in one's past and staying in touch with the values and models in which one has been educated, while also participating in a changing world. Ultimately there is no way of life that is absolutely right; whichever one we choose is, in some sense, limited and limiting.

It can be very satisfying to be alive in our era and exposed to a broad panorama of experiences and opportunities that no longer circumscribe us to our original "villages" where people were born to live and die as their ancestors had for thousands of years. If good sense shows us that the formative values we grew up with are in some ways harmful to us or if we feel we have outgrown them, we have more and more opportunity to choose to change our life styles. Yet we also need to be aware and responsible that in the passage of change there is a danger of disconnecting ourselves by insulting and repudiating the identification bonds we carry with us from our past. If we do so radically, without good and thoughtful reasons, we are, in effect, turning ourselves against parts of our own selves. Those whom we have loved and situations we have participated in are parts of us forever. If the changes we made are too wrenching, too revolutionary, and killing of the past, we will have exposed in ourselves a kind of value-unfaithfulness which will also make us less trusting of ourselves as decent and loyal people.

There is also an intuitive good sense in people which can tell them that certain fads are pure nonsense, especially those that threaten one's health if not actual life. Just because a whole group goes crazy over drugs or some other contemporary form of "Russian roulette" doesn't mean one should go along with the crowd. There is an inner wisdom based on respect and love for life that is available in us from which to judge new ideas and fads and scripts for the future.

LIFE-CYCLE MARKERS

The drama of the unfolding metaphors of what a person wants in marriage and how much s/he is prepared to do to seek fulfillment of expectations is also profoundly influenced by a series of "life-cycle markers" or time stations.

Many couples break up nowadays, for example, when one of the mates cannot bear to continue into the older more vulnerable years without the positive companionship that becomes even more important at this stage. They were able to put up with their spouse during the earlier years, say during the active period of bringing up young children to whom both of them were devoted parents despite the serious problems in their marriage, but as they face the "empty nest" of being together in their later years, there isn't enough to hold them together.

The life-cycle markers or turning points at the change of each decade are personal crises that throw open all areas of life, including marriage, for renewed choices. Since moving into the 30s is for many women a period of concern about remaining young and attractive or becoming sexually fulfilled before it is too late, many a woman whose personal metaphor previously did not include being sexually excited and in love with her husband will now feel compelled to seek changes, either within her marriage or outside of it. A man who turns 40 and feels he does not receive the appreciation and respect he deserves in the prime of his life is likely to press harder for what he wants in his marriage, either with his wife or away from her.

The diagnosis and prescription of treatment for marital problems must always include an analysis of the contextual markers or how each spouse's desires and behaviors are related to their place in the life cycle (Sheehy, 1976; Levinson, 1978).

The implicit ethic of many therapists seems to be that if a person is sacrificing in marriage too much of his/her personal fulfillment and if a move out of the marriage will not be overwhelmingly damaging to other members of one's current family, then such a move may be justified. But if, for example, there is a child teetering on the brink of psychosis, is it really justified for a parent to leave the marriage even if he/she is decidedly unhappy? In one such case, the father decided not to leave because of his overriding commitment to treatment of a precariously disturbed youngster; over the years he was able to find increasing gratification in the once disastrous marriage, along with deep satisfaction from the recovery of the child. If one of the mates becomes seriously ill, the consensus of most fair-minded people seems to be that the right of the healthy mate to seek his/her own emotional satisfaction has to be limited by a measure of honorable obligation to the care of the sick person.

These decisions are not always clear-cut or simple. This kind of situation becomes especially problematic when there has been a long history of abuse by the now sick mate and the first mate has felt trapped and powerless. The illness and weakness of the abuser may now open the doors to a sense of possible freedom as well as to the pleasure of taking a long-overdue vengeance. Who is to say what the ethically correct choice should be in these situations after the many years of abuse?

Artful caring for one another and a disciplined restraint of destructiveness all through the marital process make it possible for people to accompany one another as friends through their respective life-cycle transitions. The crises of transitional periods are then likely to result in an enrichment of the marriage by virtue of the deepening appreciation of life that can be released by these transitions and the awareness they bring all of us that no life is forever.

5

When Is a Marital Problem a Problem?

Hidden Traps in Seemingly Successful Marriages

Can there be a significant problem in a marriage even though neither mate complains of dissatisfaction? If the therapist sees a difficulty and the couple do not, is there a problem? For example, couples may present with various problems for one or both, such as vocational dissatisfaction, depression, psychosomatic complaints, and parental difficulties, especially with acting-out children. The therapist will also need to look carefully at the marriage itself even though the couple do not complain about it.

We know that often one of the two mates denies major problems that the other spouse is terribly upset about; in these instances we do not hesitate to identify the disavowal of the problem as a denial of reality. But it is rarer to see confrontations by therapists of situations where *both* mates together deny that they have a problem. In my opinion, much as "false negatives" and "false positives" are issues that must be dealt with in medicine, so in marital therapy we need to know how to identify certain "non-problems" as problems (and also to be able to identify certain "problems" that do concern some people as not-really problems).

The maturing and professionalization of marital therapy require that we know much more about what really constitutes a problem in marriage rather than going along slavishly with what the clients say. There are too many people who accept the short end of the stick and don't complain about things they should complain about; too many who live "high off the hog" and deny that they are creating a problematic world; and too many others who complain and complain when they have so much they should be grateful for having.

For example, a husband and wife are eminently capable in their respective fields of work and together they delight in building a "marriage of Greek Gods." The couple *are* happy at this time, but what are the probabilities over time that one or the other will fall from grace and falter in their never-ending quest for excellence to a point that will not be tolerable to them? What will happen to this couple when the exigencies of life impose on one or the other serious vulnerability?

> She has inherited considerable money from her family, which provides for the high standard of living she and her husband and children are enjoying. He is a college graduate who is working in the civil service as a junior clerk. He brings home a steady income that does not cover even a minor portion of the family's expenses. He is a gentle man, but also given to putting on airs of more worldly knowledge and ability than he possesses, as well as airs of wealth commensurate with the family's standard of living. However, his words hang unnaturally on him in some awkward way; there is a feeling of a "pretender" about him.
>
> Both spouses say they are happy. They are, in fact, devoted to each other, loyal, and with no major dissension. We do not know for sure about their sexual life, but there are some hints that although they are both only in their late 30s, they may have stopped having intercourse. They have four children, all of whom are quiet and nice. However, the second child, a 12-year-old boy, has become more and more reclusive during the past year and was taken for treatment to a child psychiatrist, who is concerned that he might be heading toward a psychotic state of withdrawal.

Does this couple's acknowledged "happiness" warrant the approval of marital therapists? The real life outcome in this case was that the marriage and the family deteriorated into a kind of depressive mausoleum. All the children suffered a good deal and had to struggle to find their way in life as well as they could. Both parents died prematurely.

> He is a hard-working man in a partnership managing a small manufacturing company which requires of him an enormous investment of time and effort. Thus far, after a decade of very hard work, he still has not managed to draw a good financial return from his work.
>
> She is home with their three children, one of whom suffers from a learning disorder that upsets her very deeply. She becomes increas-

ingly agitated and demands that her husband leave his company and take another job which will enable him to come home at regular hours to spend more time with her and the children, especially with the learning-disabled child. He responds to her demands by getting very angry at her for telling him what to do. Moreover, he cannot turn his back on his partner and he expects it is just a matter of time before they finally make huge profits.

This couple is singularly unhappy. The wife talks of divorce. Yet, does this state of unhappiness in itself foretell the long-range future of this couple? Can we imagine that this couple will be able to live through three or four years of bitter unhappiness, come perilously close to divorce, and then succeed in working out their situation and achieve a loving renewal of their marriage that is genuinely satisfying to both of them?

The actual outcome in this case was that the couple did develop ways of working together and some years later their marriage filled with renewed love, although, unfortunately, in the long run they did not succeed very well in helping their developmentally disabled child

OBJECTIVE ASSESSMENT OF MARRIAGES

In the existing literature of couples therapy, it is not at all clear when mental health professionals and marital therapists should qualify marriages as "troubled," "dysfunctional," or "problematic." To judge the quality of a marriage (in professional language, to establish a clinical "diagnosis") calls for looking at several quite different and often contradictory considerations. When we want to assess the emotional status of a marriage, we can well end up with markedly different viewpoints depending on the perspective from which we conduct our evaluation (Willi, 1982).

The most common popular as well as professional error is to evaluate marital health simply in terms of the subjective happiness and unhappiness of the couple. Whatever the couple report is taken at face value. If both say they are happy, so be it, their marriage is evidently "normal." If one or both say there is trouble, then the marriage is "disturbed" or "dysfunctional." The couple's report of their happiness or unhappiness is the frame of reference on which an overwhelming majority of both researchers and clinicians fall back. Yet, the conscious experience of being happy may or may not be a prelude to a couple's long-range happiness. Many people are currently happy because they are living in a state of compensation and making up for serious weaknesses in ways that protect them from facing their failings. Their successful way of life is, in fact, intrinsically weakening them further. It is a matter of time before they will learn that their underlying problems and challenges can be put off only for so much time before they come back to haunt them.

The same situation is apparent when a person seeks refuge in other psychological escapes. An alcoholic or a drug addict or a charmer who moves from job to job, for example, may report, even for long periods of time, that they are "happy," but our judgment will be that they suffer from a serious pattern of disturbance. Yet, evaluations of the quality of the marriage by the therapist rather than by the couple are not commonly accepted and many professionals object strongly to the therapist "judging" people's marriages.

Similarly, at any given time a marriage may be in distress and deep conflict, yet this in itself does not tell us whether the couple have a good or poor chance of succeeding in building a satisfying marriage over a longer term. Some distress, even if severe, spurs some couples to huge leaps of growth and to remarkably happy and rich marriages. Isn't this the hope that marital psychotherapists extend to such couples when we "sell them" our services?

Four different comparative perspectives of marriage will be considered here. The first perspective is the one we have been discussing in these last pages, *subjective versus objective*. The other comparative perspectives are *short-range versus long-range, individual versus marital versus family,* and *preserving a marriage versus encouraging divorce*. In each of these perspectives, dialectical philosophy will suggest that both or all sides of the perspective are valid, and that the contradictions between the opposing positions and the tension the contradictions set off are necessary and valuable.

Subjective Versus Objective Perspectives

The subjective view of a marriage derives from the statements of each marital partner of how the marriage feels to him or her. There are many situations when the married partners will report that they feel quite well, yet their marital situation is not desirable or healthy.

> A husband reports being quite happy with a nagging, even maddening, wife.
>
> •
>
> A husband or wife agrees to the mate carrying on an alternative sexual relationship—heterosexual or homosexual.
>
> •
>
> A wife agrees to her husband working excessively long hours and not spending time with her or contributing to parenting and family life.

•

A spouse accepts ridicule, humiliation, or brutality.

•

A spouse puts up with a major behavioral problem ("What can I do about it?") such as alcoholism, addiction, gambling, criminality.

•

A husband or wife surrenders all parenting functions to the other.

•

Couples are happy notwithstanding foregoing one or more major areas of marital experience such as not having any outside social life or no longer having sex with one another.

An objective perspective will insist that although the couples accept or even claim they like any of the above situations and say they feel safe in the marriage, they are living in emotionally unhealthy ways.

Short-Range Versus Long-Range Perspectives

Another frequent error, which in effect was also included within the above perspective but is worth fleshing out independently, is to limit the assessment of marriages to a time frame of what is happening at the present time. This way of thinking precludes the concept of a process and the possibility of change for better or worse in the future. Yet the immediate status of a marriage is not at all the same as the long-range prospects for the survival, effectiveness, and pleasure of the marriage. Continuing a present arrangement or taking steps to help a marriage keep going may succeed in keeping the couple together for a while, but at a later date they will break up. There are also opposite situations where a couple who are in bad straits will nonetheless find their way towards a satisfying reorganization in the long run.

Admittedly, we are not at a point where we have the ability to predict with any definiteness life outcomes for people. However, we are able to consider possibilities and probabilities of what may befall people and couples over longer periods of time, especially given the predictability of various kinds of pressures inherent in the normative life cycle (Sheehy, 1976; Levinson, 1978). For example, one can suspect an unhappy outcome may befall a man who is a lackey or emotional appendage to a dominating, brutalizing woman. A therapist seeing such a couple at an earlier time in their lives has profound clinical and philosophical choices as to whether or not to support the style of appeasement by the husband or to seek to invite the husband to be more assertive.

Individual Versus Marital Versus Family Perspectives

A third compelling issue in evaluating the effectiveness of marriages is to analyze for whom in the family the continuation of a marriage is good and for whom it is not. Often, it will be advantageous for a marriage to continue for one of the spouses, but not for the other. Other times, the continuation of the marriage will be crucial for the emotional welfare of one or more of the children, but to the disadvantage of both parents. Sometimes, divorce would better serve a child's needs to be freed of an oppressive marital-family world, yet it will expose a parent to considerable vulnerability. (See Wylie, 1989, including a case illustration where a 63-year-old Hispanic husband is having an affair with a younger woman. The therapist, who is strongly against infidelity, is "on the verge of catapulting the wife into a therapeutic maelstrom" [p. 28] and possible divorce by pushing the wife to protest more than *she*, the wife, herself could bear.)

Just whose welfare do marital therapists have an obligation to serve? To this day, there is a tradition, at least among individual therapists, that the one spouse who happens to arrive at a therapist's doorstep first is the one who has "first call" on the therapist's loyalty. Systems-thinking, which is at the core of the work of most couples and family therapists, should lead to a correction of this point of view, but there have been few guides to help family therapists develop a methodology for thinking about whose needs and interests they should weigh first. There seem to be several guidelines implicit in current-day thinking in the field, in effect a series of informal rules, among which are these:

1. The emotional welfare of young people takes precedence over the welfare of elders.
2. The needs of very weak members of the family, such as severely handicapped children or elderly people who are having trouble caring for themselves, supersede the needs of healthier members of the family.
3. Preserving the intactness of a family group tends to take precedence over the needs of any single member of a family.
4. A spouse's desire for greater personal fulfillment and development of potential is to be respected even to some extent at the expense of other family members' needs, but not desires for "freedom" and "happiness" that are more hedonistic or narcissistic.

The time is coming when our professions will need to examine these and other assumptions more explicitly. At this point, there may not be clear ethical guidelines for practitioners, but what should be clear is that all therapists must begin to be conscious of the need to think about these issues.

Preserving a Marriage Versus Encouraging Separation

Finally, clinicians or scientific researchers who look at the immediate outcome of treatment of couples only or largely in terms of whether or not couples stay together are bound to make serious errors. There are many "successful" treatment cases where the couple stay together, but when one looks back over the years at the quality of their lives together the preferred outcome would have been for the couple to have separated. Conversely, there are marital therapies which culminate logically in separation and divorce and these "unsuccessful" treatments really should be evaluated as successes.

The question is how therapists go about making their judgments and choices of the desired direction of therapy. Deciding what stand to take and when and how is one of the profound responsibilities of therapists. The therapy situation assigns them the authority of wise men and a responsibility for deciding how to render the services being asked of them. So it is important for therapists to know how to think about using their considerable influence. It is a myth that only the patients themselves decide whether or not to stay married, and whether or not to seek major changes in their relationship or personal development. Therapists have a very large role in making recommendations to the couple and the steps the therapist takes in shaping therapy have a definite and possibly decisive role in determining what takes place. The "clinical judgments" therapists make are, in many ways, philosophical choices or value positions, yet one hears almost nothing in professional circles of family therapists or training programs about how a therapist should go about making these value judgments with some degree of "objectivity" and "responsibility."

IDENTIFYING POTENTIAL FUTURE DYSFUNCTIONS BASED ON CURRENT COLLUSIVE AGREEMENTS*

Let us consider more systematically marriages which are ostensibly secure and free of problems, but are based on a collusive balance between the couples. The ostensible security is gained through some kind of "protection racket" to which both mates agree.

Many marital therapists take the position that marital problems begin only when the couple or one of the two spouses say they have a problem. If no one is complaining about a problem, there is none; so long as both spouses are "satisfied," the marriage is satisfying. However, there are mar-

---

*This section is adapted from Charny, (1987) with permission of *Contemporary Family Therapy.*

ital arrangements or collusions which inherently carry with them a danger of breakdown or potential dysfunction at a later date, in many cases when it will be too late to renew the growth process. This is also why I have always objected to marital satisfaction questionnaires and researches as unable to prevent false negative diagnoses. Responsible clinical work with couples should include "Marital Trap Analysis," or a careful effort to evaluate the potential of damaging outcomes in the future, and a responsible decision as to whether or not to attempt therapeutic penetration into a collusive agreement even before the couple themselves have complained directly about their lives together. These ideas are relevant for clinical work in the many situations where people present symptoms other than marital complaints, which they don't realize are connected to their marriages. They also are useful in educational and preventive settings such as seminars for "normal couples" in the community.

The marital process is so complicated that one must recognize that there can be long stretches of time when couples live comfortably in undesirable collusions (Charny, 1986c; Sager, 1976; Sager & Hunt, 1979). In some marriages, a more obvious problem will explode relatively soon. In others, years may pass, but then there will be an eruption and the long neglect of the issue will have left the couple without a resiliency with which to deal with the crisis. In still others, there may never be a recognizable crisis, but there will be consequences of the collusions which will determine much of the couple's and family's life.

A common example of dormant problems that are intrinsically serious long before either mate or the couple ask for help are couples who maintain a collusion around humiliation and domination. Often the mate who is treated badly translates the experience of being humiliated into excitement and fascination with the aura of power of the controlling spouse. These situations can last for years, yet they carry within them the seeds of likely deterioration over time.

There are also "successful" dominant-submissive relationships where a spouse enjoys little of his/her own being. This collusion can even "satisfy" both mates for their lifetimes, yet show up in a chain reaction that leads to a psychiatric disturbance in a child or even a grandchild, or find dramatic expression in the submissive mate's inability to carry on life for him/herself when the spouse dies.

In my judgment, it is scientifically and professionally wrong to limit our interventions with couples to stated complaints and not look seriously at those apparently functional and acceptable styles of functioning that are potential time-bombs. Of course, it is also true that people have the basic right to be as they are and as they choose to be. This also means the right to their collusions and it is not always clear what therapists' responsibilities are (Margolin, 1982). For example, there are a surprisingly large number of couples who live without sexuality; in some cases, they compensate for this lack through their companionship. If and when such a couple come into a mental health clinic for reasons other than dissatisfaction with their lack of sexuality—an area of experience which is clearly much more important to some people than to others—should the therapist open up this issue as well? A responsible, sensitive, and humane judgment is called for as to whether the best interests of the couple will be served by exposing and exploring their collusion. Alvarez (1983) has described some collusive marriages thus:

> Mutual assistance pacts can last a lifetime. They are not necessarily happy marriages in the accepted sense of the term—on the contrary, they are often founded on hatred or contempt or distaste—but they may be the only way the partners can get through life without crumpling under the pressure of urges they will not properly recognize as their own, like a stunt man with a wife who is frightened to cross the road. He takes the risks she secretly yearns for, while she personifies the fears he feels driven continually to conquer. The same coin, different faces. (p. 196)

INCOMPETENCE TRAPS, COMPLEMENTARITY TRAPS, AND SUCCESS TRAPS

Three types of long-range "marital traps" that can be identified are collusions around incompetence, around a complementary arrangement, and around oversuccess. I shall call these respectively: *Incompetence Traps, Complementarity Traps,* and *Success Traps.*

- In *Incompetence Traps,* the two mates accept one another's incompetence or lack of investment in what is to others a major role-function in marriage, e.g., the example we saw of the agreement of a couple to forego sexuality, or a mutual understanding to forego any emotional dependence on one another.
- In *Complementarity Traps,* there is an agreement that one of the couple will be responsible for carrying a given function, such as managing all the affairs of the family, while the other mate will remain relatively helpless and dependent on the "stronger" spouse.
- In *Success Traps,* one or both mates ostensibly shine in great competence and investment in an important area of life; it is hard to imagine that a problem is likely to result from such excellence. The couple make the

understandable mistake of letting a mate overdo whatever it is s/he is best at doing and, without knowing it in advance, the increasing success in this area itself leads the couple into a number of "traps," which are discussed later in this chapter.

Although these collusive agreements may be genuinely agreeable to both mates, they stand a high risk of breaking down at later times because, inherently, *these are agreements which stifle growth in each mate and in the couple.* It is not simply the distribution of functions between the couple that traps them, but the fact that these patterns are frozen into rigid, unchallengeable ways of being in the world that lay the groundwork for emotional problems in one or more family members or in the family unit as a whole. The collusive agreement is a balancing mechanism for both mates and seems to protect each mate, as well as the two as a couple, from anxiety and risk. However, the result is a paralysis of choice (see Koestenbaum, 1974 for a discussion of choices in the way people shape their love lives). In collusive relationships, potential traps are left unattended and then tend to grow in extent and meaning until they take a serious toll on the vitality of the marriage.

Incompetence Traps

These are potential problems that are based on the agreement of both mates to forego an area of experience, for example, not to share emotions with one another or not to have children.

There are surprisingly many instances where couples agree to give up an area of experience and seem to make a go of it without feeling they are missing anything. These couples silently and unconsciously effect a "contract" and they proceed to live their lives consciously satisfied with their arrangement. The agreement may be to forego meaningful communication or closeness, or respect for one another. They may agree that one or both can ignore any need to remain physically attractive. Or they may agree that neither will be expected to contribute too much to bringing up the children and the children will have to "grow themselves up" as well as they can.

Some decisions to maintain incompetence are based on a mate's lack of talent in a given role-skill, which is excused, tolerated, and even seen as charming by the other: "She is such a lovely scatterbrain—she couldn't care less about balancing the checkbook, but she's terrific in bed." Or both mates are incompetent in the same role-skill and the couple will arrive at an agreement to forego an area of functioning, such as two shy people who decide not to have any friends or social life.

Couples vary enormously in what they cannot bear. For some, the "red line" of what cannot possibly be tolerated will be a mate's failure to manage family financing; for others, it will be an absence of communication. Some couples want so much to do well in *all* areas that they are unable to live with any major incompetence whatsoever. Even when it occurs as a result of illness or other life circumstances, any inability to function becomes a threat to the continuation of the marriage.

In other cases, couples are able to acknowledge that they are, in fact, losing out on something desirable, but they are committed to live with each other as they are and they laugh off the weakness. Sometimes, couples wisely try to compensate for their weakness by seeking an outside resource to provide some of what they themselves are unable to generate, e.g., a couple who are poor parents but who care about their children are careful to hire a talented housekeeper-nanny to give the children some of what they cannot. Because these couples are less blind and are more open to facing the weakness in their lives, they tend to fare better.

Insofar as a couple give up on themselves as never to be able to perform and grow in a vital area of marital experience, they are vulnerable over the long haul. One of the great dangers in all such arrangements is that a spouse will suffer a serious change of heart and no longer be satisfied with renunciation of a vital role or experience area that is, after all, intrinsically appealing and even essential. There comes a day when the once acceptable minimum or absent sexuality, or meager communication, or limited companionship time is no longer acceptable.

Not infrequently, these *re*decisions by one mate take the other by cruel surprise. The change in policy by one is, in effect, a major betrayal, not unlike infidelity. The betrayed mate may have become so set in his/her ways and so unmindful of a possible reconsideration of this area of experience and functioning that s/he is literally immobilized and unable to deal with the challenge.

In our age of "future shock" and intense drive to experience new ways of life, a collusive relationship is especially likely to break down when one of the mates ventures into a new world of activities and meanings.

> The wife enrolls in social work school at age 36. Her marriage has been relatively satisfying to her and her husband thus far, although it has been a very quiet, often boring, overly secure relationship with little sexual activity. She succeeds in her studies and becomes aware of a range of relationship excitements and the possibility of sexual pleasures that never preoccupied her before. Now she is no longer satisfied with her relationship to her husband. She makes an effort to bring him with her into therapy, but he is resentful of how she has aban-

doned him for her involvement with her new world of experiences which he cannot share with her, and he refuses to go to therapy.

In no small number of marriages, the collusive agreement will have been effected by one mate because of an unknown alternative relationship outside the marriage. A familiar example of such a pattern is a situation where one mate is involved with a lover away from home and prefers to avoid sex with the spouse. Typically, the latter seems to remain unknowing and uncaring. Similarly, one spouse may replace the absence of a meaningful relationship at home with significant intimate friendships away from home. There are also instances where a husband or wife refrains from pressing the mate for a minimum level of contribution to the family economy and instead turns to an alternative source such as money from one's family of origin; the unproductive or even nonworking spouse is left infantilized and progressively more crippled.

In such situations, where one spouse is "eating out" (getting satisfactions away from home or at the expense of the marriage or family), the dangers of a possible change of heart lie on both sides: the mate who is satisfying the experience away from home may one day decide against continuing in the sterile, nonfunctioning marriage: "I wanted to leave for many years and I've decided to do it now before I grow old"; or the abandoned mate at home may finally become aware that the spouse is "married to someone else" and erupt in anger.

Many collusions in incompetence are broken down by the consequential chain of events they set off in one or more of the children. Some children's problems are mocking reflections and/or protests of the renunciation of a normally necessary and desirable area of functioning in their parents. For example, some acting-out children live out the denied passions and muted aliveness of their parents. Depressed children often reflect the renunciation of experience by their parents at home. Some of the most difficult learning problems are a consequence of collusion in pseudomutuality or lack of identity-separateness in the family.

In sum, *Incompetence Traps* are collusive agreements to forego much or all of a vital area or dimension of experience in marriage and to deny or remain indifferent to the avoidance of this area of life. Such agreements can hold indefinitely, but often they break down under the sequence of life pressures generated by what are essentially unhealthy and undesirable renunciations of basic human needs. The healthier the couple, the more they will reorganize themselves around the incompetence of one or both mates by more honest acknowledgment of the incompetence, seeking to improve themselves through mutual support, humor and understanding, reliance on each other's strengths, and bringing in outside resources to help so as to keep the important role or experience "alive" even if they are naturally deficient in that area.

Complementarity Traps

These are situations where mates trade off strength and weakness to each other, with one of the mates largely doing or being responsible for the other in the latter's area of incompetence or neglect, while conversely the other renounces responsibility for this area of experience-competence and depends on the competent spouse.

An example of such a complementary arrangement is a wife who is very unsure of herself socially and depends on her man-about-town, confident husband to stay with her and "talk for her" in social gatherings. Another example would be a husband who is very uncomfortable about sitting quietly or playing with children and depends on his wife to provide the children with closeness.

Many, if not most, couples start out with such complementary arrangements, but then respond to the natural tensions of the differences between them and the discomfort generated by the incompetence and grow towards a better balance between them. In the couples we are describing here, the pattern remains frozen and is treated as if it is not troubling to either husband or wife.

Each of the two sides to the complementarity represents a personality problem of an individual playing a role that is "buying" for him/her security through the other, i.e., at the expense of one's personal growth. It is often clinically useful to work with each mate separately on his/her role and to single out one of the two sides of the complementarity as a major source of tension, even though complementarity, by definition, is an interlocking system created and maintained by the two mates together. From the point of view of each *individual* mate, complementarity traps can be further defined as either *responsibility traps* or *dependency traps*:

1.   *Responsibility Traps*

The trap of responsibility for one's mate involves taking over for the other's weakness without expecting the other to control the weakness or to grow. Thus, a husband undertakes too much of the responsibility for the commitment to the marriage and the family while his wife continues to be unfaithful to him. Or an exhausted wife assumes responsibility for creating companionship and maintaining the relationship with a taciturn, indifferent husband who continues passive-aggressively to sabotage her efforts at relating.

2. Dependency Traps

The trap of dependency involves relying too much on one's mate's strength rather than seeking to develop more of one's own, or at least to contribute significantly in some other way that balances the dependency in this area of functioning. Thus, a wife presents herself as a helpless parent and depends entirely on her husband to discipline the children, without making any effort to learn how to participate and support him. Or a husband leaves his wife total responsibility for initiating romantic or sexual experience between them.

Functional Versus Dysfunctional Complementarity

Distinctions between functional and dysfunctional complementary relationships are often based only on what the mates themselves report. If the tradeoff seems to "work" for the couple, the complementary relationship is seen as functional—e.g., he takes care of the children and she is out in the world as the big earner for the family, but they are satisfied. If the complementary roles are accompanied by anger and bitterness, the complementarity is termed dysfunctional—e.g., he tries to provide the warmth and closeness between them despite her repeated manifestations of coldness and hurting. The tension between them eventually leads them to separate.

The fact of complementarity in itself is not definitive of a problem. Complementary relationships are virtually inescapable in the initial joining of couples and are often the basis for much of the initial attraction. No one can be competent at all matters and there is an inherent pull towards joining with another person who has greater competence in the area in which one is weak. The complementarity is potentially growth-facilitating if both mates are honest about their roles and alternate between helping one another and relying on one another in different areas of experience in a basically equal relationship.

Complementarity becomes problematic when roles are rigidified into permanent *adequate* versus *inadequate* positions. The system mesh that results may create a workable balance for some time, but the seeds of future problems are embedded in the structure of inequality—for both spouses. There comes a point when a "dumb wife" can go off to college or to business and develop a whole new image of herself. Similarly, there comes a point when a well organized husband may tire of providing for his poorly managing wife and seek the fulfillment of a more equal partner. Insofar as couples build too much of their emotional balance around their complementary roles, the entire structure of the marriage is at risk if a breakdown of the longstanding arrangement develops.

My own way of differentiating between functional versus dysfunctional complementarity is based not only on whether the balance or trade-off is "working," but also on the inner meanings of the "helpfulness." I use a category which I call *potentially dysfunctional* in order to think about collusive states where couples are currently functioning effectively without conscious complaints or dissatisfaction, but where the basic pattern of the relationship portends major difficulties in the future.

Potentially dysfunctional complementary relationships are those which are seen to enforce and augment weakness, failure to grow, and unequal status. These relationships freeze the development of both partners and invite serious complications of hidden resentment, rage, and revenge. If a husband or wife enjoys and actually seeks to be responsible for the mate's poorer functioning as a way of confirming his or her own vitality, meaningfulness, or superiority, I consider it a potentially dysfunctional relationship. This is a compulsive psychological arrangement that stifles growth in both partners because the weakness of the one mate is needed to facilitate the functioning of the other. Similarly, if a husband or wife insists on being dependent on the partner's strength in order not to develop further as an independent personality, I consider it a potentially dysfunctional relationship.

In a functional (healthy) complementary relationship, the more competent mate is comfortable in acknowledging his/her relative leadership in whichever areas and is comfortable in helping the partner without feeling superior or patronizing. The more competent partner is also genuinely interested in helping the other improve functioning as much as possible and, in any case, expects the mate to contribute other strengths to the relationship. The dependent mate in turn is comfortable in acknowledging his/her relative weakness, open to improving his/her functioning if possible, comfortable about accepting help without jealousy and anger, respectful and supportive of the other's greater strength, and sensitive to being more present and contributing in other ways to the relationship. Healthy complementary relationships are also reflected in the fact that the same couple take turns being the helper and the helped one in different areas of functioning.

It is important to keep in mind that even when a complementary relationship seemingly works for a couple for a long time, problems may show up for a child or in covert apparently unrelated disturbance for either mate. For example, a wife's commitment to the permanence of her marriage may be so great that she keeps up a brave front of family closeness and warmth and tolerates her husband's considerable indifference and distance for many years. Yet, simultaneously, while the complementary roles seem to work, there may be covert symptoms of distress in one of the children who may show behavior problems which actually are a protest of the mother's acquiescence to her husband's indifference and withdrawal. Similarly, a husband who seemingly lives comfortably with his wife's dominating leadership in their relationship may develop a psychosomatic condition that expresses his unexpressed unhappiness.

Sometimes, problems are "paid for" by the children many years later in their own marriages.

> The husband's father cared for his mentally ill wife for many years. His was a kind of patronizing acceptance and overconcern with her every need that, perhaps compassionately, did not challenge her beyond her limitations and made it possible for her to keep functioning pseudo-adequately. On the other hand, it also guaranteed her remaining a marginal shadow figure for all of her life.
>
> Their son learned the pattern to the point where, unconsciously, he sought in his marriage to recreate the same kind of patronizing relationship with his wife. In effect, he encouraged her to be "crazy" by doing crazy things to her, following which he would make himself solicitously available to protect her. The pattern worked for some time, but then something began to shift in the wife and her ensuing protest and push for equality forced a major crisis between them. This crisis proved more terrifying for him than for her; what was at stake for her was an escape from "craziness" towards being more competent and in control of herself, but for him it meant giving up the pseudo-power which was his way of confirming his existence.

Success Traps

These are the potential problems that are based on one or both mates agreeing to the other's overcompetence or overdoing in an area of strength to a point where success is used as an excuse to avoid other needs in one's personality and in the relationship, while the admired skill becomes unattractive and damaging because it is overdone.

The fascinating implication is that significant success in any role or area of experience in itself should be recognized as an emotional hazard. Success traps refer to people who put too many of their eggs in one or another basket of working too hard, overparenting, doing too much sex, being overly committed, etc.

The problem of success is that when one is very good in a given role or quality, the success naturally reinforces one's desire to have more of that same experience. According to the law of reinforcement, the more gratification we get out of doing whatever we are good at, the more we do of it, and then more and more, in order to get "strokes," reinforcement, positive feedback, and pleasure about ourselves for being so capable. The more the investment in that one area, the less time and energy are available for other areas of experience. Moreover, since these "other" areas of experience invariably include skills and roles that are problematic for us, the more we avoid dealing with them, the more problematic they become. At the same time, the more we concentrate on doing more of what we excel in, the more that skill changes in quality and meaning to become "overdone," unattractive, and a source of power and superiority over others. The ancient truth that power corrupts enters into the picture; when people get too good at anything, there is a tendency to pridefulness, hubris, and arrogance. Not infrequently that pridefulness compels continued and even greater success.

The most common success trap in modern life is the escape to one's professional or business life, thus avoiding marital and family intimacy. Another common trap is for a woman to lose herself in mothering functions at the expense of her attractiveness or relating to her husband. Any area of special strength can be taken as a haven to avoid other challenges. For example, a mate who is a warm, loyal friend and companion to his/her spouse may count on the security of this role and not develop necessary power for the role of parent and disciplining children.

Success traps are also a form of complementarity and set off complicated dynamics. There is always a danger that a husband or wife is going to be jealous of the mate's supercompetence; or that the husband/wife will be confirmed in his/her poor self-image, for how is it possible to be as good in this area as the mate? The more such feelings deepen, the more unlikely it is that the difference between the mates will contribute to growth. What often develops is a superior-inferior relationship, which, of course, provokes unconscious hostile feelings. An Italian movie, *Wife Mistress*, described beautifully the alternation between a husband and wife around the exaggerated competence of the one and the incompetence of the other. Early in the film, we see the dashing husband on top of his world, moving elegantly across the countryside, enjoying his business and many women, all the while his wan wife lay at home in a neurasthenic stupor. By the end of the film, we see the wife freed of her neurosis, enjoying herself as the manager of the business which she has now taken over. Now she is with her many lovers, while her husband is locked into a paranoidal impotence and is confined to the house.

THE FAILURE OF COLLUSIONS: PROJECTIVE BLAMING AND THE "PARANOID MARRIAGE"

When a marriage is characterized by blaming and bitter criticism of one's mate, it is often possible to track the dissatisfaction back to one of the above marital collusions where the mates had agreed, albeit unconsciously, to a way of life in which emotional growth would not be expected. Collusions around incompetence, complementarity, and oversuccess are, after all, ways in which people agree to remain as they are and not develop their personalities further. The agreements vary as to whether they ratify primarily one's own incompetence, one's mate's incompetence, one's own superiority, one's mate's superiority, or combinations of the above. However, what they all have in common is that they "freeze" the existing situation and turn away calls to new growth and more evenly balanced personalities and relationships. The underlying intention in all cases is to stop anxiety, uncertainty, and risk.

When the collusive agreement nonetheless proves not sufficient to bind anxiety, there may develop familiar marital complaints, anger, and other symptoms of the couple's need to renegotiate their agreement (Dicks, 1967; Charny, 1972). If the couple are able to respond constructively, stop their blaming, and get on with building a more balanced competence, one can only marvel at how the marriage flourishes after a difficult period of tension and crisis. However, in many cases the projective process of anger and blaming is not reversed and builds into a new phase of bitterness and chronic hate; if this process lasts and escalates, it can lead to what can be called a "paranoid marriage."

The marital system now deteriorates to a rigid system of blaming, accusation, rage, mistrust, revenge, and chronic wishes or plans for the other's disappearance or demise. Many more marriages than we would like to admit are maintained around such a system (see Lansky, 1981 about the "narcissistically vulnerable marriage"). In effect, the couple become locked into a kind of mutual paranoid state. The mate is blamed for all the miseries of the marriage and life. Unlike criticism and anger that are processed constructively by mates who turn discontent and disagreement into opportunities to develop further, the anger and hate flood one or both personalities and no longer can be explored to challenge and free the individuals or the couple to grow. Even in therapy, it is generally not possible to talk out blaming and accusations once they reach this stage.

Although the bitterness and rage clearly bring a good deal of suffering, even this terrible system often is covertly valued and its continuation may be guarded for a long time. Attributing to a mate all the misery and bitterness of one's life is hardly a pleasant experience, but it does have the distinct advantages of explaining all of one's troubles, holding someone else responsible, stimulating energies through anger, and generally confirming one's identity through the intense experiences of bitterness and rage. Even when the latter are basically justified, the temptation to fall into "living" through the blaming-paranoid process is enormous.

In a presentation of Bowenian theory, Kerr (1981) has written:

> Conflict in the marriage often provides an amazingly stable solution to the relationship dilemma of the need for emotional closeness on the one hand, and the allergy to too much closeness on the other. Conflictual marriages are extremely intensive relationships in which each of the spouse's emotional reactiveness is focused on the other spouse. (p. 243)

Such couples characteristically ask for treatment at a point where one of the mates somehow is beginning to consider breaking out of the system. Sometimes it is because the suffering has become too much to bear; other times a point is reached in the life cycle which brings home the message that time is running out and the next stage of life will be a grim one without a major change. This also happens when one of the mates has enjoyed a spurt of personal growth (often as a result of experiences outside of the marriage—at work or in a love affair) which gives him or her a vision of better possibilities and the courage to challenge the long-standing paranoid system. In most cases where the marital system has been seriously paranoid for a long time, the emerging readiness of one spouse to break out of the system will *not* trigger corresponding growth in the other mate who, on the contrary, characteristically will be incensed at the breakaway of his/her fellow slave from the mutual paranoid system. The definitive treatment issue in these cases tends to be to help the mate who is ready to grow to fulfill his/her new potential to be free. This includes helping the spouse to take responsibility for all those elements of weakness or exaggerated strength that helped create the original collusion against growth. Hopefully this will happen before they actually separate; if not, second best is in the preparation for a new intimate relationship after the separation is effected.

WHEN IS A MARITAL PROBLEM A PROBLEM?

To conclude: So long as marriages are unfolding, changing, searching processes, either blessed with pleasure and satisfaction or blessed with hopes that these will yet be achieved, the marriage is alive and basically "well" even if there are problems and even if the couple should have professional help. However, marriages that are frozen in an unchanging, undeveloping posture, even if they are to all accounts "successful" or "happy," are in trouble. Without an essence of "becoming," without the courage to be involved in working at one's various inadequacies and over-doing, without criticism, confrontation, challenge, and being responsible for one's various poor judgments, marriages stagnate and die. Marital Trap Analysis is a way of thinking about these dangers as early as possible, even before people complain.

6

Levels of Psychological Organization in Marriage

Individuality, Couplehood, and Family

> He is sour-faced and glum. She looks peaked and tight. They are on
> their way to an island vacation. He puts his hand around her shoulder
> and there is a slight twitch around her mouth in response. "I hope
> we'll be able to have a good time," he says. "I'll order a blue movie
> in our room." She smiles wanly and tries to rally herself brightly. "It's
> been a while, Dick, but who knows, maybe the vacation will do us
> good."

Who are the actors in this small vignette of marital interaction—the two
individuals who are in the scene or the couple as an interactive system? The
question is not at all absurd when one considers that to this day mental
health professionals engage in frequent debate about whom precisely they
are going to treat when it comes to marital problems.

Many insist that when there is marital tension, one or the other
spouse or, even better, both of them undergo *individual psychotherapy.*
Other therapists believe that the focus of marital treatment is the interaction of the two mates and therefore prescribe *couple therapy;* some of
these insist that therapy be only for the couple together, while others
devote many sessions to couple work, so that the core of the therapy
flows from this mode, but also see each of the spouses individually, and
perhaps quite unevenly—one spouse comes much more to individual
therapy than the other.

Some therapists do not work very much with the couples as couples, but
instead do most of their marital therapy by working on the *marital subsystem*

within the framework of a larger family therapy. Still other therapists want to see the parents of each spouse with their adult child or the parents of each spouse with the couple, in *intergenerational* or *family of origin* sessions. There are other variations as well. Framo (personal communication, 1976, 1981, 1992), one of the pioneer-originators and teachers of intergenerational work, insists on the presence of all siblings as well. So the question of who will make up the cast of characters in the marital interaction also has very real consequences for just who will be invited to work with the therapist and what level(s) of organization of the marital experience will be emphasized.

There are also many variations in creating the therapeutic drama, even within the same structural mode. Couple sessions, for example, can be devoted to working on the couple's interaction, but they can also be designed to work on the personality problems of any one mate (including going back to early childhood issues) *while the husband or wife is present*. The mate can be assigned the role of "observer" or, I prefer, "consultant," an intriguing technique because it makes the spouse a partner to the therapy even though it is very much individual therapy of the one mate that is being emphasized. This approach has aroused concern among some therapists who feel that instead of making the spouse "a partner to the therapy," it may place him/her in a one-up position as the healthy one vis-à-vis the disturbed mate in need of treatment. In my experience, this has not happened. Couples feel more warmly connected and the "consultant" spouse is far more empathic and caring after sharing such sessions. Often the consultant mate's contribution is a very powerful one that cuts through the spouse's deepest resistances because it is based on expert knowledge of the spouse and his/her family of origin. When rendered from a "consultant's" role, as distinguished from participating in the sessions as a self-interested spouse, these interventions can be even more powerful. Moreover, my own experience is that the decision to do individual sessions with one spouse grows so organically and "fairly" out of the material that has come up in couple sessions that it neither embarrasses the spouse focused on nor enhances the power of the other. It simply "is" what everyone could see should be worked on at this time, for both spouses' benefits.

On the other hand, the presence of the husband or wife can also inhibit an individual therapy. Many individuals decide they do not want their mate present in this kind of session because they feel a need for the specialness of being alone with the therapist, or they do not want to expose to their mate the issues they want to work on.

When individual sessions for one or each of the mates are the chosen mode of treatment, it is still possible to emphasize work on the marital system rather than on the individual's personality by focusing on the characteristic scenarios of the couple's interaction. Through change in the one party who is working in individual therapy, the goal is to change the system. In other words, even after the operational decision is made of who will be participating in the sessions, there remains a choice of focus in the session itself: a therapist can work on individual matters when a couple is present and a therapist can work on the couple when only a single spouse is present.

My own answer to the original question of who make up the cast of characters is, unhesitatingly, *both* the individuals *and* their shared system. It has to be the height of absurdity not to see in a husband and wife two real individuals who are saying and doing things to one another and influencing and impacting on each other. It also is evident that a husband and wife create a sequence of interactions with one another that have their own repetitive, stereotypical momentum, a kind of dance or system which determines much of how each then reacts to the other. Moreover, a couple who have children are also playing out their relationship to one another in the ways they lead the family unit, while their marital relationship is in turn highly influenced by the process taking place with their children and the ways in which the children are and are not thriving. There are many couples who come for help because they want to help their children and are very willing to work on their relationship as married people insofar as they hope in this way to improve their parenting. They should be seen either in family therapy or in couple sessions devoted to their parenting. However, if therapists push them to work on their marriage in its own right without reference to the children, these couples will flee therapy. I also think it is wrong not to recognize that adults remain children to their own parents, so that the opportunity to work directly on unresolved issues in relation to one's family of origin (e.g., should mother live with us?) can be an excellent way of dealing with pressing marital problems.

Sad to report, the new wisdom we have gained about the couple as a system or field of forces has in many cases spawned a new orthodoxy that, like that orthodoxy of yesteryear that recognized only individuals and refused to recognize couples, now refuses to recognize individuals. For many years the prevailing school of psychoanalysis ruled out the possibility of a patient talking about his or her marital problems; in a psychoanalytic session, these were treated as resistances to the 'real' therapy. Along with this cardinal rule against any marital content in the individual therapy session, there was an absolute injunction against the therapist of one mate seeing the spouse, even if the spouse or both partners would request such a session. To this day there are psychoanalytic practitioners who on principle will not agree to nor initiate a suggestion for a session with the husband and wife together.

I had occasion to see a man who had been in private psychoanalytic therapy for no less than 20 years with a psychiatrist affiliated with a major university department in the United States. His long-standing therapist had refused to see his wife even when the patient asked him to do so. Not surprisingly, the wife turned out to be the object of some of the patient's deepest fears. Admittedly, these fears derived from a childhood trauma of early loss of his mother, but they were projected with such intensity into expectations of loss of the current mate that they were causing real havoc in the marital interaction, which in turn increased the patient's anxiety even more.

Family therapy appeared in the world of mental health in the early 60s as a blessed new approach. Here was a truly revolutionary leap where patients were brought into treatment together with their family members. The new form of therapy was a new perspective for seeing and working with the problem as a couple or family problem.

Unfortunately, almost immediately this "revolution" brought with it its own successive version of certainty and tyranny. A great many new family therapists now insisted that only the *entire* family should be seen and that all requests by individuals to be seen in an individual interview were to be turned away and treated as resistances to the *real* therapy with the family as an entirety.

Kaslow (1981a) has observed that the practice of family therapy should be based on a wise selection and integration of different modes or tools of treatment; she is critical of any one-sided single school of therapy viewpoint.

> The problem arises when adherents of a school become totalistic purists—exuding a fanaticism, purporting that their way is the only right way. As has happened throughout the history of the psychiatric professions, brilliant, charismatic leaders attract those who have a longing to become worshipful true believers. They carry the gospel with them—unquestioningly—and any deviations from the master's catechism is heresy. (p. 347)

At this writing, many but definitely not all marital therapists are more flexible about meeting individuals, at least on request. However, the prevailing mode is to insist on seeing the couple as a unit. One is often treated to admonitions by teachers of therapy not to be seduced by people who want to talk about individual psychological issues—whether these be past experiences such as early childhood experiences, vivid inner-life issues such as appear in dreams and other yields of unconscious production, or a spouse who wants to meet alone to tell his/her personal viewpoint and experience of the marriage. Individual sessions for spouses are regarded as "old-fashioned" psychoanalytic treatment, and as "failures to think systemically." It is sad that so much of the wisdom we have gained from systems thinking about couples as a unit and field of forces has also spawned a new orthodoxy that blindly refuses to see in marital interaction the two individuals who are there in their real individual strengths and weaknesses (Salin, 1985; Schwartz & Pessotta, 1985).

FOUR LEVELS: INDIVIDUALITY, COUPLEHOOD, THE CONTEMPORARY FAMILY OF THE COUPLE AND THEIR CHILDREN, AND INTERGENERATIONAL INFLUENCES

One of the main tensions that therapists face in designing psychotherapy for couples is knowing how to distribute the relative emphasis on the couple as a couple and on each of the mates as a person with his/her feelings and actions in the marriage. An accurate picture of a couple always will include both the couple as a system and the two mates as individuals. Two spouses as a couple create a characteristic style of interaction or a "system" operating between them, but they are also individuals, and each of them has a distinct identity in the marital process. Systems thinking represents a major step forward in all psychotherapy, and is rightly hailed as a major "paradigm shift" in the epistemology of emotional change. At the same time, we must remember that individual husbands and wives are the ones who process the major choices in their marriages and are responsible for their consequences.

Sometimes the responsibilities of marriage and family life force a person of integrity to choose not to choose—that is, to forego their own individual needs and stay with the overriding needs of a member of the family or the family as a whole, as when one mate devotes much of his/her personality to saving the stability of the other. This would seem to be a classic instance of a system of disturbance. Yet, in a paradoxical way, this kind of deferring of one's individual needs in favor of rescuing another person, as well as the obverse of being spared falling apart by reliance on one's protective mate, is also a reminder that real individuals exist in each one of the mates, each of whom is *choosing* the system described.

What is especially interesting in the marital process is that the two poles of individuality and couplehood are drawn together in fascinating phenomena of considerable resemblances between married mates. It is generally considered that husband and wife are likely to be at the same level of emotional development and that they are likely to have similar ego structures or basic styles of defense. Giovacchini (1965) wrote: "I have come to the conclusion that the nature and depth of psychopathology are identical for the husband and wife in a long-established marriage" (p. 46). In fact, it is a basic rule of marital therapy that any spouse's complaint about the other should be evaluated first of all as a possible and probable projection of a similar problem in the complainer's personality (Dicks, 1967).

There is a balance between couplehood and individuality. People who are secure in being themselves are less likely to use the other to hide their own weaknesses behind their mate's similar shortcomings and then to complain about the very weaknesses which they secreted away in their mate. So one goal of adult development is to become more of one's own person. People who are committed to cooperating with one another and are best friends to one another are less likely to use the other as a dumping ground for their own shortcomings. So a proper goal for couples is to be committed to cooperation with one another. Individuality and couplehood are two sides of the coin of being adults in a marriage; each is real and precious, and the two together create a symphony.

Couples create characteristic styles or patterns and get into ruts. Each person chooses his/her pattern and the two fit together in self-repeating mosaics. The story of one couple, repeated over and over again, is that *he pursues her while she plays aloof, indifferent, and patronizing*. The prevailing story line in another couple is that she *loves him warmly and he is pleased by her attention and appreciation, but they both pretend not to notice that he is not as devoted to her as she is to him*. The repetitive program-template of a third couple is that *he does everything for her, and she allows him to do so*. So much of the history of couples' lives is written around the templates of their system that it is only wise to plan marital therapies that include working with the couple together to look honestly at their system.

Research shows the best results of marital therapy derive from therapies which are built substantially around couple sessions, hardly surprising considering the nature of the beast to be treated—the couple—and not at all surprising when one appreciates the power of the system that a couple creates (Gurman & Kniskern, 1978, 1981b). At the same time, too many marital therapists get locked into doing only couples therapy—in whatever combination of couple and individual sessions—and ignore the fact that couples who have children are also leaders and caretakers of a family unit that is of enormous significance to them. The development of the family and the welfare of the children have considerable impact on the evolution of the marriage, for better and for worse. It is one of the significant discoveries of child psychiatry and family therapy that mature and wholesome marriages protect children from emotional disturbances and even can succeed in cushioning children's passages through many objective problems such as birth defects, illness, developmental limitations, learning problems,

and so on. But it is also very true that any of these problems and many
other events and processes in the lives of children in turn have an enormous
impact on the parents and their marriage.

Many therapists have taken the truth that marital problems generally lie
behind children's emotional problems to the point of an unwillingness to
recognize that *parental* pleasures and worries also affect the adult man's and
adult woman's ability to sustain and cultivate their marital experience and
pleasure. In other words, the children's situations affect the parents who
are affecting the children. Parents are affected by the personalities of the
children, even the chance elements that derive from the ages of the children,
their birth order, their sex, biological characteristics, the match between children's temperaments and their parents, and so on. There are couples who
are basically very well suited to one another as marital partners and who
are also well-intentioned parents, but for various reasons do not succeed
in putting together a happy family system; over time, this failure eats its
way at the fibers of the marital process. For example, a long-standing empirical observation is that families with disabled or developmentally disabled
children and families where children die of an illness or an accident suffer
a considerable increase in divorce rate (Voyse, 1975).

Marriages also live within a larger framework that is beyond the primary
family. This framework includes the parents of the spouses—the grandparent generation, whose influence is considerable. Even the absence of a
grandparent is a fact that has substantial impact on a marriage. *For example,
a young mother loses her beloved father during her first pregnancy, she becomes
depressed over her loss, and suffers an invisible panic at being alone that affects
her rearing of that same child.* Similarly, the interfering demands of obstrep-
erous, tyrannical elders in young peoples' marriages or parenting are a
theme in countless popular stories and anecdotes; parents and in-laws can
and do ruin marriages that would have grown otherwise on their own.
Moreover, even if the grandparent generation is not playing an active role
in influencing their children's marriage and parenting, there are many
instances where young adults are unable to grow in their marriages because
they are still so involved *internally* with their relationships with their family
of origin.

In these instances, too, the appropriate focus of marital therapy should
wisely be on the unfinished business with the elders in the past. If they
are alive, and if the relationships and the logistical possibilities are such
that actual intergenerational sessions can be held, intergenerational sessions
are a wonderful opportunity to shortcut the process and get to the core of
matters more effectively than is possible when one works only with the
young peoples' side to the story, and without the emotional impact of the
actual presence of their parents (Framo, 1976, 1981, 1982, 1992).

Ideally, the proper diagnosis of a couple and the planning of treatment will be based on understanding major issues on four levels of psychological organization—each of the individuals who comprise the couple, the couple as a system, the couple within the framework of the family unit that they lead, including the impact of their children's welfare on them, and each of the mates as a representative of a continuing process with his/her own family of origin. Clinicians need to understand how each level of psychological experience can have a major impact, and need to be open-minded in approaching each case to learn where the process-foci are. If the clinician is invariably committed only to one focus or one method of intervention, many cases will be forced into a less-than-optimal treatment strategy in order to fulfill the clinician's needs rather than the best interests of the clients.

A couple are in a state of shock following a major explosion by the long-taciturn wife who has spoken up to say that she wants a divorce. He is hurt and bewildered by her wanting to leave him. She is for the most part pleased, but also frightened by her own unusual burst of spirit and strength. Both really want to see what kind of impact this crisis will have on their relationship which has been sterile for some years.

How should this couple be treated? The therapist in the case believes that the level of organization which is most relevant to both spouses at this point of their presentation of themselves for treatment is their marital interaction. Therefore, the therapist chooses couple sessions as the immediate treatment mode. In doing so, the therapist is also aware that, empirically, couple sessions maximize the possibilities of the couple staying together and not divorcing much more than individual sessions do (Gurman & Kniskern, 1978, 1981b).

In the course of the couple sessions, a picture begins to emerge of a long-term style in the husband distancing himself from intimacy, repeated use of irony, cynicism, an insistence on maintaining distance, use of a bossy pseudo-power, and a disavowal of tender, respectful, and loving feelings. The basic picture that emerges of the wife is that she suffered considerable emotional deprivation as a child—there was virtually no physical touch-loving by her mother— and she has developed a special style of forbearance and renunciation of her needs. The therapist decides that the treatment will now be extended to include individual therapy of each mate *along* with continuing couple sessions. The goal in this second phase of treatment will be to hold the couple sessions in a low-key or background function which will support the individual work before returning with greater force to couple sessions at a later date.

A FIFTH DIMENSION: THE LARGER SOCIETAL FRAME

There is another level that has not been identified in our multilevel analysis thus far. What is happening in one's community, other major identity groups such as one's religious affiliation, the larger cultural pattern of one's era, let alone in the international arena also definitely affect the marital process. Problems that require treatment not only can be cast in a context of a larger extended family system, they can also be influenced by systems of connections to larger and larger contexts of the societal system and even international events. It is the responsibility of the psychotherapist to look at these successive stages of interpersonal connection and the larger systems in which couples are embedded. Otherwise, the family therapy which "saved" psychotherapy from a narrow solipsistic view of individuals that denies the presence of other key people in the individual's life ends up creating another fairytale world, still focusing only on too-small units of reality.

Too many therapists treat the process of marriage as if it stands unto itself and hold husbands and wives responsible for their wins and losses as if they are all their own doing. In part, this is a statement of the responsibility that every couple really does carry for their outcome regardless of broader events, but it is also a superficial way of ignoring the broader events of society and history that affect marriages strongly. For example, if a couple lives in a community where it is possible to walk the streets at night safely and to relax at home without fear, the context supports the marriage, whereas living in an armed fortress and in constant fear pushes people up against the more panicky and more nasty parts of their personalities. Similarly, a community which retains its tradition of open contact between people, uncomplicated social visiting, get-togethers, and parties will create an entirely different climate for couples than a community where contact is strongly regulated by stereotyped roles and rituals that maintain distance and reduce expressions of warmth and friendship.

Admittedly, this level of psychological organization—what we are calling "a fifth dimension"—is likely to be more puzzling to many therapists. It is very hard for therapists to conceptualize how cultural and societal perspectives impact on the lives of a couple. However, the fact that these are difficult conceptual linkages to make does not excuse a refusal to think about larger events on the part of many therapists who refuse to deal with anything beyond their consulting rooms.

For example, many of us believe that the ultimate watershed event of our century is the Holocaust. Yet to this day, I have seen and heard of many therapists who are totally unable to relate to the impact of the Holocaust, even for patients who were *direct* victims and therefore carry deep within them crucial memories of cruelty and barbarity.

A Holocaust survivor in her sixties, who is herself a practicing psychotherapist, told me on the occasion of her belated first visit to Israel that she had been in therapy with several well-known therapists in the United States and none of them had asked her to track the implications of her experiences in what she euphemistically called "the war"! Now that she was in Israel, she was suddenly overwhelmed with deep reminiscences of everything that she had undergone as a Jewess in the Holocaust.

* * * * * *

I remember the therapy of another woman who was coming to couple sessions with her husband. Both were survivors of the Holocaust. The main purpose of treatment was to help them in coping with a psychotic child in his early 20s. We reached a point one day of such bitter, mistrusting remarks towards me by the woman that I had no choice but to focus on the issue of her transference towards me. I insisted over and over again that she tell me what was so troubling to her that day. Finally, she reluctantly explained that her mind was occupied with a story that would explain why she was angry, but it would be better for her not to share the story with me. It took a good many further requests and encouragements before she agreed to tell the following story:

When she was 10 years old, she and other Jews were escaping from the Nazis. They paid a Christian to lead them over the border. The guide led them safely across the river not too far from the border, but once they had crossed in safety, he abandoned them. Shortly thereafter, they were picked up by the Germans. They had reason to suspect that not only had the guide deserted them, but that he had sold them out to the Nazis for another fee. They were then taken to the concentration camp where they suffered the remainder of the war but miraculously survived. "What I feel when I pay you for this therapy," said the woman, "is that you are that same guide we paid to get us across the border, and you don't really care either!"

I don't know when I have been moved more deeply by a "transference complaint"! To my ears and heart, the story she told bespoke the overwhelming reality of events in the Holocaust which no one who endured them can possibly forget, and hence the dominating role of the Holocaust in this woman's life and that of the couple.

In therapy the realness of these issues of the larger world calls for a special sensitivity on the part of the therapist and specific variations of technique.

Let us say a wife is the daughter of Holocaust survivors. She and her husband are bored with one another. The husband complains that his wife is too practical and forever busy with "doing things right." They don't seem to have any fun together. A responsible therapist would know that many children of Holocaust survivors characteristically suffer from denial of joy and playfulness, as if they cannot enjoy life too fully in the presence of what their parents went through. Theirs is often a combination of a kind of survival guilt—their own and/or the intergenerational transmission of their parents' guilt at surviving—and a direct conditioning by their post-Holocaust depressed parents not to be too joyful (Davidson, 1980 and forthcoming). In the face of the accumulated hell their parents suffered, how can they be frivolous and enjoy themselves? It may be much more productive to steer the therapy to the wife's relationship to her parents and, specifically, to the meanings of the Holocaust in their family life than to work too soon on current marital interactions.

As we move toward the end of the 20th century, contemporary couples clearly are responding, even if unconsciously, to the growing reality of nuclear and other ecocidal hazards which threaten to destroy so much of human life and which also affect marriages. It is not farfetched to speculate that some of the epidemic of cynicism and disillusionment with marriage and family life, as well as some searches for alternatives through meaningless styles of sexual experience and trivial encounters, are also statements of a panic about the destiny of life. The human animal has been increasingly exposed as a selfish, destructive, insane creature, and in this context it is hard to love, to trust, and to commit oneself to stay in long-term marriages.

It is also true that if people come into therapy and actually want to talk about preventing nuclear extinction and not about their marriages and themselves, or about whatever ideology or efforts to solve injustice in this world, it is the task of therapists to lead them back to the level of experience that psychotherapy is most designed for—human relationships and inner experience. It is true that neither therapist nor patients can solve the problems of society in the therapy room beyond a certain point of spiritual commitment to seek to be as constructive citizens as possible. This, too, is one of the sad, existential truths to be learned in therapy.

7

Defining the Goals of Marital Therapy

In introducing an issue of the *Family Therapy Networker* devoted to couples therapy, editor Richard Simon (1988) observed that overall "couples therapy remains a puzzle."

> Despite its prominence in clinicians' practice, couples therapy, with the exception of a few highly structured models, still seems to lack a clear method. Most couples therapy I've seen bears the stamp of the clinicians' personal style far more than any coherently spelled out theory or technique. There is a sense of winging it, of knowing a few ideas from here and there, while spicing things up with some inspirational rhetoric about "intimacy" and "growth." Most therapists I know admit that their work with couples is the most confusing part of their practice. (p. 2)

The seemingly simple solution to the problem of setting goals for couple therapy that many therapists like to adopt is to treat those specific problems for which people seek help. I reject this definition out of hand just as I would expect a physician to refuse to offer every treatment that is requested, even when people are complaining about a problem that is genuinely troublesome to them and deserving of relief. Consider, for example the following situation:

> The couple has been married five years, but they have yet to achieve a satisfactory basic sexual relationship. She is tense, inhibited, and barely able to allow him to enter her after long periods of no contact between them at all. He is a sweet, eager-to-please, and understand-

ing personality, someone who seems to be able to maintain a positive, optimistic attitude about everything, but now he is beginning to run out of patience.

What treatment should be offered this couple, given the above information? The natural inclination of laymen and many professionals as well is to hope that help can be given to the couple to become sexually functional. Presumably, this would involve teaching them to work together, for him to help her overcome her fearfulness, and for her to learn to relax and work through whatever emotional conflicts have made her unable to embark on a path of personal sexual development. Perhaps then this couple will be able to live the proverbial happily ever after. However, clinical wisdom teaches us that if such a couple are given couple therapy plus or including sexual therapy, it is likely that (a) other major issues will turn up as the underpinnings of their inhibited psychosexual interaction, and/or (b) once the couple achieves sexual intimacy, major distress of another sort could develop between the husband and wife, even to the point of possible breakdown of the marriage (Levay & Kagle, 1977a). Jane Brody (1980) described in a *New York Times* article cases of "successful" sexual behavior therapy which led to couple divorce *because* of the successful therapy.

What happens in the process of treating a couple's inability to function in some area is that serious flaws in the character and personality of one or both mates are likely to be discovered which have led them into their impasse. When the impasse is removed, the underlying flaws are seen and experienced more vividly than they were so long as the symptom of marital insufficiency held everybody's attention. Thus, to continue the previous example:

> He is a Mama's boy in the sense that as a child he came to an inner conclusion that mother's authority could not be challenged even though she was an unpleasant kind of personality, often cold and rejecting. Thus, he turned himself into an all-pleasing, optimistic kind of person, as if in charge of his life, but at the expense of some important part of his "backbone" of courage and masculinity.
>
> She is the daughter of a frighteningly volatile and angry mother. She reacted by closing herself up in fearfulness and tightness that also became a suit of armor against hurts slung at her by her mother. She really wants to learn to open up and be sexual, but what happens for her with her husband is that she finds him too much of a boy to be able to help her in her fright. As therapy invites her to experience and risk a new degree of openness, she looks at him and realizes that he is not the kind of man who can help her to fight the nasty mother

she had, that his pleasantness is built on being accommodating and avoiding conflict rather than on self-respect and an intention to tackle problems, and she becomes increasingly disenchanted.

When couples ask for help about a given problem, we do not know what their real problems are until we complete an objective diagnosis and assessment. In this case, for example, the evaluation should lead us not to a prescription of sexual therapy nor to any kind of couple therapy that is intended to bring the couple to greater tenderness and sensuality as a first goal, but to a serious look at what has been holding each of the partners back as an individual from being able to generate a momentum towards development of his/her natural sexuality.

Even so, the problem doesn't end there, for in countless instances of couple therapy there develops a situation where the emotional needs and welfare of one spouse are not consistent with the needs and welfare of the other. In the above case, for example, it is possible that the wife's potential for unfolding into mature sexuality is greater than her husband's potential for retracing his steps and becoming the kind of person who really takes autonomous and expressive stands. As she grows, he will be less and less satisfying to her. Or the situation could go the other way where he will prove capable of learning to put his foot down and take stands and not be propitiating, but much as he would have wanted her to grow to be able to move ahead with him in life together, she could prove permanently crippled by her needs for self-protection against maternal rage and rejection and need to remain a limited, embittered woman with whom he will not be able to stay.

CLINICAL PROBLEMS, PRAGMATIC CONSIDERATIONS, AND ETHICAL VALUES

I find it useful to differentiate between three aspects of the problem in conceptualizing the goals of therapy:

1. *Clinical Problems.* These are the identified problems that the couple is complaining about. I also add here anticipated problems, as seen either by the couple or by the therapist, that represent potential dysfunctional or limiting aspects in the couple's future marital experience.

2. *Pragmatic Considerations.* Here I have in mind the available resources and limitations of the people requesting treatment, such as financial resources, logistical availability to scheduled treatment sessions, ideological considerations such as a religious point of view that might make cer-

tain types of therapy unacceptable, degree of emotional strength available to sustain stresses of ambiguity or confrontation of one's weaknesses, life-cycle considerations or demands inherent in the life timetable of a couple or family, such as having to move to another city at a certain time, and so on.

3. *Ethical Values*. These are the implications of the treatment process and its outcomes for the physical and mental health and welfare of each and all of the family members. Thus, given the current symptom pattern, what are the implications of continuation of these symptoms for each spouse, for the marriage, and for the immediate and extended family? And given the impact of a proposed therapeutic process, what will be the impact on each person and unit in the family? Ideally, one would hope that what is good for the couple qua couple will also be good for each of the mates as individuals and, if they have children, for each and all of their children. In reality, however, there are often serious discrepancies between the needs of individuals, couple, and family.

These different frames of reference must be considered when one is thinking about the various people and groupings involved. Referring to the couple as a couple, we are talking about the potential continuity and quality of a marriage. At the same time, there is a drama of the potential of each of the mates as a human being in his/her marital/family experience compared to the potential of each mate were he or she to leave the present marriage and family. Will he be able to grow while living in this marriage and family structure, or would he do better if he left and went seeking a different kind of experience with another woman? Will the wife be able to grow healthily while living in this marriage or would she be a healthier person if she sought a different kind of living experience? Similar considerations attend the welfare of each of the children of a couple—each child's potential for his/her self within or outside the framework of the present family as it is now or if there were a divorce or separation.

There may be no way to summarize how to go about evaluating the conclusions to be drawn from analyzing the combinations of clinical, pragmatic, and ethical considerations when formulating the goals of treatment, but therapists should be trained to think actively of these several considerations to a point where they are able to analyze from these points of view, knowledgeably and responsibly, the multifaceted picture of any couple in treatment and to utilize this information in selecting the goals of therapy.

There should be no one set of standard goals for all the couples who come to us. The traditional psychoanalytic-psychodynamic point of view that each person should look deeply into his/her self and grow in personality is not necessarily good medicine for all; brief therapy models that specify a number of sessions which are focused on removing the major symptoms about which a couple is complaining are not necessarily the correct choice for all; learning to communicate freely and completely should not be prescribed for all couples. Each case must be evaluated on its own merits. The therapist must be prepared to defend the choices that s/he makes, not in the name of an ideology, but in the framework of the analysis of the couple and their picture of strengths and weaknesses, resources, and limitations. (See Haley, 1980 for a sadly accurate ironical portrayal of would-be marital therapists who have no treatment plan whatsoever.)

The following is a case illustration in which these concepts are applied:

> The quality of the marital experience was near terrible. She had insisted they come to therapy because of her husband's violence towards her, which she could no longer tolerate. He came because she insisted, but clearly was not about to enter into therapy willingly.
>
> They fought a great deal. They rarely spoke with one another. They rarely shared experiences with one another. Sexual activity had ceased almost entirely, even though they were both very attractive people in their thirties. It also emerged that the husband had regular female companionship arranged in his daily "professional schedule."
>
> What both husband and wife shared, however, was a deep commitment to their children, and to their family. Divorce was inconceivable to either of them since it meant leaving the children. Neither was dissatisfied with the emptiness of their experience together. In fact, just coming home, being able to see the children, and simply sitting around and watching TV with them seemed to fill some deep yearning for family togetherness for both of them. The therapist asked for the children to come in with their parents for a series of exploratory family sessions. In these sessions, it became clear that the children were consciously, even obsessively, fearful that their parents might divorce and clung with desperation to both mother and father, enjoining them explicitly never to part.

What should be the goals of treatment in this case? It is all very well to argue that the present couple relationship is obviously disturbed by any normal standard and it is even right to argue that the marital/family structure is inherently a pathogenic one that will foster disturbed children. Nonetheless, here was a group of adults and children who felt strongly that being together was more important than anything else. In this case, the three ways of looking at the couple's needs for treatment that were introduced earlier can be summarized as follows:

1. *Clinical Needs*. The presenting problem of the husband's violence needs to be treated. Other problems which the couple does not complain about include a lack of sexuality, the husband's routinized deception, the wife's renunciation of demands for herself, including any natural power with which to stand up to his violence, and a lack of activities together.

2. *Pragmatic Considerations*. The wife was successful in forcing the husband to come for therapy around the presenting complaint of violence, but there are no indications of motivation to undertake to improve their marriage and grow for themselves in other ways. Certainly, there is no desire to risk trying to grow or, if they are not able to, then to separate. On the contrary, there is a message of desperation about the possibility that they might be forced into a separation they do not want.

3. *Ethical Values*. The husband appears smugly confident that he has pulled together the kind of world of work and sexual pleasures that he wants and a marriage/family structure that is important to him without his having to suffer emotional intimacy with his wife. What will happen to the husband if he is forced into intimacy? There are indications that he is really afraid of going crazy if he has to be accountable in a close relationship. Maybe he would. The wife seems organized in a martyred kind of self-denying personal style. She enjoys a very active work life which apparently nourishes her sense of identity sufficiently to help her remain oblivious to how much indignity she suffers in her marriage. What would happen to her if therapy pushed her to a confrontation with the extent to which she disowns her basic self? The answer isn't clear, but what comes through strongly is the sense that she has long since given up on any strong definition of her personhood. Finally, the children make it very clear that they suffer desperate fears of a breakdown of their family.

The conclusion that seemed appropriate to the therapist in this case was to set as a decisive goal the limiting of all violence. Among other things, the wife was "trained" in the husband's presence in couple sessions to call the police if her husband struck her. Then the couple were counseled that there were strong indications that they would always remain limited in the degree of intimacy and genuine communication they would be able to achieve, but that they should purposely plan to increase the number and variety of activities that they do together, such as going to the movies and visiting and receiving friends, in order to add to their sense of themselves as a married couple. They were told that their real forte was their love of their children and their devotion to their family, which they will have over the years, but they should accept the fact that they are not going to be close friends. The recommendation was made that no further marital therapy be attempted once the violence was under control.

Of course, it would be entirely legitimate to argue against the therapist's conclusions and handling of the above case. The point of the illustration is not to show that the one and definitely correct answer was reached, but rather to illustrate a way of thinking where the therapist holds himself accountable for being able to explain his professional decisions as to how he designs the therapy.

I believe that many marital therapists refrain from acknowledging and using the authority assigned to them by virtue of their professional role and seek to conceal the fact that they have a significant role in deciding what treatment to offer and how to design the therapy. A sloppy tradition has developed of offering therapies based not on assessment of the clients but on an automatic acceptance of the patient's manifest complaints and requests, automatic identification with whichever spouse calls first for help, the therapist's treatment ideology, the client's ability to pay, and so on. I think that psychotherapists need to formulate each case's needs based on each situation—which is no more than what we ask of all other professionals such as physicians, lawyers, and accountants.

Willi (1984) has written how goal setting in marital therapy is also a function of the *particular* value-attitudes the therapist adopts. He distinguishes between three value systems:

> An *ethical value system* is based on a conception of good marriages vs. bad marriages, where good marriages are considered a function of unselfishness, compromise, sacrifice, and duty.

> A *medical value system* puts the burden on those conditions and processes which will keep people psychologically healthy vs. those conditions expected to lead to psychological illness in any member of the family.

> An *emancipatory value system* is based on the goal of a growth-oriented marriage as opposed to a stagnant one.

Willi observes that, by virtue of their professional identification, most therapists are operating, in effect, from the point of view of the last value and often overidentify with it at the expense of people's needs. In any case, he cautions that "in couple therapy, a therapist can find himself involved in difficult—for him sometimes almost insoluble—conflicts between these various value systems" (p. 103).

Figure 2 illustrates a worksheet for thinking in a somewhat more organized way about these issues with couples who come for marital therapy. It is a framework for questioning, thinking and seeking consultation and

FIGURE 2
WORKSHEET FOR THINKING ABOUT THE GOALS
OF MARITAL THERAPY FROM MULTIPLE PERSPECTIVES

COUPLE _____ THERAPIST _____ DATE _____

FOCUS	1a CURRENT PROBLEMS H HW W	1b POTENTIAL PROBLEMS H HW W	2 PRAGMATIC CONSIDERATIONS H HW W	3 VALUE CONSIDERATIONS H HW W	4 TREATMENT GOALS H HW W
01 FAMILIES OF ORIGIN	*essential* *optimal*	*essential* *optimal*	*essential* *optimal*	*essential* *optimal*	*essential* *optimal*
02 CONTEMPORARY FAMILY OF THE COUPLE AND THEIR CHILDREN	*essential* *optimal*	*essential* *optimal*	*essential* *optimal*	*essential* *optimal*	*essential* *optimal*

03 COUPLE SYSTEM	essential optimal	essential optimal	essential optimal	essential optimal	essential optimal	essential optimal
04 HUSBAND	essential optimal	essential optimal	essential optimal	essential optimal	essential optimal	essential optimal
05 WIFE	essential optimal	essential optimal	essential optimal	essential optimal	essential optimal	essential optimal

addresses current and potential clinical problems, pragmatic and value considerations as discussed above. It sees the couple as a system, each of the mates as individuals, the family unit including the children, and each spouse's family of origin. The chart invites the therapist to think along each of the various perspectives about the needs and welfare of the couple and their family. Each of the four levels of organization—the couple, individual spouses, the contemporary family of the couple and their children, and families of origin—is looked at along the lines of current clinical needs or the major problems of dysfunction that are seen today: probable and expected clinical problems given the dynamic structure of the couple; pragmatic considerations, or the givens and constraints of resources on the various tiers of the marital/family structure; and ethical values, or the likely implications on each of the tiers of the couple's outcome—most often the implications of their staying married vs. getting divorced, but also other issues such as what is likely to happen to the health of a mate if s/he does not get help. Using the worksheet, the therapist can enter a potential goal focus for therapy in many of the squares.

It is also useful from the outset to differentiate between two levels of goals for therapy: correcting or arresting serious damages or dysfunctions and maximizing growth and development. The goals of limiting and correcting dysfunctions are identified in the chart in the first two columns of present and future clinical problems as "essential"; the second set of goals for maximizing growth are identified in the chart as "optimal." Obviously, it is not always clear how to separate which goals are essential and justify taking the risks that are inherent in the therapy attempt to achieve them from the goals that are optimally desirable but not necessarily essential. The latter can be foregone if there are indications of resistance or that the attempt to reach these goals could lead to someone in the family paying too high a price.

ASSESSING THE DEPTH OF MARITAL PROBLEMS

There are many marital problems that look alike, but really represent different kinds of structural problems. I like to think of three possible levels in looking at a presenting symptom:

Level 1: *Developmental Block or Delay*
Level 2: *Dysfunctional Style or Habit*
Level 3: *Psychopathology*

Developmental blocks or delays are, in effect, complications in the growing up of a person who, for one of many possible and even trivial reasons, may not have been able to learn how to perform a given function at a certain point in development. This is the kind of problem which is "easiest" to treat in that it may respond to relatively simple instructions and encouragement to try directed exercises.

Dysfunctional style or habit involves the development of specifically wrong or damaging habits in the course of original efforts to solve a given developmental task. These now have to be undone as a precondition for any possible learning of alternative or new ways of doing things.

Psychopathology refers to problems that are compelled and continued by deep inner, often unconscious processes and characterological patterns that will not respond for the most part to retraining or instruction for new behaviors without more penetrating treatment of the inner structure of the personality.

Figure 3 presents an illustration of a single symptom that can be referred alternatively to each of the three levels. In this illustration a case of premature ejaculation is described in three different ways, which enable us to see that the same symptom can mean very different things.

The illustration of developmental block involves a shy man who has not tried hard enough on his own to learn possibilities of control of his ejaculation, and a woman who has not made a natural "fuss" in response to her husband and expected him to learn and grow. Although it can be argued that there are also evidences of psychopathology or disturbances in character because both the husband and wife are too nice and don't ask enough of themselves, nonetheless the power or structure of the symptom of premature ejaculation is rooted more in the man's failure to learn how to control his ejaculation than in an escape from or failure to use his power. In planning therapy, the therapist expects that the couple may be able to respond to a few sessions of behavioral sex therapy with considerable progress which they will be able to sustain.

On the level of a dysfunctional style or habit, this illustration describes a couple who are given more and more to avoiding sexual activity. They came for therapy after several months during which they had an agreement that the wife would only masturbate her husband and that they would cease their unsuccessful attempts to have intercourse. The planning of therapy in this kind of situation calls not just for behavioral sex therapy, but for a probe of this couple's interactional style which led to their collusion in giving up intercourse. In this case, what we discovered "underneath" the sexual problem was the wife's long-standing rage about the husband giving up (with a million rationalizations) on earning more money; by imposing a "no intercourse" rule on him, she was taking her form of revenge.

In the illustration of psychopathology, there is a picture of resignation of a man to his inner passivity and to an accompanying unconscious rage at

FIGURE 3
ASSESSING THREE LEVELS OF DEPTH OF PROBLEM

	DISTURBANCES OF NATURAL DEVELOPMENTAL PROCESS	What level of problem is getting in the way of the natural need and potential to learn, practice and perfect new skills?	Illustrations of levels in several cases of premature ejaculation
Level One	DEVELOPMENTAL BLOCK OR DELAY	Complications owing to failure to learn skill at point of original and usual developmental opportunity.	Shy man and sweet agreeable mate; he does not try hard enough on his own to learn possibilities of control and she does not relate to his not learning.
Level Two	DYSFUNCTIONAL STYLE OR HABIT	Problem owing to inadvertent development of wrong or dangerous habits in effort to solve original developmental task.	More and more he and they shy away from sexual activity; alternatively, they undertake mutual masturbation more often than intercourse.
Level Three	PSYCHOPATHOLOGY	Problem that is compelled by a deep emotional process or characterological pattern that cannot be solved by retraining of behavior pattern alone.	Resignation to inner passivity and anger at woman and unconscious needs to encourage/allow her to become involved with another man; his self-respect and her respect of him drop to a low and he succumbs to unconscious rage and severe depression.

women that leads him to be secretly satisfied about ejaculating prematurely, even though consciously he is interested in successful full intercourse. Therapy planning here should take into account a need to penetrate deeper psychological patterns in the man, quite likely through some form of psychoanalytically oriented individual therapy along with couple sessions. In the latter, the behavioral sexual tasks should not be prescribed before there is evidence of meaningful change in the man's feelings and use of himself vis-à-vis his wife (and his inner world of "woman").

Many failures of treatment are the result of a failing to differentiate between different levels. If a man and a couple are ready to benefit immediately from behavior sex therapy (Masters & Johnson, 1970; Kaplan, 1974), a prescription of psychoanalytic treatment which will take a long time to complete is insulting and demoralizing to the spouses and their marriage. It is something like doing psychoanalysis for a child with a reading problem: by the time the child is ready to learn how to read, he will be several years behind in his educational skills and the price is enormous. The same goes for couples who do not catch up with their basic sexual functioning because of an overly long treatment.

On the other hand, efforts to do sexual-skills training with someone who needs work in regard to basic personality issues will lead to a high rate of failure in treatment in the short and long run; these, too, are demoralizing to the spouses and their marriage. Back in 1917, Karl Abraham (1957) wrote a brilliant analysis of the psychodynamics of premature ejaculation, noting that it is based on a combination of passivity, narcissism, and rage at the woman. In my opinion, this psychodynamic paradigm is true to this day for cases of premature ejaculation that are not more simply at the level of a developmental block or a dysfunctional habit pattern. What is also true today is that a systems-oriented couple therapist can work at an integration of individual and couple therapy; both modes are useful for teaching and correcting passivity, narcissism, and hostility, as well as facilitating and relearning more positive emotional transactions between the spouses that should speed up the therapy considerably.

Once the basic diagnostic picture has been assembled with regard to the level at which a problem or dysfunction is consolidated, there follows a natural logic or way of thinking about the level of therapy or remedial work that is indicated. If the couple's problem is essentially a function of a developmental block or delay, the most rational way to help the couple is to provide them with new opportunities to learn. Therapy then becomes, for the most part, a process of teaching, training, coaching, encouraging development, and renewing natural learning processes leading to more skillful adult functioning in marriage. Techniques which exemplify or are especially appropriate to this level of therapy include counseling, information and advice, recommendations for revised behavior, behavior modification programs, "homework" or "exercises" and follow-up supervision by the therapist, and teaching the couple skills such as communication skills, negotiation skills, and a framework for arriving at shared solutions rather than solutions imposed by one or the other.

Insofar as the assessment is that the couple problem represents a repetitive dysfunctional style or habit—that is, incorrect behaviors which have become consolidated as a way of being in the world (e.g., the couple demand one another's full attention, but more often than not they are disappointed, hurt, and angry at "proofs" of the other's unavailability)—then the implied requirement of treatment is, first of all, to limit and block the incorrect habits. Techniques that are appropriate for this level of problem resolution include: instruction and practice in inhibiting the current behavior; redirection of behavior from the current pattern to a prescribed alternative; reframing of the meaning of an ongoing behavior so that it changes meaning because of the different context or significance which is assigned to it (Fisher, Anderson & Jones, 1981; Weeks & L'Abate, 1982; Weeks, 1985); behavior modification techniques to assist in the inhibition of the existing behavior and/or to reinforce the desired replacement behaviors; rational-emotive therapy techniques to underscore the self-defeating consequences of existing behavior such as those that are based on an irrational need to do things entirely well or those that thrive on anxieties about appearing well in the eyes of others (Ellis & Harper, 1968); and techniques that invite and teach an existential yielding to being and becoming what one "really" is and can be rather than a caricature of a person locked into a rigidified ritualistic behavior (Yalom, 1980).

If the diagnostic assessment of the couple's problem is that there is more of a psychopathological problem, that is, a pattern that is compelled by deep emotional and structural processes that will not be solvable or changeable by educational or retraining methods, the implication for treatment is that techniques for psychodynamic penetration of the personality are called for. Techniques which express and which are conducive to such personality work include: evoking and intensifying greater anxiety (Minuchin & Fishman, 1981); inducing or prolonging the existing state of crisis in order to motivate more serious encounters of the patients with themselves (Napier & Whitaker, 1978; Whitaker & Keith, 1981; Whitaker & Bumberry, 1988); the pursuit of core issues such as fears of separation, loss, and mortality; invitations to and exposures of underlying emotions of dissatisfaction, anger, and hatred (Bach & Wyden, 1969; Charny, 1972b; Whitaker & Bumberry, 1988); techniques which invite unconscious associations and flows of imagery; work on dreams; analysis of the basic style used in relationships in general and in intimacy in particular; confrontation of one's major weaknesses and unfairnesses; awareness of one's undeveloped potential; a call for responsibility for one's inner attitudes and behaviors; and an assessment of a person's ability to arrive at choices and decisions and to sustain a commitment to them.

SUPPORTIVE VS. CONFRONTING TECHNIQUES

In all of the above there runs a continuum which differentiates between supportive therapeutic techniques and confronting techniques. In supportive techniques, the therapist is positive, offers the patient structure, direction, and specific advice in a context of warmth, encouragement, and understanding. Such therapy is rooted in a humanistic view of the potential development that awaits in people if they are treated with deeper regard and acceptance.

In confronting techniques, the therapist seeks to unsettle patients, increase uncertainty, doubts, and confusion, promote anxiety and invite or intensify the crisis which brought the couple into treatment, expose the patient to darker sides of his/her behavior and personality such as indifference to others, exploitativeness, or nastiness, remove the patients' refuge in self-deception, pomposity, and narcissism, all in a context of firmness, professional realism, and a kind of parental sternness. Such therapy is rooted in ethical imperatives which differentiate between desirable and undesirable, mature and immature, healthy or constructive behaviors and emotions and sick or destructive behaviors and emotions.

Teaching and retraining techniques tend to utilize supportive techniques, while techniques for blocking existing behaviors, especially highly pathological ones, seek to penetrate into unconscious personality processes and rely more heavily on confrontational techniques (in addition to the bedrock of a positive relationship or "joining" which is necessary in virtually all therapeutic work). However, there are also many techniques for teaching and counseling that are confrontational in their style and structure and not supportive, such as when the traditional stern teacher or therapist places strong demands on the student or patient to study, practice, and demonstrate mastery of given material or a skill: "*I want you to be friendly and appreciative to your wife when you come home and suppress all the resentment and criticism that comes up in you.*"

Similarly, techniques for penetrating into deep recesses of the personality and unconscious are often intrinsically supportive and not confrontational, such as when the therapist relates to the patient empathically, encourages the telling of deeply painful memories and experiences, or gently guides a free-associational process reinforcing the idea that all associations are human, therefore natural and in themselves not pathological.

Figure 4 presents a framework which combines thinking about the relative distribution of supportive and confrontational techniques with the three levels of problem-resolution techniques previously discussed.

FIGURE 4
CHOICES OF SUPPORTIVE VERSUS CONFRONTING TECHNIQUES ON DIFFERENT LEVELS OF CONFLICT RESOLUTION

	Ego-Organizing, Strengthening, Supportive Techniques	*Anxiety-Promoting, Unsettling, Confronting Techniques*
First Level of Conflict Resolution Techniques TEACH, DEVELOP, RENEW BASIC SKILLS Communication Negotiation -"No Lose" -Give & take Commitment Follow through		
Second Level of Conflict Resolution Techniques LIMIT, BLOCK INCORRECT HABITS: REFRAME, REDIRECT, RETRAIN Reframe-relabel runaway habit Conditioning & behavior modification techniques Correction of performance and appearance anxieties Existential yielding to being what one is and the flux of inner process and marital process		
Third Level of Conflict Resolution Techniques IDENTIFY AND CONFRONT PERSONALITY AND CHARACTER WEAKNESSES AND PATHOLOGY: TREAT TO ACHIEVE PERMANENT (2ND ORDER) CHANGE Evoke and intensify anxiety and crisis over: separation, loss, mortality, dissatisfaction, anger, hatred, rage, psychic violence Correct major weakness and unfairness and take responsibility for remaining weakness Listen to unconscious and apply to life relationships Renew choices in one's life		

SELECTING AND PRESCRIBING THE TREATMENT MIX APPROPRIATE TO EACH COUPLE

How does one go about selecting and creating the appropriate mix of supportive and confronting techniques for each couple and each individual? Virginia Satir is reputed by one therapist to have taught that you must keep your arm around the patient while slugging them (but unfortunately the therapist didn't have an exact quote). Carl Whitaker (Whitaker & Bumberry, 1988) has written about the dialectical selection and integration of supportive and confronting techniques thus:

> It's much like the dilemma faced by all parents. You must be able to encourage and support, as well as discipline, your children. Finding a good balance is difficult; remaining at that level is impossible. It has been said that it's not really a question of succeeding or failing in raising your children. That's not the choice. The real choice you have is how you are going to fail. Will you be too strict or too soft? Too controlling or too flexible? No matter how you slice it, failing is part of the job. Yet the task of finding a workable balance persists. (p. 39)

The hallmark of virtually every ideological camp or "school" in psychotherapy is that it prescribes from the outset the same level or grouping of techniques of treatment for virtually *every* patient that comes down the street. Psychoanalysis insists on uncovering psychodynamic techniques and considerable confrontation; reality therapy insists on confronting each patient with the damage that he is doing to others and to himself in real life; behaviorism calls for conditioning or behavior modification techniques to change incorrect behaviors and to reinforce selective behaviors; family life education, couples communication training, marital enrichment and encounter groups, and peer counseling emphasize reopening wholesome experiences of communication and togetherness for couples; brief therapy experts insist that all cases be limited to such-and-such number of sessions focused on resolving a current problem or making a new choice; PET groups provide a standard curriculum of learning to listen, speak, and negotiate no-fault decisions with children without paying attention to other issues such as family coalitions, scapegoating, dynamics of pseudomutuality, or evidence of significant psychopathology in the children.

With regard to the continuum between supportive and confronting techniques, there are several schools of therapy and many therapists who tend to adopt fixed positions from the outset. There are no few who would never offer patients anything but goodness, acceptance, understanding, tolerance, and so forth; others invariably confront every patient with greater complexity or absurdity and insist *a priori* that any kind of counseling, instruction, or advice is superficial and counterproductive to therapy. I propose that both supportive and confronting techniques of treatment are in themselves entirely valid: each is an art form in which serious training is required to develop a good level of professional skill; each is a highly meaningful grouping of techniques that can offer powerful help. However, each is differentially appropriate and inappropriate to various patients and to the combinations of their problems and resources and their therapist's skills and personality in using different techniques.

WHOSE MARRIAGE IS IT?

What happens in the setting of goals of couple therapy can also be understood using a "commercial model" of salesmanship on the part of the therapist and the decision of the consumers or patients whether or not to purchase. Since the customer has the option to accept or decline the offer of therapy, one can say that the therapy is up to them and that the outcome of their marriage is in their hands. On the other hand, insofar as salesmen can have many dirty tricks up their sleeves, let alone lie about the products they are selling, there are dangers of unethical practices and swindles, especially considering the fact that therapists are invested by lay clients or patients with extraordinary magical and priestly qualities which give them many opportunities to con the unsuspecting believers.

When a couple and their therapist agree on a treatment plan, all would seem to be well philosophically and ethically and each party carries an appropriate share of responsibility for the ultimate outcome of the treatment. However, a host of problems arise when there is a basic disagreement between the two mates and the therapist. The therapist may be in agreement with one of the spouses but not with the other, or in disagreement with both spouses who may disagree or agree with one another. The situation where both spouses agree may at first glance seem to be the simpler since presumably the couple are then free to pull out of the proferred treatment they both don't agree with and seek treatment they both want. Even here it is not so simple since there are many times when patients remain in treatment out of a basic respect for the professional or out of inertia and fearfulness of leaving a professional even though they disagree with him/her. The problem then remains that the therapist is pulling in one direction and the couple in another. Is this legitimate when the marriage, after all, obviously belongs to the couple and not to the therapist?

In the situations where the two spouses are in disagreement and the therapist agrees with one spouse, how is a therapist to know that the coalition between the therapist and the one spouse is not a form of bullying the mate to give in to the power of the coalition? I remember one "successful" therapy where, together with the wife, I "succeeded" in bringing the husband back home from his intention to leave for another woman. The marriage has since persisted as a long-term and apparently reasonably satisfying one, but I have various indications that the husband has never forgiven me for helping to break up his escape plan and dream of the other woman.

The only answer I can come up with about these situations is that therapists must be able to demonstrate that their motivations for adopting a given position and their methods of arriving at conclusions in their professional work satisfy a number of criteria which define the responsibilities of practitioners to the people who seek their help:

1. In defining a treatment plan, the therapist is motivated by considerations of helping more than by considerations of selling or personal gain, financial or otherwise.
2. The therapist does not overidentify with any one marital partner (especially not in an automatic way with the spouse who may have been the first to contact the therapist), but evaluates the couple's problems, needs, and hopes from a systemic point of view that includes seeing the roles both have in the problems and respecting the rights of both spouses to seek better lives for themselves.
3. The therapist is prepared to explain and "defend" the sequence of his/her thinking and the range of issues that were included in arriving at the assessment and choice of the proposed treatment.
4. The therapist also evaluates the welfare and needs of the children and each spouse's family of origin in connection with treatment of the couple.
5. The therapist is able to propose a reasonable range of flexible alternatives if for one reason or another the preferred treatment is not practicable, especially in response to new information or changing conditions of the couple.
6. The therapist is open to examination, criticism, and protest from the patients, seeks feedback from peers, supervision, and consultation, and is responsive to the opinions of the other professionals.

> Her conception of the marriage was that she wanted him fully loving and involved with her. She had suffered a great deal in her childhood, and she hoped that as an adult she would at long last have a reliable intimate relationship in her marriage.
>
> His conception of the marriage was that it should be a positive social and sexual sharing, as well as an operationally effective unit for family life, but that tender emotions should not be expressed. He had forsworn such emotions in his childhood. In a great many ways, he had

developed himself as an unusually resourceful "frontiersman person-ality"; he did not like to feel sadness, regrets, yearnings, appreciation, or love. In therapy, he was not averse to providing the material from which a reconstruction could be made of his childhood, which sug-gested that a witchlike invasive mother along with a weak father who did not challenge his wife or contain her had taught him to escape from intimacy. His dream material suggested that were he to open himself to greater intimacy or penetration of his feelings, he would feel faced with serious danger.

What should be the goals of marital therapy in the above case? It would be a nice fairy tale to report that simple processing of the differences in feel-ings between this couple led to a nice happy ending where the husband agreed to meet his wife's needs without feeling threatened. However, that is not the way of the unconscious when a person is convinced that grave danger lies at the other end. In this case, the husband progressed in therapy enough to make his wife happier, but only up to a certain point, and then he planted his feet firmly on the ground and said, in effect, that he had made his final offer. The wife still felt miserable; in fact, she was even more confused because for a while she had let herself enjoy the pleasure of the progress her husband had been making towards greater sharing and close-ness. Now she was disappointed anew, with a painful feeling of letdown after having felt better.

What should the therapist do in this situation? One possibility is for the therapist to help "close things down," recognizing the gains that were made and encouraging the couple to be satisfied with their degree of greater friendship and closeness. Another very different possibility is for the ther-apist to identify with the wife's demands as legitimate.

In this case the tension grew as both spouses made it clear that what could develop if either were pushed too hard would be the dissolution of the marriage—though they both wanted to stay married—because each was rapidly approaching the point beyond which he or she could not go. Whom does the therapist seek to please? Whom does the therapist dare to displease? For me, the answer to these questions is that the therapist's choices must not be guided by concerns about pleasing or displeasing cli-ents, but must grow from a genuine professional commitment both to reducing emotional suffering and to maximizing personality functioning and development. The case is a good example that very often therapists must take stands that are going to be unpleasant to at least one spouse and sometimes to both.

In this instance it seemed clear to me that the wife's displeasure at being emotionally alone without intimacy was rooted in the natural meanings of marriage and was, therefore, more justified than her husband's fears of being pushed into intimacy—although I did not doubt that he was genuinely afraid of very real psychic suffering that would follow on reconstruction of his mother's invasiveness and negativity in his inner world if he allowed his wife in closer. It also seemed to me that from the point of view of development of potential, the wife was working hard to overcome her own misery from a childhood in which no one had taken care of her, but that her husband was pitching his oppositional strength behind resistance to developing his personality any further. Although his requirements of psychological defenses against closeness were understandable, to my mind they were not connected with efforts at recovery from the damages of earlier life experience, so that again I felt that it was right to support the wife's goals for the marriage.

Doing so meant taking risks, of course. There was a considered possibility that the husband would walk out of therapy. More important, there was a considered possibility that the husband would organize himself to leave his wife. The question would then be one of whether or not she really had gained from the assistance of the therapist, or might she have been better off if the therapist had compromised and helped her to accept limited goals for the marriage without attacking the husband's defense system to a point that he could not tolerate?

Obviously, one can judge retrospectively the correctness of the goals chosen for therapy on the basis of the outcome of the treatment—just as when a patient dies in surgery, the techniques used by the surgeon undergo critical review. However, in the work of psychotherapists it is very important not to be limited to choices of techniques that will avoid risks of loss, for much of the healthy living and growth our clients want us to help them achieve involves taking intelligent risks. To design a therapy that will be only pleasing and not disturbing to patients' defenses is immoral if it means shortcutting the possibility of more profound growth that could take place if the therapist had the courage and conviction to stand behind the showdowns with defenses. Moreover, appeasement often leads to illusions of therapeutic success. I have seen couples whose marital therapy was ostensibly successful because the therapy was superficial and did not challenge real core issues separate and divorce some years later after experiencing a kind of boredom or non-life that might have been avoided had greater risks been taken in the conduct of therapy. I have also seen couples 10 years and more after I had exercised the "wisdom" of supporting an accommodation between them return with the pain and despair of a seriously disturbed child and a later-life marital crisis, making me feel ashamed that I did not do a fuller job for them back then.

The helping professional's traditions of reducing suffering and aiming to increase the range of a person's use of his/her potential are complementary to one another. When more than one patient is involved, as in couple therapy, these two goals extend to both participants and to all the family members who are related to them. Insofar as there are conflicts of interest between the two complementary goals of pain-reduction and growth with regard to different members of the family, I believe that one must think out clearly the implications and prognoses of different courses of action, weigh the alternatives, and then arrive at a judgment of what promises to contribute maximally to all concerned.

To which goal does one give preference? Since human life is the ultimate value, certainly the protection of actual life will always be first in importance. Since actual suffering is so unpleasant, there is much to be said for giving a high priority to the correction and reduction of pain. On the other hand, one cannot justify the automatic continuation of a marriage whenever one spouse's life is at risk or a spouse is suffering terribly. For example, sometimes the threat to life or the source of great emotional pain is a function of extortionist or terroristic threats of self-injury, illness, madness, or death; many of these threats cannot be honored as such. In general, if serious possibilities of a better life beckon for one spouse but at the likely risk of much pain and worse for the mate, the choice of treatment goal requires much careful thought, but one cannot rule out automatically favoring the stronger spouse's growth goals. There is often no clear or simple answer, but an ethical professional will struggle long and hard with the contradictions and poignancy of such choices (Willi, 1984). Having made a decision, the ethical therapist will stand courageously behind it and work at turning the risks involved into stepping stones towards growth.

Some couples are helped precisely because their therapist has the courage to take a stand. In part, the therapist's strong leadership gives the patients an opportunity to experience good parenting that helps them grow. The therapist's strength creates a role model for the patients to reach for more mature parts of themselves. The fact that the therapist demonstrates an ability to work through a process to a point of choice between difficult dilemmas can facilitate the patient's learning how to better choose goals in their lives. I believe that in many cases there is no alternative but for the therapist to accompany a couple towards some kind of showdown of choices where the therapist him/herself has taken a clear stand as to what is desirable for the couple.

If in medicine the guiding values which help make many decisions about treatment goals and treatment procedures are the maintenance of life vs. death and the improvement of physical functioning as opposed to deterioration and chronic dysfunction, in marital therapy the guiding criterion should be the maintenance of psychological aliveness in the marriage.

Marital therapists are prejudiced in favor of the "life of the marriage" and in favor of those spouses who are committed to the marriage and to deepening and expanding its quality. However, different aspects of commitment will often be at war with one another. Frequently, one spouse will insist sincerely that the first requirement for continuation of the marriage is that the mate be loyal and then perhaps other changes for the better can follow, while the other will insist on real changes and improvements in the quality of the relationship first of all; and if not, there can be no commitment to the marriage. Both parties are, in effect, colluding to defeat growth so long as each hangs on to their emphases on only one aspect of their marriage, one to promises of security and the other to signs of an improved relationship. The one spouse's insistence on feeling secure may be justified, but if it is held up as a rigid precondition it can also be a way of not giving attention to the legitimate needs and complaints of the other mate. The other spouse's insistence on efforts to improve the quality of the marriage may be justified, but it can also be a defense against making a commitment to the mate.

Whom should the therapist support in these situations? My answer is neither spouse alone, but the combination of both spouses, for if the two spouses together are able to join and combine the important emphasis each is promoting, they will succeed in capturing the essence of what a healthy marriage is.

When a therapist takes a position like this and, in effect, stands against the shared collusive system of the couple that aims to keep the marriage superficial, there is always a chance that the couple will leave therapy, perhaps angrily, and possibly also move towards a separation. In effect, the therapist is insisting on a goal and process that are at a higher level of development than either mate is ready to seek. Has the therapist "failed" under such circumstances? My own belief is that the therapist would have failed if s/he had agreed to the splitting of the different values of marriage, devoting the marital therapy to "improving" functions such as cooperation and communication without honoring the one spouse's need for the mate to make a commitment, or by accepting a commitment to the marriage from one spouse that was not accompanied by his/her work at improving functioning in areas of dysfunction. If the therapist's attempts to bring about an integration of the reasonable goals of both spouses fail and the couple do separate, there is every reason to be sad, but I do not believe the failure of the marriage should be made synonymous with the failure of the professional work done in good faith on behalf of respecting the needs of both spouses and on behalf of a more mature marriage system.

8

Formulating a Systemic Challenge for the Couple Along with Challenges for Individual Growth

Coming for marital counseling is often satirized as a humorous event. In real life, however, couples often enough arrive in considerable distress and even in what we might metaphorically call "emergency room" condition.

Acute emergency room situations in marital therapy include threats of loss of the partner such as when one of the spouses has announced a desire or intention to divorce, discoveries of infidelity, mental health crises such as threats of decompensation and breakdown, fighting that has gotten to a powerful pitch of emotion and an impending sense of disaster, and eruptions of violence. Of course, there are also numerous situations when a couple come for help very upset because of or in response to breakdown in one of their children—drug problems, criminal behaviors, dropping out from school, and so forth. These are family therapy problems that are not our direct focus. Here we will restrict ourselves to the sense of despair and urgency that couples experience about their marriages.

In these urgently upsetting situations, it is especially unfair to invite a couple to sit down to speak and for the therapist to offer them nothing but a version of the proverbial analytic silent treatment. Such therapy implies that speaking in itself is magically helpful, that the couple must begin to learn that there are no clear answers, and that the therapist can help them only to discover that answers there are in themselves. There is always some

126

truth to this point of view and it is certainly correct that some relief from anxiety is engendered "simply" by coming to see a therapist, but such treatment is rarely sufficient in the "marital emergency room."

When people come in "bleeding" or in "shock," the therapist's first responsibility is to stop whatever runaway process is overwhelming them and give the couple a sense of structure by putting up a stop sign for the acting out or going too far or too fast that is taking place in the marriage, as well as by providing emotional first aid to whoever is in panic and despair that are too painful to bear. The therapist functions as a kind of replacement parent for the fearful, confused couple who are at a point of lack of control over their lives. This, in itself, makes it possible to reduce some degree of acting out that is taking place. Many couples are only too pleased to assign the therapist parental meaning and then welcome the directions the therapist will give them to end the cascading intensities of their hurting one another.

Violence must be ended immediately. This is an important subject to which we return at greater length later, but here I would summarize my experience that the most effective treatment technique for stopping marital violence is to express understanding that there must be very real reasons for the rage that is erupting in violence, but that violence and physical injury to a human being are wrong and must be stopped (Charny, 1967). If the couple has not been resorting to violence in a chronic way but is suffering from a recent eruption of violent behaviors, this intervention will generally bring an end to the acting out and give therapy a chance to get going. However, if the violence is more chronic, my experience is that the therapist must recommend to the spouse who is the victim a hard line of insisting that the violence stop or the police will be called. Often enough, the victim spouse who has not been able to stop the violence heretofore will not be able to adopt such a position right away and will resist the therapist's proposal, but hopefully the therapist's emphasis on the necessity of calling the police will become the beginning of a process which over a period of time will enable the victim to develop the conviction and ability to stand up to the mate's violence. Once the victim spouse conveys to the aggressor this decision to end the violence with real resolution and determination, most violence ceases.

When the presenting problem in the "marital emergency room" is a threat by one spouse of separation or divorce that is terrifying the other, the very act of coming together for therapeutic consultation provides a certain amount of relief from the feared aloneness. In these situations, I congratulate the couple for coming to evaluate their different wishes and intentions for their marriage. I suggest that even if eventually there will be a separation or divorce, a therapeutic review of what is happening may be able to help them to arrive at more joint conclusions about their future. If they jointly decide to separate, this may make the aloneness that one of the mates now dreads somewhat easier because it will be his/her decision as well that they should go their separate ways.

When one mate responds with actual or implied threats of emotional and mental symptoms such as depression, threats or evidences of mental breakdown, or possibilities of retaliation against the mate through an emotional regression, I express sympathy for this suffering and a readiness to help reduce and overcome it. However, I make it clear that I will not be a party to any implied threats of regression or use of regression as revenge or power, nor will I encourage the mate to surrender to any threats.

In all "emergency room" situations, I encourage the couple as much as possible to resume their basic family tasks—especially to take care of children together, to see to it that meals for the family are continued, and to take care of the myriad small tasks of family management that need to be dealt with every day. I promise the couple that a continuation of family functions will make them and their children feel better, but will in no way be used to defer looking at the serious marital strains about which they have come. I caution them that if they allow the snowball of trouble to get out of hand, they may work themselves into such a state of disorganization that it will not be possible to construct a useful therapeutic process.

JOINING THE THREE CLIENTS—HUSBAND, WIFE, AND THE COUPLE

Beginning marital therapists are often concerned with whether they are going to identify with or be more sympathetic to one of the two spouses. I think that a therapist should try at the outset to identify not only with each spouse but with both of them together, namely with the marriage itself. Most people marry hoping that their marriage will be rewarding and long lasting; when a therapist relates to the couple-union with respect, it touches something in each of the mates. Even when the marriage has gone very badly and is headed for breakup, people still want to have the history of their marriage respected in some way. It is something like talking about a child to its parents—even a difficult child is *theirs*.

"Joining" with a couple as they begin therapy is an art form of building bridges of interest, understanding, and respect with each of the "three clients,"—the husband, the wife, and the couple. Questions about the marriage, the couple's shared experiences in the past, their milestones, hopes, and joys, the story of their initial attraction, their disappointments, problems, and current despairs should all be addressed. Similarly, information about the spouses as individuals should be tracked—their work, their dreams in life, their achievements and disappointments, and of course their personal feelings about their marriage and its future.

Many spouses present their case at the outset of marital therapy almost as if they have come to a Solomon, each hoping to be exonerated as the good one while putting the finger on the mate as the bad one. The therapist's message early on is that marital difficulties go beyond a simple addition of complaints to a more complex, shared pattern in which there is a system ongoing where each mate is triggering and being triggered by the other. The therapist conveys in a variety of ways that any marital history is for the most part a joint creation of the two people who, wittingly and unwittingly, have entered into and are repeating a specific "dance" or pattern where they are playing on one another's weaknesses and reinforcing one another's problematic habits, including the serious behaviors that are causing them the most problems.

There is a message of hope in this "systems point of view." Many marital problems that at first look very difficult will prove more easily treatable because they are outgrowths of cyclical, escalatory processes that neither spouse really wants to be taking place. There is also a message of relief for some of the guilt and shame of people who know that they have gone too far in hurting their spouse when they learn that in some sense they have also been responding to circular patterns which have been setting off the worst in them. One should add, however, that a systems point of view should not be taken to an extreme where it wipes out the need for acknowledgment and responsibility for each spouse's individual actions and bad motivations.

SHOULD THE THERAPIST HELP THE COUPLE TO COMMUNICATE DIRECTLY WITH EACH OTHER OR NOT?

Therapists who have not been trained in couples therapy characteristically approach couples with a belief that the essence of marital therapy is to have them communicate with each other. The truth is that many couples are totally unready to communicate with each other even in the therapist's office. When they are invited and stimulated to speak to one another, they often add new fuel to the fire of their previous marital communication.

The logical error at the heart of this treatment strategy is that the fact that healthy couples need to communicate with one another does not mean that one starts distressed couples communicating with one another before they are ready to do so. Therapists who do get couples to speak to one another prematurely soon find themselves presiding over rage-filled diatribes and demoralizing, raucous fights. Many of these couples then leave therapy prematurely because therapy has exposed them to their worst and proved impotent to give them a new direction. Heartfelt communication between couples is to be left to that stage of therapy where the couple are capable of clarifying problems with one another respectfully, searching for mutual solutions to their problems, and experiencing and conveying caring for one another.

In many cases, marital therapy is begun and maintained for some time around helping each spouse say what s/he needs to say to the therapist and not to the mate who, however, is present and listening. The therapist receives these communications in ways which convey a readiness to understand and take in respectfully whatever each person has to say—including hurt, anger, yearnings for love, and so forth. Not only is the other mate listening to this information which the therapist skillfully evokes and enlarges, but he/she is privy to seeing how the therapist is a good listener and conversationalist with the spouse. In other words, the second mate has an opportunity to see the therapist modeling wholesome conversation with the spouse, even with regard to difficult emotions. (For some couples who come to therapy, it will have been many a moon since a normal conversation took place between the two of them.)

Segraves (1982) presents a structured format for beginning therapy in which he gives each spouse uninterrupted time to tell his/her story. He tries to make sure that both spouses express their views for a roughly comparable period of time. He is then careful to paraphrase what he has heard—in other words, to reflect back or summarize the information and messages he has heard from each party. If what a spouse said was inflammatory and provocative, he attempts in his reflections to modulate the provocative elements while retaining the essential communication and information, thus again modeling the importance of respecting the essential message a person is delivering. He also tries to reach and reflect the underlying pain in each spouse. Segraves' goal in these early interviews includes restoring hope for a possible shift to a better way of interacting in the future.

ACKNOWLEDGING PERSONAL ERRORS

A familiar picture of marital therapy is that spouses come to a counselor with their complaints, disappointments, criticisms, and demands for compensation from the other. An existential/dialectical framework of marital therapy says that there are likely real justifications for such feelings, but also that there is invariably another story in the marital interactions of each of us, namely of our own faults, weaknesses, and errors. Each of us has contributed a certain number of weaknesses to the marital pattern in the way of poor functioning in certain important areas of marriage and in respect to certain unattractive qualities of character and personality that accompany even some of our most effective functioning. From this point of view, marital therapy calls for the therapist to help each spouse not only to express his/her complaints against the other but to actively seek to identify his/her own weaknesses as mates and people. Once a husband and wife are engaged in this kind of experience, they are no longer quite so acrimonious, judgmental, superior, or vindictive; in fact, they are more *human*. For the spouse then to hear criticisms is more palatable insofar as the criticisms are now coming from a human being who is humble and acknowledging of his/her own shortcomings and not from a monster of some sort.

If one mate can do it, perhaps the other may be able to do it as well. In other words, if one of the spouses is able to look at his/her own self and acknowledge his/her significant contribution to problems in the marriage because of basic shortcomings in personality, then perhaps the other will feel less threatened to do the same. The capacity of any spouse to relate to his/her own shortcomings will remove some of the onus from the other and the fear that exposing weaknesses will lead to humiliation and condemnation.

Therapists are accustomed to a procession of couples coming to complain about one another to the "parent" therapist. Relatively few therapists seem to bring up in the early sessions each mate's contributions to the problems. What generally happens is that the therapist is "understanding" and accepts complaints as rendered in the first sessions. Only after several sessions does the therapist hold up an interpretive mirror to each mate's weaknesses, especially if there are indications that one or both have difficult kinds of personalities to begin with and are not open to criticisms of themselves. However, when the therapist begins to move in the direction of such clarifications and confrontations, an antagonistic atmosphere may develop with clients who do not want to hear anything about their own faults. Often such clients then feel betrayed by the therapist, for after all they came to seek justice about their spouse's problems and poor behaviors and now the therapist is turning on them with criticism.

Although it can be very difficult to do in the press of the first session, which includes an inevitable outpouring of bitterness, anger, and whatever else each mate brings to say about the other, I believe that it is important to introduce from the beginning of therapy the theme of genuine criticalness and an ability to receive criticism about one's failings and limitations. While it is true that at the beginning of therapy only a small number of people will be able to respond meaningfully to direct questions about their contributions to their marital problems, the fact that the therapist makes it clear at the outset that this is a basic part of the work to be done in therapy sets a direction that can help reduce feelings of outrage and betrayal later on.

I like to frame the importance of self-criticism in existential/dialectical therapy from the beginning:

> I want to hear from each of you what your disappointments, problems, and angers are at this point in your marriage. I would guess that many of the complaints that each of you have will prove to be justified. However, our experience with marriage shows two other things to be true along with the fact that most people's basic complaints are legitimate. One is that without knowing it, couples get into a dance pattern with one another and each contributes to bringing out the worst parts of the other, even reinforcing the worst parts of the other that they would most like to get rid of. The second is that, without exception, we human beings have many shortcomings and each one of us proves to be a poor mate in some vital areas of marriage. I would like each of you to learn about these shortcomings in yourself and your contributions to bringing out the weaknesses in the other, along with your expressing your complaints to one another clearly and strongly.

Unfortunately, there are many individuals who are terrified to be wrong. For them to admit error is to give others an opportunity to take advantage of them, or to be made fools, or to be put in some kind of catastrophic position. Many people rarely admit to any kind of insufficiency, even to themselves.

Some stages of the life cycle reinforce this attitude, as in the bravado years of adolescence when anybody who shows any kind of weakness is "chicken." So, too, certain cultures reinforce this attitude—the shared culture of adolescents as well as certain societies that insist on men who are tough, rough, and able to drive home their interests in love and business without being soft or considerate of others. Some societies convey unambiguously that might is right and weakness is disaster. There are also ideologies which foster or demand invincibility, arrogance, certainty, and use of one's self as an instrument of a larger ideological absolute which is never to be questioned. In days of old, Spartan and Roman society had many of these features; in modern times, certain dictatorial regimes, fundamentalist religious faiths, and a variety of cult movements show this orientation. Mitscherlich & Mitscherlich (1975) analyze the German culture following the horrors of Nazism as a culture in which people were unable to mourn and to feel guilt. These are apt concepts for marital errors as well as for a national style.

It is not surprising that it is "impossible" for some people to relate to their errors and weaknesses. Is existential/dialectical therapy ruled out for these people? Encountering the mixed picture of their weaknesses and strengths is, after all, what they need. Might their fearful opposition to self-disclosure of weakness even lead them to welcome skillful and sympathetic presentation of the importance of their meeting up with their weaknesses?

My experiences with such people in therapy indicate that sometimes they convey (even if indirectly) that they appreciate very much a straightforward, firm, but also sympathetic approach to the fact that they are playing strongarm roles. When dealt with firmly, some of them turn around to become charmingly cooperative with therapy. I do find that when the aggrieved spouse is strong enough to insist on therapy and the therapy is conducted with a fair-minded determination to set the record straight, not simply about what each spouse is doing to the other but about what is "off" and distorted and weak in the basic character and way of being of each person, some of these "never-wrong people" are able to make important changes in their behavior for the better.

Of course, not all such personalities are able to make such turnarounds to acknowledge in good spirit and humility anything that is fundamentally at error or lacking in their personality and character. I venture to say that some of their spouses who long for genuine intimacy in their marriages will have to think either of replacing their partners or of yielding to the fact that they will never enjoy a full intimacy.

ACCEPTING AMBIGUITY AND INCOMPLETENESS

To be married is to encounter both in the other and in oneself many sides of our humanness that are not attractive and that we would wish did not exist: selfishness, smallmindedness, revengefulness, cowardice, pomposity, cruelty, and so much more. Ideally, we are able to love both ourselves and the other as wonderful and beautiful creatures overall even though both have many undesirable characteristics. The classic state of love that is attraction and infatuation at their blindest, where the other person is idealized, is always doomed to disappointment because there is no preparation for the fact that every partner in this world will soon be revealed as disappointing and lacking in character. It is far better to be prepared by knowing a good deal about the foibles, quirks, insecurity, and unfairness of the other; yet one loves this person despite, and in a sense even because, these human qualities are parts of his/her overall beautiful self. When the time comes that one must fight some of these obnoxious qualities, at least there will be no surprise and, therefore, there will be less demoralization to add to the real hurt and concern that will have developed in response to a mate's bad qualities.

> Her parents had died at relatively early ages. Both of them had been colorless, "small," routine-bound people living on the edge of a total greyness that had threatened to swallow her as a little girl. She had one sibling who had responded to the poverty of spirit in the family home by dutifully becoming a mentally ill adult who went in and out of hospitals until she, too, died an untimely death.
>
> She had found her solution in early childhood in fantasy. By the strength of her own imagination, she peopled her world with beautiful, idyllic colors. Her experiences were recorded as if they were poems. All her contacts with people were graced with unending smiles and charm. Everyone said of her that she was such an unusual and wonderful little girl. When the time came to marry, she married a prince of a man who could do no wrong. If her parents were grey, he was orange and red with deep hues of blue and green backing them up. An outstandingly successful professional who led a fascinating life, he was for her a Prince Charming who finally took her away from the desert of her childhood.
>
> At no point did she allow for the fact that he was human and that the day would come when she would be enraged with him for so many of the qualities she now loved in him: his devotion to his work, which would take him away from her so much of the time, and his wonderful insistence on excitement in life which would throw up a barrier between the two of them because she would require a great deal of quiet rest at home in the safety of the palace she had created there. Disappointed, she would take to her bed, cry and mope.
>
> In this case, the vicissitudes of life were such that a time came when they were also in serious financial straits. She refused to work and contribute to their budget because, from her point of view, it was his responsibility to take care of her totally. He complained bitterly that she didn't understand any of the reality pressures in his life and that she couldn't take any criticism from him. In fact, all she "understood" was that he was trying to return her to the greyness that had threatened to engulf her in her childhood.

Is it possible to teach people in therapy to tolerate ambiguity and incompleteness? People like to think of therapy as a process for releasing hurts and getting rid of them. Can we also utilize the psychotherapeutic medium to help clients to accept that all of life is a sequence not only of pleasure and love but of inevitable problems which intrude on our finest moments and threaten to bring down the structure of our existence, including our marriages, even our extended family ties, and also our very communities and societies? The destiny of every human being hangs on a thin string. Nobody knows when disease will strike. Nobody knows when a cruel accident will destroy life—in one fatal second, a fateful burst of windshear can force a majestic airliner to the ground and kill all aboard, in one unbearable stroke of luck a motorist can be crushed in a dread collision. And nobody knows when our most fateful "social contracts" with our spouses, treasured belief systems, or governments will be violated in cruel and seriously damaging ways. What we all need to know is that all of these are possible—even quite probable—in the course of life.

Existential/dialectical marital therapy calls for the discovery and development of tolerance for the intolerable bad fate and injustices that we cannot control in our destinies and in the destinies of our loved ones. A good sign that such a philosophical underpinning of compassion for ourselves, our mates, and our marriages is taking hold as the therapy proceeds is that an "existential humor" begins to color the sessions. This humor is not based on "jokes" or canned stories of people in situations with funny lines. It is a whimsical, bemused, and sardonic humor which touches on the never-ending play of life and death; strength and weakness in everything that we do and everything that happens to us. It is an ability to poke fun at the arrangements we are all busy making or avoiding for our certain funerals. No matter what we do, we can't win, and that's the biggest joke of all on all of us. Whitaker (Whitaker & Bumberry, 1988) writes:

> You never really "get there." The healthy family is one that is dynamic, not static. . . . I want them [families] to learn to not only tolerate but also enjoy the anxiety and pain that make living real. (pp. 198, 210)

FORMULATING THE MAJOR PROBLEM BOTH AS A SYSTEMIC COUPLE PROBLEM AND AS CHALLENGES FOR INDIVIDUAL GROWTH

As much as possible, towards the end of the first session I try to give the couple clear feedback as to how I see their problems, as well as their resources and potentialities.

Obviously there is a great deal that I cannot possibly know or know with responsible assurance by the end of a single session. People and marriages are much too complicated and our knowledge of psychology is far away from understanding a great deal of human behavior and experience. Nonetheless, I feel very strongly that I want to make this effort to give people at least my emerging professional interpretation. In part, this insistence grows out of my conviction that professionals owe clients information about the ways in which the professionals perceive the clients' situations and intend to intervene. When I am a medical patient, I insist on knowing the doctor's interpretation and intention; when I am receiving legal services, I have learned that I cannot leave decisions about the legal procedures or even the style of their implementation to the sole responsibility of the attorney, or I may be setting the stage for events that are going to affect me in ways that are not at all to my liking.

The idea that clients deserve and professional people should be required to give information about their observations, opinions and intentions expresses for me a basic ethical responsibility of any service-provider. In addition, this attitude is also connected to a philosophy of activating clients to participate in and shape the kind of treatment they are going to get.

The dynamic advantage of reporting back to the couple as early as possible includes bringing both the clients and the professional provider more alive to the task of creating an authentic treatment experience to which they both must contribute.

The need to prepare a cogent and meaningful report for the patients creates a different work atmosphere than when the therapist operates with priestly authority without being required to disclose his/her knowledge. The challenge to formulate a responsible and clear diagnosis to the clients makes for a therapist who is likely to be more genuinely involved, intuitive and alert. For the couple, receiving clear information about themselves means that they are going to be stimulated by the feedback process to engage in more serious decision-making about themselves and to generate greater energy, thoughtfulness, and spontaneous efforts to improve their situation.

In my experience, the clients' evaluation of the therapist's evaluation is often a very significant "moment of truth" in that clients themselves most often know what is going on with them even if, in most cases, they have not been able to formulate these matters consciously and express them. On hearing the therapist's formulation, they are able to perceive with intuitive wisdom the correctness or incorrectness of the professional's formulation. I find that the resulting feedback from the clients to the therapist is an invaluable step either in validating the diagnostic process or in raising serious questions for further thinking and reformulation by the therapist.

I also believe that an early formulation of the problem by the therapist is directly helpful. If psychoanalysis taught us that patients become "crazy" when therapists do not speak to them—and this was the technical purpose of the use of silence (Menninger, 1958), the other side of the coin is that patients really enjoy being given information respectfully by therapists. One meaning of a therapist offering patients a summary of their problems is that it is a gift of a sort—an expression of the active presence and involvement of the therapist with the people who have come to consult him. In addition, in our day and age, people feel they deserve to have information about their condition from the professionals who take care of them; I believe that this new norm is valid.

Formulation of the problem also conveys to clients that whatever the difficulty at this time in their lives, it need not remain so forever, for the pattern of their difficulty can be mapped and the sequence that brings it about understood and set up for intelligent change (Wile, 1979, 1981). By translating the repeated events that the patients are complaining about into patterns that can be described and make sense, the therapist conveys to the couple a sense of their possible control of heretofore not understandable and uncontrollable behaviors. Moreover, the specific cognitive concepts which are given to the patients, such as advice to use greater power or to make an effort to trust more, become tools for stimulating and directing their efforts at change.

DEFINING THE PROBLEM AS A COUPLE PROBLEM

Most lay persons listening to a marital problem tend to assign the primary responsibility to one of the mates and to see the other as more of a victim. Today, modern family therapy has given us a new perspective of the extent to which problems are derived from the interacting and interlocking contributions of both mates to a problem *system*. Even if the treatment interventions are intended to operate on or through one of the mates, the therapist designs interventions to the impact system of interaction between the partners.

The concept of a system means looking at the way two partners dance together to the same tune even though outward appearances suggest that one is producing and directing the show. Thus, the husband who is unrelentingly abusive of his wife, insulting her, humiliating her, bossing her around, using her sexually, perhaps even beating her, is obviously running the show, yet his wife is a very serious participant in the creation of the script as she allows her husband to continue in these ways. Granted, there are some instances in which the woman really is unable to consider separating from the man. Insofar as the wife is from a traditional culture and may be lacking in resources for making a living without the husband, and when age, illness, or special family conditions create real barriers to her taking a stand for herself, it is not fair to assign the victim wife *equal* responsibility for creating a victimizing marital system. I have seen capable, college-educated, modern women resign themselves to situations along these lines out of pure fear that their man might kill them if they left. Nonetheless, even in all of these difficult situations, one still should look at the extent to which the victim-wife should and could fight back against her victimizer husband. The implication that follows is that the extent to which the wife could defend herself but does not is her contribution to her role as a victim.

Of course, complex psychological and philosophical questions are involved. If victims *cannot* break loose from the situations in which they are being victimized because they do not have the personality resources needed to make and follow through on choices to free themselves, is it right for us to consider the victims responsible for contributing to the system of events in which they are participating? Is it fair to say that they are *choosing* to participate in the system? If they are, in fact, compelled to do what they do, is it appropriate to talk about their having a significant, let alone equal, share in that system? Still in the ultimate perspective, situations in which two people complement and confirm each other's positions take place only because the two are there and make them take place the way they do. In marriages, repeated fights are ultimately the choices of both mates to fight; repeated stretches of silence and non-talking are ultimately the decisions of both mates to be silent; and repeated poor sex is a function of the agreement of both parties to repeat a stereotyped, unsatisfying pattern of making love. What this means is that most of the time a marital therapist can shed important light on a couple's major complaints, even if the complaints are largely being brought by one of the mates about the other, by redefining the problems as *a shared system or pattern which each of the two mates helps create and confirms.*

Sometimes the systemic interaction is not that obvious. There are nasty situations in which the ugliness of one spouse who is beating on the other makes that spouse the predominant actor and manifest victimizer. It is unfair to assign shared responsibility to the victim in these situations with the same moral and emotional weight that one addresses to the victimizer. Many times, too, the victim consciously knows that s/he is trying everything possible to stop the victimizer and it doesn't make sense to say that the victim and victimizer share in the problem "fifty-fifty." For example, a husband fails to work or is unable to maintain gainful employment; the wife, who used to encourage and support him, has gone on to criticize and berate her non-provider husband. It doesn't make sense to attribute to the wife's current attacks on her husband the reasons for his lack of motivation to work successfully, nor does it make sense to attribute to the wife's original acceptance and patience with her husband's problem responsibility for his not working back then. Even if her contribution to the husband's lack of motivation to work were clearer, the basic problem of not working is still his. More than likely, the history of this husband will show that he always had difficulties performing in work or studies or participation in home life, and it hardly makes sense to attribute these earlier events to the wife who wasn't even in the picture.

However, even when the husband has always been the way he is, there is now a pattern of shared influences and forces at work between husband and wife which needs to be understood. In the situation described, the shared patterns would include the fact that the wife originally selected this man to be her lover and husband despite his poor history of performance; no doubt, there were other indications of his problematic character traits. In that sense, she chose a man who predictably would show in the future an inability to perform. Moreover, at whatever point the wife became convinced that her husband's failure to seek and hold work was very much his problem, she had a variety of choices open to her. Insofar as she chose to stay with the status quo of his not working, she became a partner to the system and a co-participant and creator of the ongoing events.

Yet I also believe that any number of marital and family therapists have allowed their excitement with the new systems thinking to lead them into an intellectual trap which has its own price in clinical work, namely an inability to see each mate as a person in his/her own right. The increased power of seeing couples as systems who cue, reinforce, and validate one another in circular sequences of interactions is so considerable that it is understandable that therapists become excited with this new way of thinking, but many go too far to the point where only systems thinking is considered valid and reference to individual dynamics is neglected.

Layton (1989) has described "the more optimistic vision of marriage" that is possible when one views the couple's interaction and the growth of both spouses as individuals as complementary.

> At its best marriage operates dialectically: the mutual supportiveness of the couple engenders the foundation for each individual's risky thrusts out into the world. As each partner grows in power and independence, the other partner is challenged to grow, and in changing becomes a new person with whom to fall in love again. As each partner grows and takes on new challenges, the old life-long fears and inhibitions rise up again, placing new demands on the capacity of the other to respond supportively and intimately. Marriage and family life are a dynamic and flexible context for growth, a "win-win" relationship in which each person is invested in the strength of the other. In such a dialectic, it is understood that an adversarial stance weakens

not only the other but ultimately weakens one's own context for growth as well. (p. 11)

It is important that professionals respect both sides of any complementary process and understand that the denial of either side is factually untrue and even weakens the appreciation and ability to work with the side that is being emphasized because, ultimately, complementary pieces draw their meaning from their apposition to one another and not only from their own selves. Moreover, much of the history of ideas in psychology is a constant replay of movement from one polarized position to the other—nature-nurture, free will-determinism, conscious-unconscious, behavior-experience, to name but a few of the major dialectical issues in psychology around which many well-educated people jump on one or the other extreme bandwagon.

The interaction of a couple in their system is a complex, fascinating symphony of many issues. However, at the beginning of treatment it is important to identify *one* major problem theme, preferably one that has to do with the issues that brought the couple to request professional help. The goal is to show the couple the paradigmatic pattern of how they are both creating, allowing, or surrendering to the situation that is disturbing them. Such a description carries with it an invitation to hope that the never-ending, repetitive chain around their necks can be broken.

Usually each of the mates coming for therapy believes that it is the other mate who is making life terrible and has to make the changes. The systems paradigm tells couples that some degree of change can be effected by either mate and that even the aggrieved or complaining spouse can help change the marriage to some extent even if there is no change by the other spouse who they feel is "making all the trouble." The systems concept also tells clients that couples who can be inspired to work together to effect changes can reshape their marriage most effectively of all.

Here are examples of formulations of a couple's problems as a shared system pattern:

Case 1
You (the WIFE) allow yourself to have this exciting potion of a love affair with another man. You defend it by saying that it adds to your life and does not compete with your marriage, but in the process of your open affair, you are pushing your husband's lack of security in himself to a new height. If he denies his natural feelings of jealousy and agrees to share you with another man, he becomes less of a person and a man for himself.

You (the HUSBAND) pretend so much to be a strong, independent man that you tell yourself you can allow your wife to have her other pleasure without it threatening you, but it is very obvious that you are nervous, your body is throwing up fairly strong symptoms of psychosomatic problems, and your head is full of revenge fantasies. What is also happening is that your wife is proving to you that you don't know how to admit that you are vulnerable and wounded, and you don't know how to fight back. I think that you (the HUSBAND) need to admit to yourself that you are crushed by your wife having this affair and that you want to stop her from continuing her affair and return to being a man who can hold on to his woman.

I think that you (the WIFE) need to make a choice between your two men. Even though your feeling will again be that you don't want to give up either of them, you must choose one of them. If it's your husband, you have to go on to find out whether you can make your relationship with him more alive as well as secure.

Case 2

You (the WIFE) want so much more emotional response from him, and so you love-talk him, caress him, and invite him to you, but it doesn't take very long before he pushes you away. Either he doesn't respond to you or he subtly conveys distaste for you or he quite openly turns down your overtures. Then you are crushed with proofs of the very feelings that you were trying to overcome by making so many overtures for more contact, namely your deep-down feelings that you are not lovable or deserving.

You (the HUSBAND) have good reason to be sensitive to the invasive, pushy, demanding qualities of your wife (and I gather these are reminiscent for you of a previous experience with a female who demanded that you do things for her more than for yourself), but in the process of pushing her away so that she doesn't gobble you up, you are creating a degree of hurt and a pattern of marital discontent that can lead to a permanent, devastating coldness between you.

Somehow, the two of you need to work out a better basis for regulating closeness and distance. I think the key to it lies in you (the WIFE) being careful not to press your husband with obligations and you (the HUSBAND) learning to appreciate your wife's wishes to be closer to you without your feeling trapped.

The formulation of the system problem should be challenging of major change on levels of both behavior and emotional development. It should deal with forces that are presumably within potential reach of the players in the marital system, albeit with the aid of further therapy. The language of the challenge should be related, if at all possible, to the major presenting problem that brought the couple into treatment. The formulation should speak to how therapy represents an hour of opportunity not only to solve an immediate specific problem but to enable genuine emotional growth.

Some marital therapists seek to redefine couples' problems in a way which will "reframe" their problem to make it appear far more hopeful and in relatively easy reach of their corrective efforts. For example, in the above two illustrations, reframing can be done thus:

Case 1

You (the WIFE) have been glad your husband has been letting you have your affair, but I also think that you are going to be much happier if he is a strong man and is able to insist that you stop and be loyal only to him.

You (the HUSBAND) have tried to be a real nice and understanding guy and let her have this extra pleasure without being an old-fashioned male chauvinist, but it really will be better for both of you for you to let some old-fashioned husband possessiveness and power take over.

In this formulation, both mates are told they have the same goal, no analysis is made of the interplay between pseudo-strength and loss of power in the husband, and the wife is not given a further sense of her need to make a choice between the two men.

Case 2

You both want to be close to one another and you can avoid unnecessary impasses simply by establishing together how close you agree to try to be on each day. You (the WIFE) have to discipline yourself so that you will seek only whatever goal the two of you are able to agree on and not try to go beyond it towards your ideal of a wonderful romantic totality. You (the HUSBAND) will be able to feel safe from being obligated to perform for your wife because you will have a full vote in deciding how close the two of you will be each day.

In this formulation, both mates are directed to a very concrete joint behavioral task. There are fewer references to deep personal issues. The wife is not reminded that she fears/expects to be not lovable. The husband is not asked to learn to reinterpret his wife's psychology.

Proponents of brief therapy argue that such reframing and other techniques for changing the immediate patterning of the couple's behavior are often sufficient to re-start the couple on a more successful road. This being the case, they argue it is unnecessary and perhaps destructive, as well as exploitative, on the part of therapists to keep such couples in longer therapies. My own feeling is that even when a brief system-intervention succeeds in redirecting the couple, it is prudent to follow the couple for a period of time to see whether the problem which was successfully solved does not lead on to other issues. There are many cases where effecting correction of a major symptom—inability to be close or a sexual problem—leads the couple on to a discovery of an underlying dislike or rejection of one another that the symptom simultaneously expressed as well as concealed (Brody, 1980).

DEFINING THE PROBLEM AS A CHALLENGE TO EACH MATE

If a marriage is going poorly and it is clear that each mate's behavior is contributing to the problems of the marriage and to their inability to overcome their problems, it is likely that each of the mates has his/her own psychological problems. Granted, one can speculate about a rare situation where the "fit" of two spouses is so wrong that, notwithstanding the fact that each is basically a sound person, the marriage does not succeed. However, even in this kind of situation one would want to question why such totally unsuited people agreed to get together as life partners. More than likely, therein will lie a tale that will point to the problematic needs of each of the partners.

When I see couples, along with the formulation of the system problem, I seek to formulate for each spouse a central personality issue which needs attention. In the above cases:

Case 1

(*To the HUSBAND*) The fact that you have not reacted to your wife carrying on with another man and even feeling she could get away with this—she even thought she could have your agreement to her open affair—means that you are suppressing some vital part of yourself, your power. I don't know why. I don't know if you feel that you don't deserve to demand for yourself or if you are afraid to use your power. I don't know if you suppressed your power in your original family. I would suspect this was the case. It is clear to me that you have cheated yourself seriously in your marriage and you ought to examine where this comes from in yourself and correct it as soon as possible.

(*To the WIFE*) The way in which you insisted that you must have

your own way and that you have a right to have both your own, independent way and also your marriage means to me that you have been
spoiled by someone and that you have come to believe you can pretty
much call the shots in any relationship. On the other hand, it also sug-
gests to me that you do not really trust anybody enough to invest
yourself fully in a relationship. I wonder if your being spoiled and your
not trusting both lead back to some faulty experience in the way you
were brought up.

The definition of the couple's system problem and the definition of the
individual problems clearly syncopate with one another. The husband is
being advised that he must demand his wife's loyalty to him and not give
in to her insistence that she can have both her worlds. He is also called on
to take a look at where and why he renounces his legitimate power. The
wife is instructed to make a decision as to whether or not she wants her
marriage because she will not be able to continue counting on her husband
to be weak and curry her favor. She is also advised that her readiness to
exploit her husband reflects her own inability to trust and to commit herself
to one relationship.

Case 2

You (*the WIFE*) must have some reason from your early background
that you are ostensibly out to get "everything" from your husband
but, in fact, expect and set up the result so that you get nothing.

You (*the HUSBAND*) have a real complex about a woman demanding that you serve her and you go to offensive extremes to protect
yourself against feeling obligated to the woman. Which woman in this
world first obligated you to serve her? I think you need to find out
and to see how you handled her, as well as how you handle your wife
now.

After the couple are offered both systemic goals and individual growth
goals, it is important to monitor their responses to both challenges, including keeping an eye on the possibility that progress in one area will be
used as resistance to undertaking the second goal. Some couples will seize
on immediate system-change possibilities and thus block or limit the therapy from penetrating more personal problem spaces in one or both of
them as people. The therapist then has to work hard to try to maintain
the tension of invitation to the personal growth issues that are being
ignored. Other couples will do everything to allow themselves to escape
into long-term psychodynamic work on them as individuals while
avoiding making any real changes in their marriage. Here, too, the ther-

apist needs to maintain a tension which calls for changes in the marital interaction and not agree to one half the package of spouses working only on self-improvement.

THE INTERFACE BETWEEN SYSTEMS WORK AND PSYCHODYNAMIC THERAPY

Perhaps the old psychodynamicists were right in believing that once a person saw his/her transference repetitions of childhood hurts and patterns in adult relationships, s/he would be able to act more constructively in marriage. However, it took ages to get to this understanding; in the meantime, marriages went to hell.

Perhaps modern systems theorists are right to be excited about their understanding of the circularity of mutual reinforcement of negative patterns. However, it turns out not to be so easy to break up ongoing negative interactions of couples because they are fed by streams of memories and engravings in people's unconscious impressions of their definitive experiences in their youngest years.

The fuller goal of marital therapy should be to help people to see how they themselves help bring about that which they fear or resent the most in their mates who are also doing things that are going to bring about that which they fear or resent the most. These interlocking patterns are extensions of the weaknesses with which both spouses left their childhood homes.

The best way to overcome repeated circular patterns is to stop the automatic, unconscious repetition of a pattern of the couple's scenarios *and* for individuals to work at and grow in the feelings they carry in their basic self-image. (For understanding marital projections, I have gained the most from Cashdan, 1988; Dicks, 1967; Segraves, 1982; on intergenerational transmission from Framo 1976, 1981; and on the battle with poor self-image from Satir, 1965.)

There have been many observations that many people marry the living reincarnation of the worst insult they suffered at the hands of one or both of their parents. They thus expose themselves to certain torture and, most likely, a disastrous marriage. On the other hand, other people very carefully marry the "opposite" of their most hurtful parent in what would seem to be a more healthy marital choice. Yet, given the dialectical principle, we know that this opposite will turn out to have attached to it a shadow-presence of the noxious quality or at least a related noxious quality that is similar to what one is escaping. In other words, there is probably no escape. Virtually any human being we will marry will have certain qualities that will have the capacity to elicit our most available weaknesses of personality and character.

I do not mean to deny that some marital choices are far better than others and some are far worse, but I suggest that all marital choices carry potential problems in the sense that all marital partners will have parts of their personality that will trigger in us our weaknesses and defenses. Optimally, in therapy each partner should learn what it is in him/her that is most vulnerable, how s/he responds to this vulnerability defensively and often assaultively, what it is in him/her which invites or evokes the weaknesses of the other, and what to do to stop negative cycles in the marriage.

Segraves (1982) has made a worthwhile attempt to document the interplay between couples and how each mate brings to the marriage "an inner representational system" (or built-in transference pattern of misperceptions and expectations that the mate will repeat one's parent's hurtfulness): Each engages in "eliciting behaviors" which draw the other mate into characteristic "evoked behaviors" and, altogether, the back-and-forth flow represents a system of "interactional behavior." The first purpose of therapy is to teach both mates better discrimination, so that they do not experience and interpret the other's behavior as negatively as they are wont to because of their inner expectations. Segraves calls on the therapist to interpret repeatedly how the spouse is not the same as one's projected or anticipated image of a hurtful parent. The other purposes of therapy then are to teach each mate to identify his/her influence on the spouse; to teach them alternative ways of responding to provocative behaviors; to teach the couple as a couple to work together to be able to communicate and clear up tensions, relabel events that might otherwise trigger escalations of distress, learn to prevent escalation, and be able to offer one another, reciprocally, comfort, reassurance, and constructive interaction.

There is no doubt that some couples develop an ability to process tensions and conflicts successfully in ways that enrich them.

A TRIAL PERIOD OF THERAPY

All of therapy is inherently a trial, beginning with tension and uncertainty that attend the beginning effort to create therapy when nobody knows whether or not each of the mates will be ready and able to enter into therapy sincerely, and whether or not there will be a good match between the couple and the therapist.

First and foremost is the inherent question as to whether or not both mates want to keep the marriage more than they don't want to. Many cases of couples who present themselves for marital therapy are already beyond the point of no return; at least one of the mates wants "out" from the marriage. Sometimes this spouse comes in order to be "fair" and give the other the support of a therapist and a chance to cry and yell. Other times, coming to therapy is a brief reawakening of desires to save the marriage and nostalgia for the good days in earlier years, but the die is nonetheless cast for the mate who has already decided to leave. After getting some of the nostalgia out of his/her system s/he makes the final position clear. Some couple therapists, especially those who are idealistically drawn to saving marriages if at all possible, are likely to misread such situations as more optimistic than they are.

Many couples arrive at therapy at a point where no decision to divorce has jelled in either spouse, but where the deterioration of the marriage has reached a point where it is unlikely that a spirit of trust, joy or love can ever be rekindled. However, since neither spouse has yet made an inner decision to leave, in theory there is still room for hard work to repair the marriage. However, again I would comment that serious estrangement, hatred, overt disloyalty, chronic disrespect and humiliation, an absence of commitment, failure to cooperate in everyday tasks, an absence of shared activities, cessation of once normal sexual activity, chronic neglect of childraising by a parent, and incitement of children against the other parent are among the indicators of a poor prognosis.

As emphasized earlier, one of the telltale indicators and determinants of marital outcome is the extent to which each spouse is ready to commit to working at the marriage. Another important indicator is the extent to which a mate really likes and cares for the other spouse and wants to be with him/her. Many people want to continue their marriage as an institution, so to speak, in its symbolic and structural continuity, but really don't have much feeling for the person to whom they're married.

In the trial period of marital therapy, I address a good deal of attention to issues of commitment and caring and to the extent to which each spouse will be ready to invest in therapy and the reconstruction of the marriage. The following is an example of a situation where the therapist chooses to question whether the couple will have the ability to work through their marital difficulties even though there are some nice aspects to the marriage. Such a framing may depress some couples and it may challenge others, paradoxically, to work harder:

> You have both been suffering a great deal. There is no doubt that you (HUSBAND) feel basically and chronically unloved and uncared for, and there is no doubt that you (WIFE) feel that he does not have any tender feeling for you and devotes the best parts of his personality to other people and not to you or to the children. For me, it is fairly

clear that there is a vicious cycle operating between the two of you in
that each of you is convinced of the other's lack of caring, you feel there
is nothing for you to treasure in this marriage and then you feel you
have nothing you want to give in return, and round and round it goes.
It also seems clear to me that there are various times when you both
make contact with a certain kind of loving for one another, that your
family means a great deal to each of you, and that if possible you really
would like to love and be loved and keep your marriage.

Unfortunately, although this is all very treatable, I am not at all sure
that either of you has the will or an inner optimism to give you the
strength to go through a long treatment process, to ride out the many
disappointments and objectively horrible times that you must still pass
through before one or both of you gets to have a bigger heart and can
help build a new kind of caring and confirming of one another. I feel
sad about this, because I think that you not only both want to have
your marriage, but that you are each married to a basically nice person
and that you could have been well-suited to each other. But I really
doubt that you are going to be able to have the stamina to exercise
the leadership that will be needed to save this marriage.

Having set a force in motion through a particular intervention, the therapist watches objectively how all the players react. If, for example, a person
reacts to this formulation despondently and says that there is no point in
trying because even the therapist does not believe there is any hope, the
"medicine" of that intervention may have been badly chosen and the therapist may want to try to change the "medicine" by directly encouraging
the spouses to work at their marriage. If a spouse fails to respond to the
challenge to work at the marriage with any kind of feeling for the mate or
for the possibilities of staying together, and in fact makes it even more clear
that s/he is determined to leave the marriage, the very failure to use the
"medicine" constitutes further diagnostic information that at least for this
person the marriage is probably dead and over.

Similarly, the therapist needs to keep a watchful eye on his/her own self,
on the feelings set off by the interaction with the couple, and on signs of
an overriding personal motivation such as a need to rescue a marriage
under any and all circumstances or a seductive identification with one of
the two mates at the expense of the other. Therapists must ask themselves
how such feelings originate in their own psychology and look honestly at
their relationships with their current family and their history with their own
family of origin.

Sometimes, a focus on the poor condition of the marriage will set off a
powerful paradoxical effect in the couple. They will not only touch old nos-

talgias of hopes and memories of better times, but may inspire themselves to new levels of graciousness, cooperation, understanding, appreciation, and sensuality that had not been seen in the marriage. It is not an easy professional decision to make as to whether such paradoxical effects should be purposely set off and strengthened when they appear. Sometimes, the paradoxical reactions are genuinely healing, but I have also seen a number of marriages come to "false life" through the induction of powerful paradoxical reactions, only to succumb shortly afterwards to their intrinsic poor level. In other words, the paradoxical injunction that the couple may not have the strength to recapture and rebuild their marriage may help save the marriage or it may speed up and confirm its death.

In the final analysis, coming to marital therapy is an opportunity to take honest stock of the condition of one's marriage, of whether or not its inherent dignity and appeal have been kept alive and both spouses have in them real desires to continue living together. If both husband and wife want each other and are prepared to work in therapy, a great deal can be achieved. If one or both do not really like each other and/or the structure of the marriage has been badly damaged, there are still some possibilities of arresting the deterioration and working out an accommodation that will stave off an undesired divorce, but the quality of the marriage will likely remain marginal or poor. If one or both mates are dead set on divorce, consciously or even unconsciously, then that is the likely outcome and the therapist would do well not to get caught up in an illusion that the therapy can achieve a happy rebuilding of the marriage. Finally, I would comment that the ethical thing to do in situations where a therapist does not believe s/he can help a couple work towards a desirable goal is to say so and terminate the professional service.

9

Bringing Together and Separating

Similarity and Complementarity as Basic Organizing Principles in Marital Therapy

Marriages can develop into basically decent and satisfying processes despite their imperfections. For this to happen, a couple need to be friends who feel sufficiently at home and at ease with one another that they are able to rely on one another for qualities and skills that each one lacks and to share and enjoy their differences. In this chapter I will be working with two key concepts of *similarity* and *complementarity* to describe how couples can combine sharing what they have in common with being enriched by the contrasts and differences between them.

SIMILARITY

Similarity refers for the most part to objective sociopsychological characteristics of each spouse. These are relatively describable and measurable manifest characteristics of a person, such as basic intelligence, education, work experience and skills, social class, personal attractiveness, sensuality, religious attitudes, political orientation, and other values or activities such as music, sports, or traveling.

Mates who are sufficiently similar to one another are likely to be able to get along better and succeed in creating a lifestyle that is compatible

and meaningful to both. Couples who differ from one another in important social-psychological characteristics such as ethnic origins and religion
or who come from markedly different levels on the societal ladder are
especially vulnerable under circumstances of heightened stress. The fact
that there is too little "glue" in their system is then likely to be felt more
vividly, and the possibilities of alienation from one another as a stranger
and "not-of-my-kind" grow. On the other hand, couples who do share
greater similarity are more likely under stress to be able to comfort and
be comforted by one another and by their contexts of shared identifications
and routines.

As usual, a dialectic principle is at play and it turns out again that
there can be "too much of a good thing." Couples can be too similar
to one another and the fact that they organize their lives without any
real differences or "coloring" and do the same things with one another
over and over again can create very difficult psychological problems
because of their lack of differentiation. It is hard for many people to
understand what goes wrong with such couples who are so "wonderfully" in tune with one another. The couples themselves who report their
problems are often confused as to why they are in trouble when they
apparently have "everything." But these couples may suffer from boredom, sameness, an absence of excitement and passion, and difficulty
in generating creativity.

> They were the best of friends. Each morning they started the day over
> a long cup of coffee and a warm conversation that would be the envy
> of many couples. He respected and appreciated her very much, as she
> did him. Both came from similar European backgrounds, shared the
> same religious and ethical values, and were colleagues in the same
> profession. They came for therapy because their eldest child was a
> demon at school. He was a reasonably behaved child at home, and
> they couldn't understand why he was so obnoxious and aggressive
> at school until it became clear in family therapy that the child was
> "exploding" with all the denied energies of being rebellious and neg-
> ative that he didn't dare play out at home with two so-nice parents
> who couldn't possibly understand his boyish aggressiveness.
>
> Although the couple hadn't come for help for a sexual problem, as
> long as they were seeing a therapist they also brought up a fact that
> puzzled them: Although they were young and loved each other, they
> were rarely excited by one another and had sexual intercourse as rarely
> as once or twice a month. Neither was especially upset by the dearth
> of sexuality, but they were aware enough to be puzzled by the
> phenomenon.

COMPLEMENTARITY

Complementarity refers to the counterpointing of opposite and contradictory characteristics within a person and between two mates, such as sociable/shy, generous/self-centered, aggressive/gentle, male/female. These traits generally refer to emotional characteristics, whereas similarity as discussed above refers more to objective sociopsychological characteristics. However, complementarity can also exist around objective traits—for example, she is better educated and more intelligent than he is and he looks up to her intelligence—while similarity can also be identified around personality characteristics such as their both being so sweet and kind. Ideally, each trait in an individual is backed up by a degree of connection or access to its counterpart. If not, the individual tends to be rigid and one-sided; the good quality that is overemphasized can become a source of stress. Thus, men who remain "only masculine," driving, and powerful, but are unable also to be tender and receptive are likely to become unattractive lovers. They often suffer sexual dysfunction because they do not integrate into their masculinity something of the universal female characteristics that are in their being. Women who are loving, receptive, nurturing, understanding, and unable to adopt any "masculine" toughness, drive, or aggression may appear lacking in color and power and will be vulnerable and weak in the face of a variety of life tasks. The interpenetration and interlocking of complementarities yield new and ever-renewing experiences of sexuality, love, excitement, and discovery of the poetry and drama between a man and a woman.

Within an individual's personality, too little complementarity means too little tension and challenge; there is either acceptance of one's self as a limited person in overly humble or helpless ways or overacceptance of one's self in unattractive and boastful ways, with a resulting hubris and smugness that weaken the personality. Similarly, too little complementarity between spouses means too little tension and challenge, and too little conflict in the relationship. The couple are almost always placid and seemingly without problems, either at the level of acceptance of underachievement or at the level of smugness with their unquestioned success. They do not experience themselves challenged by one another to grow. They do not confront one another critically and generally do not insist that a mate change even an obvious weakness. They are in a collusive agreement not to "rock the boat." These are marriages where there is no risk of loss of the relationship as is the case with people who take chances on raising issues with one another. Typically, such couples consider themselves as satisfied, happy, safe, and better off than other couples who are troubled, but in truth they are likely to be harboring concealed future symptoms (Wynne et al., 1958; Minuchin, 1974; Minuchin & Fishman, 1981; Sprenkle & Olson, 1978; Olson, Sprenkle, & Russell, 1979).

> They are both in their early forties. Both are successful hardworking academics, and both are committed family members. Marriage is a central value in their lives and with it their devotion to their children.
> They both have always been shy and uneasy in making contact with people. He cultivates a kind of sarcastic and cynical quality in his way of speaking and conveys to people very quickly that he does not trust himself to like or be liked by them. She conveys a sense of having taught herself to be more charming and interested in people, but she, too, never quite relaxes in a conversation; and one senses that it is still an effort for her to be sociable. Together they have created a way of life that is restricted pretty much to rituals of family events and other formal social functions. They have not made friends with whom there is any kind of spontaneous visiting or sharing of activities. Even between themselves, conversation is forced and basically uninteresting. As they enter into mid-life, she becomes panic-stricken at the thought of growing old with her husband in their stilted world.

Couples who are too involved with one another also may be prone to psychosomatic illnesses (Dicks, 1967; Minuchin, Rosman & Baker, 1978). These are also couples who may grow old early; they seem to dry up at a relatively youthful geriatric age. Lack of zest and individuality also makes older people more prone to deteriorative phenomena because there is insufficient vitality in their way of being with their mates and with other people. These couples also suffer the consequences of symptoms in their children, in my experience including serious learning disorders (see also Green, 1989 on how parents in the overorganized, enmeshed family are too involved and controlling and the child reacts with performance anxiety, procrastination, and passive-negativism), or cases of full-blown mental illness such as schizophrenia (Wynne et al., 1958), the reason being that the parents' lack of vitality does not encourage vitality in the child. The way in which the couple mesh together in a diffuse state of surrender of their independent individualities leads to weaknesses in their children (Bach & Wyden, 1969; Dicks, 1967). The children may be very "successful" in school and otherwise, but inwardly they express the lack of energy or vitality of their parents. More often these children are too good, not sufficiently playful and bad, but sometimes they act out in order to try to bring life into the family.

Sexuality is generally far below average, whether in frequency or potency or both. The marriages are characterized by boredom, indifference, and in some cases flights to outside activity. As the years pass, a number of these marriages are marked by a sudden decision of one spouse to abandon the marriage, a decision which comes as an overwhelming shock to the other. Efforts at therapy are invariably unsuccessful and the mate does, in fact, leave in pursuit of this turnabout decision to seek a better life before it is too late.

These undifferentiated couples also show risks of early death of the second partner soon after the mate has died, because independent coping skills have not been developed, and when the security of the sameness that was built by the two mates together is ended by the death of one partner, there is a sense that there is nothing to live for and no way to have the energy or know-how to live for oneself.

Complementarity is a potential starting point for growth if it launches a learning and growing process between equals who trade off strengths and weaknesses with one another without one spouse remaining (or becoming) the superior one and the other the lesser. The greater the basic equality between a couple, the more they are likely to profit from the give-and-take between their differences. But if the couple is unable to experience an underlying basic equality, their differences are likely to become pathways towards the consolidation of superior-inferior positions. Even if the couple are comfortable with this relationship, it is a potentially serious trap for them.

Very often, battles of excessive complementarity are joined around the very traits that first attracted each spouse to the other. When the couple prove unable to harness their difference in a cooperative, egalitarian relationship, these once-admired traits backfire on them.

> He used to find her a fascinating woman, but now he can't bear her charm and seductiveness. He has the uneasy feeling that she is cheating on him, even if it is only in the way she is so playful with other men. He fears that an affair could develop at any moment because she needs constantly to prove her worth by being charming and admired.
>
> She doesn't like his lack of drive to better himself instead of staying year after year at the same job level. When she first met him, she thought how wonderful it was that he was so relaxed; here was a man who would be quieting to be with. Now she sees that his relaxed style comes from his passivity and not from mastery of life.

Too much complementarity within any given individual's personality means that person will suffer, variously, too much excitement, anxiety, disorganization, and inner conflicts. Similarly, too much complementarity between a couple is characterized by sustained high tension and explosive conflicts. At the better times of the marriage, these couples enjoy as well as suffer intense alternations between love and hate. However, their insults to one another may drive them to a point where they must seek relief in some form of separation from one another. Although they are likely to return from these separations to the enormous pleasures of reunion, over time repetitions of this sequence leave them worn out and demoralized. Disloyalty and infidelity, certainly emotional and also sexual, are frequent and often serve as the focus of major crises and breakdowns. Intense anger sometimes bursts into actual physical fighting. Ultimately, these couples run a high risk of exploding with such intensity that their marriage is shattered or they exhaust themselves through their intense ups and downs until one or both no longer wish to continue the relationship.

BRINGING TOGETHER AND SEPARATING: TAILORING THE TREATMENT TO THE NEEDS OF THE COUPLE

The logic of dialectical treatment is that once one identifies the extreme or polarized side of a dialectical process in which the patients have taken refuge and overorganized themselves, the purpose of therapy is to reduce the extreme and/or introduce the missing or weakened side of experience.

Couples who cling too much together need to be helped in treatment to separate more; and couples who are too far apart need to be brought closer together. Byng-Hall (1985) writes: "The main aim of therapy is to change the thresholds of anxiety about distance, thus freeing intimacy and autonomy to function again. I aim to give the couple new experiences of closeness and distance" (p. 3). Similarly, marriages in which there is an absence of or too little conflict need to be led towards increased conflict, while couples who clash with one another too strongly or too often need to be brought towards greater unity.

The concepts of similarity and complementarity help us to organize a treatment plan based on a series of decisions as to whether to concentrate on bringing a couple together or on separating them in different functions. In each case, we ask what is the extent of similarity between a couple—that is, the extent to which they share characteristics of personality, character, values, interests, and activities. We also ask to what extent complementary processes are active—that is, the extent to which the couple are effectively pooling their differences in different functions.

The natural developmental flow in healthy couple relationships is that in any given function the stronger partner at first contributes more of his/her talent and the weaker partner receives and enjoys the offering. Then there is movement towards some expansion or learning of greater skill by the weaker partner along with acknowledgement of his/her relative weakness as well as an ability to continue relying on the mate's leadership in this area. Couples who are too similar to one another and/or lack or avoid complementary processes through which they can assist one another will need to be treated along the axes of reducing similarity and increasing complementarity, so that they can hope to grow with the help of each other's differences. Couples who are lacking in similarity to one another and/or show unduly intense, pervasive, or unstable complementarity need to be helped in treatment to increase their similarity and to reduce and redirect the flow of the complementary differences between them.

Needless to say, couples vary in similarity/complementarity with regard to different areas of functioning. Their respective roles can vary so that in one the husband is "on top" and the wife is in the "bottom" position and in another they reverse roles. Here, for example, is a brief sketch of a case where the undue complementarity of the man's overestimation of himself and the woman's underestimation of herself needs to be corrected; at the same time the wife's retaliatory independence and the husband's clinging to his wife need to be loosened.

> He thinks well of himself, but in no small part in compensation for inner feelings of inferiority. She doesn't think highly enough of herself, but fights like a tigress at every indication that he may not think well of her. He is really upset at indications that she doesn't value herself because they scare him with reminders of his own shadow. She compensates for her poor feelings about herself with thrusts of demonstrative independence from him, including veiled threats of infidelity. He then clings to her angrily but fearfully, and desperately tries to put her back "in her place."

I find it useful early in therapy to conceptualize where a couple stand overall in regard to similarity and complementarity. Without intending to oversimplify the complexity of couples, one can make an overall characterization of a couple's prevailing style. This makes it possible to formulate an overall therapeutic goal of working to bring the couple closer together or to try to separate them emotionally from one another.

THE IDEAL PARADIGM OF COUPLE TOGETHERNESS AND SEPARATENESS

When one designs treatment, it is useful to have a picture of an optimal process against which to compare a given couple's movement. Ideally, a couple will fall in love and choose to marry in great joy, without small voices telling them that they are really asking for big trouble. They will be similar to one another in many qualities such as intelligence, vitality, attractiveness, basic values, religious identification, and a cluster of interests and activities. They will also be respectful and appreciative of an intriguing number of differences between their personalities, areas of talent, and things they like to do. Overall, they will be charmed and grateful for each other's uniqueness without feeling rivalrous or resentful. During courtship and for some time into the marriage, the happy couple will make their way with satisfying trade-offs: "You do for me and I'll do for you." These exchanges will take place in different areas of their lives. In some, the husband will carry the load with his natural skill for these functions and the wife will rely on him admiringly and gratefully; in others she will carry the load and he will rely on her admiringly and gratefully. What could be more convenient and fairer?

However, in time, surprising but insistent indications of tension begin to emerge in those very areas where each had been so pleased with the other. There may be signs of jealousy in one spouse that the other is so capable and has "something" (competence, skill) that the spouse envies. There may be frustration and anger at being left to feel inadequate in the presence of the other's talent, as well as feelings that the more competent mate should have been doing a lot more "teaching" or showing the less knowledgeable spouse how to overcome limitations. There may also be the more competent spouse's anger at being obligated to compensate for the other's weakness. There are also cases where there is disappointment at discovering that the ostensibly more capable spouse is not as talented as originally expected and cannot provide the leadership that was counted on. In short, a variety of difficult and even serious tensions can develop around the originally attractive sharing of differences.

The emergence of such tensions is desirable. An absence of tensions would mean that the couple are settling into and consolidating a collusive arrangement where one is assigned the role of superior and the other the role of inferior. A fixing of roles means stagnation, no learning or development, and no challenge to growth in the relationship.

The negotiation of the couple's tensions is neither easy nor a simple straight-line process of steady growth. There is much pain and confusion along the way and periods of feeling badly. No matter what is done or tried, each mate discovers that s/he is hurt by the other, even deeply. Through the vale of hurt and tears there then follow resolutions and reformulations that announce new intentions to learn to do more for oneself, not to be so dependent on the other's strength, not to be dependent on providing for the other in the area of his/her weakness or to allow oneself to slide into benevolent superiority that is injurious to both mates. Having decided to become more for oneself (e.g., *I'm going to develop myself sexually and not wait for you to make me feel good*), there is paradoxically a renewed freeing of each mate to appreciate more the qualities and helpfulness of the other. In effect, the couple move through cycles of separating from one another and coming back to one another in renewed enjoyment of one another. This paradigmatic sequence is to take place in one after another areas of marital functioning—managing finances, sexuality, or the development of unused potential in one's career. At its best, the process leads couples to new affirmations, "I do for me, I gain so much from you, and it is my pleasure to encourage you to do more for you."

Step by step over years, each partner's pattern of growing becomes a delight and an inspiration to the other, each in turn is confirmed by the other's development, and the couple together develop a pride in the growth-sponsoring world they together create ("we can see that we are a good team because we help each other become stronger people"). In such a marriage, husband and wife see each other as they see themselves—attractively vital, developing personalities. Each of the mates supports the other and is supported, teaches and is taught, challenges and is challenged, appreciates and is appreciated; each enjoys increasingly warm glows of self-respect, pleasure at the other's increasing self-respect, and joint pride in the marriage.

SEPARATING: REDUCING SIMILARITY AND INCREASING COMPLEMENTARITY

When the therapist assesses the couple as too similar, accommodating, and enmeshed with one another, the goal of therapy is to emphasize and encourage differences and independence in activities, ideas, and feelings.

Therapist to a Spouse:
Why don't you take some time to get involved in your hobby? It's all right if you need to be away from home to pursue a hobby. Perhaps you can choose together two times a week when it would be most convenient for (spouse) to go out.

* * * * * *

It sounds like you really want to go to this convention but you (other spouse) really are not interested in letting him/her go. Would there be anything wrong in your taking the trip alone?

* * * * * *

You have a very strong interest in this activity but have never given it sufficient time in your life. I think you've been following your spouse around so much, even to places and activities that are not really you, and I also think you will probably be much more satisfied if you develop this real interest of your own.

* * * * * *

The views you both hold about the coming election really are not the same. In fact, if you were both working for political parties, you would be on different sides of the fence. Is that something you'd be willing to admit to yourselves and talk about with one another?

Many times in therapy, it is clear that couples are holding on to each other so tenaciously that one or both are foregoing the development even of simple skills for independent living. However, the prescription and encouragement of these skills should not be taken lightly. For some couples to experience differences and move to a realignment of status can even pose a threat to the continuation of their marriage.

> They were an attractive couple with one child. Both were college graduates. He was out of town a great deal on business and yet she had never learned to drive. She busied herself with their child and home and waited all too patiently for his return. They both made a joke of her not driving, but neither showed any inclination for her to learn. They had come for therapy because he was periodically uninterested in her (unconsciously she also knew that he was involved with other women), and there was a subtle but disturbing air of his degrading her and her hanging on to being insulted and injured and then feeling self-pity and humiliation.
> She made the decision in therapy to learn to drive. Although this in itself obviously did not lead in a direct line to the outcome that soon followed, one could not help but observe that after she learned how to be more of her own person in the world, she resented him for his superiority and his distancing himself from her and their child. He, in turn, became even more involved with other women who would agree to be his emotional slaves now that his wife was no longer simply his "little woman" at home. They divorced.

Just how far the therapist should go in pushing a couple towards greater separateness is not always clear. To the extent that the therapy succeeds in stirring up feelings and impulses towards life and power that have not been experienced for years, there will obviously develop crises in the psychic integration of one or both individuals and in the couple as a unit (Jackson, 1969, 1972). One has to carefully assess the justification for stirring up such troubles. Some couples will be very appreciative of the therapist's opening the door to a new way of living that gives them the opportunity to enjoy growing through sharing their more real selves with one another. Others will become too upset to tolerate therapy, will do everything possible to reorganize around their previous style of adjustment, and will leave therapy.

Technically, it is not really hard for the therapist to evoke differences between a couple, exposing the dynamics of differences they would be feeling if they did not suppress their individual spirits and personalities. The therapist need only ask any of a variety of questions like these:

- What are some of the things that make you tense and angry, even though you may not say anything about them?
- Are there some areas in which you have a different point of view?
- Do you have a dream of some sort for yourself, some area of activity, perhaps a vocation or a creative hobby, that you have not developed? What's your spouse's feeling about this dream, do you think? Do you talk about it?
- How do you feel about (spouse's) family?
- Do the two of you argue? Is s/he a fair fighter when you argue?
- Do you ever have bad thoughts about (spouse)?

In each case, expressions of individuality and differences between the spouses are to be stimulated in the dialogue around such questions. The potential differences are always there. Ideally, the atmosphere of working on these differences should be one of respect and good humor, but often the dialogue pushes couples to real fights. In doing this work, the therapist needs to be prepared for the fact that intense anxiety can be generated and quite unattractive parts of people's personalities may be unveiled. In many cases, a person or a couple will not want to experience such discomfort and will seek to withdraw from the therapy. Insofar as the therapist is able to enlist the couple's understanding and agreement to the difficult process that s/he is introducing, the prognosis for the therapy improves.

> With your agreement, what I am going to be doing is leading you through a variety of ideas and attitudes and also feelings where the two of you really don't think the same way, in fact where you have serious differences. My goal in doing this is to help you bring some more life into your marriage, so that you'll be more individualistic and more your real selves instead of fuddy duddy and homebound, if you know what I mean. I have to warn you that you are likely to become more uncomfortable in the course of these experiences. The truth is I can't really do this work effectively with you unless I have your coop-

eration, including your permission to make you more uncomfortable. What do you think?

Sometimes it is possible to help couples by inviting them to think imaginatively of how *another* husband or wife would express differences to a spouse.

> Can we try a situation where you (the husband) play the role of another husband who would not like the way (the wife) organizes these visits by her family and would be telling her so? Let's see how it will feel to both of you to have this kind of conflict and whether you will know how to go about such a conversation.

Couples who come to therapy with problems of not being their own selves can be pushed by such experiences in treatment to very real crises and even to doubts about the desirability of continuing their marriage. To begin to think for oneself that one's own personal feelings, goals, and dreams are valuable is a heady experience that restimulates the long-since blocked developmental adventure. Like young people who hear a call from inside themselves that it is time to leave home and go away, some spouses in these situations are drawn to fantasies of starting a new life. Obviously, the ideal goal is for husband and wife to awaken to new interests in their real selves and embark on the exploration of greater vitality and vividness in life together.

> She was a pale, plain-looking woman, still quite young, but she carried herself and behaved like a woman who was old before her time. He was an anxious, eye-blinking, balding young man who resembled a raspy older man who had seen the best years of his life slip through his hands without any great pleasure of achievement or excitement. Together, they were a pair of old folks and it was this feeling that had brought them into therapy. They were devoted to one another, their marriage and family were of profound importance to them, but they knew that they were becoming tired before their time. Both sensed that they were missing out on feeling alive sexually. They also knew that they lacked courage to stand up to various trials of life, such as in the husband's work situation which was very unsatisfying to him but about which he felt he could do nothing.
>
> In therapy, they were invited to stop being consistently pleasing to one another and to be far more honest and expressive about what each one thought. Protected by their commitment and their basic good will towards one another, they embarked on their journeys. He particularly

faced up to the considerable anger he had stored up towards his bosses and colleagues at work and was able to speak up more forcefully at work, with rewarding consequences. She was particularly interested in discovering new sexual feelings that she had jealously become aware other women enjoyed, but which she had never experienced. Over a period of time the couple bloomed.

BRINGING TOGETHER: INCREASING SIMILARITY AND REDUCING UNDUE COMPLEMENTARITY

It would seem to be an easier task to bring couples together to share experiences and activities than it is to get couples to go out into the world as more separate people. Yet it turns out that being together can be as frightening and intolerable for some people as being separated and alone can be for others. By the time couples who are far apart or warring get to marital therapists, even if they are eager for commonsense advice and direction to bring them closer together, many of them find it hard to act on such advice.

Spending time together is an essential component of successful marriages (Charny, 1986c). It may not be all that is needed, but it is basic—what philosophers call necessary but not sufficient. When I explain this subject to couples, I generally sketch a comparison between two couples. One couple start out in marriage loving each other very much, but then are each driven into a frenzy of activities in each mate's "success" tracks until they have very little quiet anchoring time with one another. The other couple start out with little romance and emotion for one another, but over a period of time build up a track record of sharing many simple tasks such as shopping, going to their children's school together, and spending unhurried time eating, walking, talking, let alone in more organized social and recreational activities. It is intuitively clear to virtually everyone to whom I pose this comparison that, over the long haul, the second couple have a chance of ending up more in love and more satisfied in their marriage than the first.

Nonetheless, even couples who sincerely welcome direct counseling on how they can build more activities together often prove unable to fulfill the "prescriptions" they are given. There are powerful forces at work in some people that impel them to stay on their own course of distancing themselves from another person. Some couples are habituated to getting violently angry at one another and playing out repeated choreographies of remonstration and revenge. They prefer or are driven to spoil possibilities of being together in order to "prove" that sharing time and space with their spouse is unbearable and untenable.

Couples who are too far "gone" and basically on a road to divorce at the time they come to therapy are likely to respond paradoxically to prescriptions for being together. They may show a misleading positive response in therapy at the point when the therapist brings them together, such as in creating a weekend away in a hotel. The couple may report that they had a wonderful weekend, something they haven't had in the longest time, and a honeymoon feeling develops which is especially misleading to younger therapists who are only too happy to see the couple respond with warm pleasure and evocations of memories of earlier happy years. Yet, what can then follow, predictably, is that within a week or two following the phenomenal weekend the decision to divorce is consolidated. The overriding yield of their experience in being together still is proof for one or both mates that there are compelling reasons to move on away from each other. Ideally, even those couples who are going to divorce will benefit from being in therapy long enough to learn what destroyed their bonding, including each one's major contribution to the system that created such disappointment and bad feelings that they must terminate the marriage.

Couples who are assessed as living too much off their differences with one another, especially those who are in intense conflicts, need first of all to be directed to control the damaging attacks they are making against each other. Violence in particular must be forbidden and the underlying emotional needs for violence treated in depth. (The subject of curtailing violence will be treated in the next chapter: It is so frightening and pervasive in American life that one cannot but help refer to it in a number of contexts in the book.) Similarly, abusiveness, vituperativeness, humiliation, and sadomasochistic rituals need to be labeled and limited as soon as possible. I find that young therapists are likely to be afraid to take clear stands against the continuation of abusive behaviors lest they offend the clients and lose them, but the fact is that couples cannot work and grow to be more humane and mature so long as someone is "getting away with murder."

Clinical methods for managing violent actions include teaching the victim-spouse to call the police and press charges against the mate if s/he is violent. This is a dangerously provocative step, of course. If possible, it should be negotiated as an agreement of the couple beforehand, so that it is not an imposed solution to the problem, but is anchored in an understanding between the mates. The intent should not be to punish and humiliate, but to assist the development of real control in advance of possible violence. In my experience, negotiation of such an agreement effectively ends most violent acts. Loss of control because of drinking or drugs requires different management techniques which I will not enter into here, but the overall principle is no less than the first order of therapy is to get destructive behavior sequences under control.

Couples who are locked into undue complementarity are likely to fight too often or too intensely or both. These are the couples who gain a tremendous amount of relief of their personal tensions through blaming one another. In their case, even when the blame in itself is objectively valid, the basic intention of the blaming is not to help the other spouse to bring about change for the better, but to protect oneself from one's own weakness. Anger is a basic and valid emotion, but it can be exploited as a way of organizing one's shaky personal ego or of giving "meaning" and "life" to an otherwise shaky marital relationship. Like a government that goes to war to take its citizens away from revolt, couples can fight in order to stay together.

Among the "garden variety" problems of too much complementarity and too little similarity are couples who create collusive situations where one is Big and the other is Small. A large variety of qualities can be organized in the service of this structure. Among the most common are smart-dumb, organized-inept, attractive-ugly, healthy-sick, good (or decent)-bad (or indecent). At a higher level of abstraction is the fact that on *both* sides of the complementary position there is pursuit of an insistent, rigid way of expressing oneself and organizing one's life. Each spouse becomes stuck on his/her way. There is a rigidification of a hierarchical relationship in which there is little interaction towards negotiating or influencing one another.

Many of these couples are not going to come to marital therapy for themselves, but do end up in therapists' offices because of derivative problems for a child. Some couples agree that both spouses will play the superior one in different life areas; in both cases the superior or elitist one remains aloof and above the lowly other.

> She is a beautiful, lively woman who loves to display herself to the admiration of other men and women and is a pillar of numerous community functions and organizations. He is proud of his goddess, raves about her, and displays her. He does not ask for her to take care of him because he is a super-independent man who cannot expose his power to being dependent on a woman. They collude to avoid intimacy which they both fear as dangerous.
>
> However, serious problems begin to develop with the children who also are not getting their dependent needs and yearnings for closeness met; as a result the couple come for therapy. In the process, the husband begins to want his wife to be doing more for him and the children instead of just seeking her own self-aggrandizement. Faced with his requests and with his underlying anger that she is not taking sufficient care of him or the children, she responds as a woman who is unable to suffer criticism of any sort. She has no tolerance for dissatisfaction with anything about her and is revealed as a person who will

threaten to take her own life if and when her feeling that she is the ultimate beauty is ever threatened. They fight—seriously, increasingly, bitterly—until she leaves him for another man.

The single most complicating aspect of complementary battles between couples is that there is a corresponding complementary battle taking place within each of the mates, so that any relentless position taken by one spouse in the marriage is backed by the terror each has of surrendering to shadowy inner fears. Spouses take out on their mates not only their anger and dissatisfaction in the marriage, but also their fear of being pushed to deal with inner issues which they feel they cannot face. Thus, in the previous illustration the pockets of resistance to change in each of the spouses are these:

> She must be the social queen or she will suicide-die of the insignificance that threatens her from within where she does not believe anyone has ever cared for her.
>
> * * * * * *
>
> He has to allow her to be a queen in her glittering world so that she will be too busy to take care of him because he cannot bear to be mothered.

Ideally, reduction of undue complementarity is developed through the reduction by each complainer of his/her own inner complementary struggle that is contributing to the couple system of too much complementarity. The battle in therapy is often drawn around conquering a focal projection by each mate on the other through which that mate is concealing the real inner fear: *I blame and attack you for "x_1" behavior of yours which mirrors my own denied inner weakness "x_2".* In the example above, these positions would be as follows:

She: I refuse your demands for more attention to you and the children, because I do not deserve to be cared for.

He: I blame you for not giving me and the children more, because I fear being taken care of by a woman.

Given an ability to look at one's own part in the marital turmoil by virtue of facing up to one's own inner dilemma, each spouse may be able to learn to accept him/herself as a person; then there is less need for projective attacks on the other. If the focus of energy and attention is shifted from blaming the spouse to trying to resolve one's own dilemma, there can be some relief of tension in the marital system. If, moreover, there develops a measure of grace towards one's spouse and a readiness to help him/her deal with and grow out of his/her parallel dilemma, what was once an area of fierce marital battles can become a framework for increased friendship and appreciation of the privilege of being able to be meaningful helpers to one another. A rewarding empathy can develop between the two spouses as they discover that they are each fighting a similar, internal battle. It is, of course, far easier said than done. Relatively few couples go all the way in therapy to emerge as genuinely creative couples. Few people go all the way to see themselves in the spouse, to recognize in their anger at the spouse the reflections of their own weakness and struggle.

There are various possibilities for reducing powerful marital clashes. One way of helping fighting couples is to develop with them an understanding that marriage is an overall process and not a steady-state of pleasure. The concept that conflicts and marital fights are useful and desirable up to a point is helpful, since it both legitimates some of the fighting and invites a rational approach to reducing overly intense fights. George Bach's (Bach & Wyden, 1969) seminal work on fair fighting is helpful in guiding people toward accepting guidelines for being fairer and more controlled in their fighting. Even when people don't understand the projections to which they are responding inside of them, a commitment to fair fighting means that they will take responsibility for stopping fights before they get out of hand. The metamessage of the fight becomes that the intention is to improve the marriage and not to destroy it.

One concept that I find especially helpful is that some measure of injustice, unfairness, and betrayal are, unfortunately, basically natural and must be expected in life by all of us (Charny, 1972a, 1972b). It is disappointing and even frightening to find how unfair the man/woman we have chosen to live our lives with can be. But once we understand that there is no person who does not have this trait, including oneself, there is almost no choice but to develop a more tolerant resignation to the human condition which we all share and perhaps a greater appreciation of what one's partner has to give despite such unfairness in his/her personality.

Another concept that I find very helpful is to know that we all become upset in our marriages and feel wounded by our spouse. Therefore, a first level of management of distressing emotions is to not be so distressed over being distressed. If we "go crazy" about feeling wounded, our discomfort and distress are intensified many times more. Better that we should simply accept the fact that these feelings are all a part of life (Ellis & Harper, 1968).

Increasing tolerance for frustration, ambivalence, and ambiguity, especially if added to acceptance of responsibility for one's own parallel conflicts around one's hidden weaknesses, can turn around a tumultuous marriage to a reasonably stable and satisfying one. Needless to say, the course of therapy towards such a corrected position is a hard one that requires considerable persistence and devotion on the part of both therapist and patients.

Couple sessions shorten the course of such therapy remarkably when compared to the older option of working only in individual sessions with each mate. In individual therapies, many months and often years were required before the individual could see his/her own role in asking for and reinforcing the noxious behaviors they most complained about in the mate. The intensity with which a beleaguered spouse protests the behaviors which hurt and offend him/her the most actually reinforces these behaviors. It is as if the complaining spouse actually is honoring the power of the offender, thus increasing motivation to use that power to make one's mate squirm again. The subliminal message of the hurt mate is that protesting these injustices is emotionally satisfying—so please repeat them so I can have the chance to protest again.

In couple sessions, the cues are right there to be identified and dealt with as they occur. Segraves (1982) has given very helpful guidelines for combining psychodynamic and behavioral-cognitive techniques to stop a mutually reinforcing pattern of disturbance between two mates. His goal is to break up characteristic repetitions of disturbing paradigms in which each mate (a) invites a characteristically noxious response in the other who (b) responds to this eliciting or inviting stimulus blindly and proceeds (c) to provide the confirming noxious behavior which (d) reinforces the mate's original expectation which in itself is derived from the memory-echo of what was most problematic in one's childhood experiences. Round and round it goes. In marital therapy the couples play out these interactions and the therapist's goal is to teach them to see how they are locked together in a system and to introduce new ways of behaving. However, I do not agree with Segraves that it is possible to do such therapy work in only 20 sessions, at most, which he assigns to the whole course of marital therapy: To learn one's own role in expecting-inviting what we fear the most from the other and to see how we confirm for the other what s/he fears-expects the most generally takes repeated understanding and practice of the corrected behaviors over a longer time period. There needs to be time for regressions in the treatment and recovery from these guided exercises in the sessions, much homework between sessions, vacations from therapy, a period of reduced sessions when there is progress, and follow-up sessions still later.

Finally, I would add, even if briefly, that the difficult processes of couple therapy call not only for wisdom in choosing whether and how to bring couples together or to separate them in various areas of functioning and experience, but also for meaningful protection and a kind of "parenting" of the couple by the therapist. Couples are involved in a mysteriously difficult process and, whether or not they know it and admit it, they are frightened. Moreover, all of us human beings are involved in the mystery of being alive while heading towards death and in the maddening complexities of being talented while being frustratingly limited and handicapped in many ways. We are frightened by our unknowingness, weaknesses, and mistakes whether or not we know it. The therapist makes more learning and change possible through firmness, respect, caring, and comforting.

10

The Treatment of
Destructive Communication

*Teaching Couples How to Be Best Friends
and Their Real Selves*

The single most frequent complaint about marriage is the absence of communication or the poor quality of it (see, for example, Greene's [1970] cataloguing of marital complaints).

At the same time, perhaps the single most common error in marital therapy is the effort to bring couples together and teach them communication skills when there are many reasons and signs that they are not prepared for such communication. Not only will the effort to have the couple speak with one another fall flat if they are not really in a position to share their ideas and feelings with one another authentically, in many cases the "proof" that will follow in the therapy sessions that they are unable to communicate will become an added insult and disappointment that therapy, too, can't help them communicate with each other.

I also think that a good deal of the professional literature on couple communication encourages an overly mechanical sequence of couples saying and hearing words or sending and receiving information in properly polite ways, but misses the truths of sentimental and emotional meanings of communication. There are any number of "packages" of communications skills in the literature which structure periods of communication for couples (e.g., 15 minutes each after you come home from work) and specific communications tasks such as how to reflect feelings and statements conveyed by your mate (variously called "active listening," "reflection of feelings," "positive listening"), which can be somewhat helpful. However, I think these tasks represent largely instruction in technology and not necessarily in the spirit of communication. No matter how one says the "right things," there are or are not present genuine feelings of interest in sharing oneself with one's spouse; both parties feel this level of genuine interest instinctively. (Writings about enhancing positive communication between couples include Epstein, Baldwin and Bishop [1983], Gordon [1970], Miller [1975], and Satir [1967, 1977].) Another problem with much of the material on teaching couples to communicate is that it is restricted largely to working with positive feelings and there is little recognition and even gross denial of the powerful dilemmas of anger and hate. Satir acknowledges hatred perhaps a little more than the others, but her whole style was always that the well-rendered "good" feelings would certainly banish the bad, which created a romantic conception of people for which she was so loved. In this sense, I do not believe her writing about couples reflected much of the real complexities of husband-wife interactions.

Communication between spouses is vital as an antidote to the "empty spaces" of loneliness that overcome many marriages, as well as to the emptiness that needs to be overcome inside of each of us. Sharing oneself with another and experiencing that person's interest, caring, and pleasure in response is a powerful process of being confirmed as a meaningful person; our own genuine interest in the other adds a further, no less powerful dimension of being confirmed as a result of being able to confirm the other.

Communication is also vital as an opportunity to hear oneself in the course of telling about one's life and thoughts, thus facilitating a crucial self-observing machinery for monitoring one's own self and evaluating strong and weak points. The communicative process also encourages the serious critical review by one's mate who, more than anyone else in the world, is in a position to understand the nuances and real motivations that lie behind even one's most successful activities. Couples who develop a mutual trust which allows each one to tell the other essentially the full truth about him/herself and who experience critical observations by each other without the criticism constituting an insult or rejection are deeply privileged. Genuine feedback offers each spouse invaluable information for personal growth, while the authenticity of the relationship between the couple builds a deep sense of security—far more than rubber stamp, unconditional acceptance can ever provide.

Strangely enough, angry marital communications also make possible a profound sense of connection between a couple and give meaning and purpose to their lives. There is excitement in the battles. Marital battles are antidotes to boredom. Anger-provoking communications also can stimulate considerable responsive strength; the angered person can become the more resolute, tough, and purposeful in response to the attacks. Moreover, destructive communications can bond people because they, too, are antidotes to loneliness and emptiness. Over time, many couples get addictively hooked on destructive communications. Whatever the "benefit," the problem with repeated destructive communications is that, slowly if not more quickly, they wear away the "surfaces" and "bodies" of each spouse and the structure of the marriage. They can hurt. They can kill spirit, hope, justice, optimism, joy.

TYPES OF DESTRUCTIVE COMMUNICATION

There are many types of destructive communication. Following are a number of types for which we will discuss treatment:

1. Blaming
2. Insulting
3. Disrespect
4. Hatred
5. Rage and Violent Anger
6. Actual Violence
7. Patronizing and Emotional Enslavement

Blaming

This is probably the most common form of destructive communication between spouses. Simple instances of blaming a spouse unfairly for things or situations which s/he really was not responsible for are obvious enough assaults on the blamed person. Less obvious are the many situations where there really is reason to be critical of one's mate, but where the criticism is not rendered so much in a tone that calls for correction of the misdoing or to convey one's hurt and upset as it is to dump a kind of fault-finding or demeaning on the other. Basically, the message is that the other person is the one responsible not only for the particular mishap or problem at hand but for much more, in a sense for all the anxiety that the blamer suffers in life.

The process of blaming is an everyday variety of the horrors that follow from the universal defense mechanism of projection. All of us engage to some extent in projections on to others of the terrible burdens of anxiety that we suffer. To learn to master the anxiety that is endemic to our human condition, to be responsible for it in ourselves, and to overcome it through genuine growth are among the great challenges that few of us can meet as fully as we would like. One of the simplest alternatives to anxiety is to lay the burden at another person's door. One might even consider the positive sense that the marital experience invites and allows some projections on to one another as an opportunity to learn more about our ways of projection; the safeguard lies in the supposition that one's mate will reject one's projections appropriately and the process that will follow will make possible an increased ability to spot one's dirty actions (projections) at work. To apologize and withdraw one's projections from the other is an experience that then adds to the dignity and emotional strength of the person who is big enough to correct him/herself and enriches the marriage relationship. So again, existentially, there is considerable value in doing some "bad" and "wrong" things if the errors are moderated and if they are used dialectically to learn more about how not to be destructive.

The therapy of blaming is deceptively simple insofar as the therapist's "umpiring" of blaming that takes place in the office is accepted by the clients. They need to be capable of accepting the therapist's ground-rule definition that blaming is an exploitative dumping on the other that differs from expressions of criticism and anger that are straightforward and respectful. However, the therapy of blaming is notoriously difficult if and when clients are enraged and bitter or characterologically committed to the use of superiority as an escape from anxiety. Self-righteous people are notoriously difficult to convince that they are not simply complaining and correcting their spouse as is their right, but also getting their "I'm O.K., you're lousy" positioning off on the other. In this regard, mental health professionals can be among the most resistant clients. What is crucial in the therapy of blaming is to differentiate clearly between acceptance of a spouse's right to be angry and critical and the subtle but devastatingly projective use of anger to put down and entrap one's mate.

Insulting

Some people seem to get married in order to have the opportunity to have somebody they can pummel with insults. To the extent that humiliation and demeaning are characteristic of the couple's relationship from the outset, I have little faith in the possibilities of these marriages lasting, nor can I as a therapist offer any kind of conviction that they should.

> They were both college graduates, handsome and vibrant. He had completed graduate school and embarked on what was to prove a brilliant professional career. They were also very interesting people with rich cultural interests and each was involved in state-of-the-art activities in their daily lives which gave them a good deal to talk about.

Yet when with them, one was immediately struck by the fact that he turned to her every few minutes with a contemptuous leer and would spin off yet another insulting remark about her incompetence, stupidity, or unattractiveness. She seemed to absorb everything he dished out without flinching—and related to his ugliness towards her as if it were no more than a minor annoyance, if not routine communication. For students of the marital sexual process, it is also interesting to note that this couple engaged regularly in anal intercourse at his insistence and her acquiescence. In this respect, as in the matter of verbal communications, she didn't know that she felt insulted. Eventually, after too many years and several children, the system of insults wore through her zone of not knowing to a point where it was personally and socially untenable for her to keep up a marriage to a man who treated her continuously with contempt. Nonetheless, even then it was he who initiated and executed the divorce as the final insult.

Insulters are bullies and bigots, in my opinion. Applied sociologists have taught us that in the larger world bigots need to be stopped firmly as early as possible and if possible with a value statement such as, "It's un-American to speak the way you do." In a couple relationship, a statement can be made which combines an I-statement of being hurt with a value-comment on the insult such as, "It's insulting to me for you to speak to me that way." The therapist essentially needs to do the same thing and put his/her weight into a refusal to allow insulters to continue speaking in their bullying way during the session. In the process, there is also a modeling effect for the insulted spouse, first of all to increase awareness of being insulted since there are many who dull themselves into unknowingness, and secondly as an example to them of how to use some degree of power to insist that the insults cease. Where necessary, the insulted spouse should back up his/her stand with real sanctions.

Therapist: I can't agree to your speaking to your wife this way. You sound to me like you're talking to a child or to a retarded person in whom you have no trust. Even if you are right in the content of your criticism, you sound ugly.

Disrespect

The purpose of identifying this type of destructive communication separately from the previous one is to look even more closely at inner meanings of communication in addition to the obvious outward expressions.

Disrespect refers to a basic lack of respect for the essence of the other person as an attractive, intelligent, deserving human being. There are many marital situations where there is no outer insulting, outer civilities are respected, courtesy prevails and even gallantry, but the inner message—which is always experienced by people for what it really is—is one of essential disrespect. A spouse may be carefully "correct" about not speaking disrespectfully to his/her mate, yet tell the therapist openly how the spouse is an idiot, weakling, ne'er-do-well. Interestingly, the obverse is also true: there are many clinical situations of considerable expression of negative emotions and attitudes, but inwardly the actively insulting spouse (one or both) has a deep respect for the other. This is an important positive prognostic sign that can override much though not all of the damage that is being done by the overt insults.

I have come to dislike therapy where the couple are ostensibly practicing corrective communication exercises while the truth is that at least one of them has no respect for the other. I find that such cases may go through a period of illusory improvement, but the truth will eventually out. In my judgment there can be no meaningful bonding in marriage without respect for one another.

Given indications of serious inner disrespect, the treatment issue is no longer one of stopping overt expressions of negative feelings as was the case with blaming and insulting, but rather one of developing an authentic discussion of the nature and degree of respect that each mate really feels for the other. Once it becomes apparent that there is too little respect, some of the hidden power of that disrespect is neutralized by virtue of the issue being brought out into the light of day; now there is also a basis for discussion of whether and how respect might be increased. With younger couples, I question whether it will be possible or worthwhile to continue the marriage without real appreciation of one another. With older couples, if I feel that the treatment goal is to reduce distressing dysfunction and help stabilize the marriage at a workable level of security and satisfaction, I will not probe the issue as much but will emphasize interventions that call for greater overt expressions of respect. Even here, however, if one spouse is secretly despising the other or communicating to the children, friends, or the therapist that the other mate is "worthless," there is no alternative but to address the destructiveness of the psychological humiliation.

Therapist: Virginia, I can't help but question what you think in your heart about Alan. Do you honestly respect him? Is he a worthwhile and admirable person in your mind? I get the feeling that your inner statement about him is not only that you are very disappointed but that you find it hard to think a good thought about him.

Hatred

The emotion of hatred itself is natural and inevitable in human beings; therefore, it is present even in an excellent marriage (Charny, 1969a, 1972b; also see on the inevitability of angry feelings an amazingly early piece by Winnicott [1965, originally published 1949]). Hatred refers to powerful emotions of imagining and intending harm to others. It goes beyond disrespect or devaluation of the other. In fact, one can hate someone who is respected.

Those who are in tune with inner emotions know that hating thoughts and feelings spring up inside of us even without any objective cause at various moments when we are at some short end of our own stick, touched by our own anxieties and deepest fears of mortality and nothingness. We often turn naturally to wishing others badly as an expression of fear and protest over the bad fates that are visiting or waiting to descend on us. Whitaker (Whitaker & Bumberry, 1988) wrote, "For the longest time I used to carry around a list of the six people I wanted dead. Then as they died off one by one, the list shrunk. I suppose it's time to make up a new one!" (p. 184). The first line of therapy of natural hatred is to teach spouses the inevitability of such emotion, tolerance for it inside of oneself, and restraint in expressing these feelings to one's spouse. Better to ride them out like a wave in the sea—in which case the emotion will pass by. Where necessary, spouses need help to learn "thought stopping" or how to consciously turn off an unjustified hating thought as bad and irrelevant.

An additional protection against the unnecessary damages of hate feelings is for couples to learn that if one spouse does express anger and hatred that seem to arise from frustration and fright, they should not take these emotions personally, because they are not intended to be personal. Most couples will also need help to learn and accept that angry *feelings* are not the same as *actions*.

Another problem in our lives as couples is that spouses' hatreds often are not synchronized with one another. If one has been full of warm, loving emotions and then gets slapped in the face with hatred, it becomes an unsettling experience that sets off feelings of having been betrayed and "repaid" unfairly. This is what marital therapists hear so often in the complaint, "How *could* he/she say this to me after I have been so loving?!" It is important in marital therapy to teach couples how each will be more vulnerable to being hurt by anger and hatred after experiencing and expressing positive, loving emotions, and how one should discipline oneself not to overreact at such times, but to ride out the spouse's rage, while limiting any excessive expressions of hate in response.

One saving grace of the dialectical principle is that it guides us to knowing that hatred in itself is often an expression of deep caring and wishes to love, and that behind some hatred lie feelings of unrequited love. One cares so deeply that one wants to obliterate the other who does not return one's caring! Therapy of this type of hatred often begins with a reframing by the therapist: *"Your caring about (name of spouse) is so intense that you hate him/her for not responding to you the way you wish."*

Most hatred in marital relationships is nonetheless more than a natural venting of an existential substrate of negative emotions. It does not simply represent embarrassed feelings of unrequited love. As the name implies, hatred is often an expression of genuinely angry wishes. Like it or not, we human beings have been given a natural machinery for anger and hate of anyone we perceive is hurting us. The positive functions of such feelings obviously are self-protection and self-defense. The negative dangers obviously are that our anger is often unfair, excessive, and destructive of our own and the other's peace of mind.

Much hatred is a response to someone we feel is doing us harm and its substantive meaning is that it is a real protest against serious marital wrongs and hurts. This should *not* be dealt with by reframing the hatred as a desire to love the other, but, rather, the severity of the underlying anger necessitates an agenda for a careful and honest review of the basic record between the mates. The "accounts" on which these angers are based need to be rendered pretty much in full, faced by both spouses, and negotiated. It is insulting and even "crazy-making" for a therapist to tell clients that they have to get over their excessive anger without giving them a fair hearing as to whether there is a rational basis to their anger and without helping them to clarify first with themselves and then with their spouses the reality of their protest.

In therapy, the therapist insists that these hating feelings be heard by the other mate and responded to concretely and understandably as they relate to specific complaints. At the same time, the spouse expressing hate is also counseled to control and monitor his/her feelings so that the mate will not be so overwhelmed or frightened that s/he is unable to handle them.

Many spouses need to have some recognition by their mate of the fact that they have suffered at their hands, along with some expression of regret about their suffering, before they are able to go on to "close the account." Shifting the focus from old grievances to the future often is not possible until past accounts have been dealt with in a way that feels fair. In my opinion, it is a mistake to insist only on "here and now" therapy of what is going on between a couple today if major hurts in the past still rankle. Of course, it is often hopeless to let couples in therapy fight about old grievances that cannot be remedied and it is almost always correct to begin with current anger and hatred. But when a couple is ready, dealing with old accounts can make the difference between a full new start and a patch-up job that is always vulnerable to the reemergence of old hatred.

Rage and Violent Anger

The power to express intense anger and to become enraged is in itself a sign of a vibrant personality. There are many couples whose relationship with one another has withered because they have not had the emotional stamina to experience and express powerful feelings to one another. On the other hand, intense rage and what I term violent anger (but not actual violence) are terribly frightening. Intense rage sets off legitimate fears that actual violence may follow. It is also frightening at some core level of experience because it is so total and consuming. While the extreme of emotion also may convey that the rage-filled person cares very deeply and there may be room for some such reframing in the therapy, violent anger also underscores the fact that there has to be some kind of major correction or quieting or else the marriage could end. Intense and violent rages lead to later stages of turning off and terminating relationships.

When there is intense rage, the temptation for the attacked spouse, as well as for the therapist, is to respond too much to the ominous form of the rage and not to respect its content and causes. The therapy should focus on sorting out what it is that means so much to the enraged spouse until the issue is understood at its fullest. Intense rage is often treated as if it were already the equivalent of violence, but if there has been no overt violence, there may be no danger at all of actual violence. The couple might even be congratulated for dealing with their intense emotions without resorting to overt violence. What is most important is that the therapy create a fair and full hearing of what is setting off the rage, as well as limit the style of expression of rage.

> He was beside himself at her temperamental on-again, off-again histrionic moods and manners. He wanted so much to love her; however, while some of the time she was charming and it seemed that heaven on earth was within reach, within a day or two there would come another attack from her. At times, her contempt seemed to know no bounds. In some of these situations, he would finally crack and blow up into an enormous rage, scream, cry, and curse. One day, in a height of desperation, he gave her a slap across her face as if to assert his husbandly control, but also with some kind of hope that this might somehow set things straight and end the bad dream of her nastiness. For her the slap was nothing more than more proof that she had to fight against him even harder. For him the failure of the blow to set things straight was the end of another phase of hope that he would ever find a way to reach her. He resolved never to hit her again and insisted

that they go to a therapist to whom they each told the story of the violent emotional peak they had just reached.

In the therapy session, he tried to get across how much he wanted to make contact with her. She, in turn, told how he was so demanding and critical of her; the ultimate insult was the violence. The therapist then "ruled" that the husband had been in the wrong, that he was immature in his emotional demandingness and intensity, and certainly in his act of violence. She was triumphant. He was surprised at the therapist's one-sidedness. He did regret the extent of his emotionalism and resolved to master it, but at the same time he was even more worried that the therapy was not going to help them because there was no recognition of her chronic style of hurting and rejecting. They returned for two more sessions, which were largely repeats of the first, and then *she* announced that she would not come again since there was no point.

Overt Violence

Overt violence has to be stopped first of all; then, it needs to be understood for what it is exactly.

If actual violence takes place right in the therapy office—a situation which does occur on occasion—I intervene immediately and powerfully with an insistence that the violence must be stopped: I say that it is wrong to hurt people physically, but I also add immediately that the intense feeling of rage that has triggered the violence has to be understood and I will do everything I can to help.

In containing overt violence, the therapist needs to be absolutely sure of his/her own conviction that moral integrity calls for the protection of human life and body. It is from the power of this integrity that the therapist draws power to insist to the patient that actual violence as a method has to be stopped. If the clinician's intent is to get a situation "under control" for control's sake, the demand for nonviolence will be perceived as serving the clinician's needs and will not help the violent individual effect control. Along with insisting on the integrity of the nonviolence, the therapist must convey no less sincerely the intention to give the patient's anger and desire for violence a full hearing and to work on the issues which are enraging him/her. It is the combination of the two messages which makes it possible to stop people who are mad with seemingly uncontrollable rage. I have had any number of experiences with violent persons who were definably mentally ill and even brain damaged, but still have been able to reach them with the above combination of messages (Charny, 1967). (However, this method of treatment does not work with psychopathic people who resort to violence as a method for gaining specific financial and tactical goals, nor is it sufficient in situations where the violence is drug-related or derives from an ideology such as a cult.)

Many therapists are confused and impotent in the face of overt violence because they do not know how to combine the two principles of prohibiting the violent acts and respecting the feelings behind the acts. The moral injunction or authoritative insistence on stopping violence is a legitimate tool in its own right, but in the face of intense fury—which in its extreme sometimes can also pick up a suicidal momentum and/or a homicidal intent—the power of this message by itself is limited. On the other hand, a therapist's sincere invitation to talk about the feelings that are triggering violence will seem like a silly and useless approach in the face of someone who is on the verge of doing actual violence. It is the combination of messages that has therapeutic power: Telling the violent spouse not to harm another human being *and* stating that the raging feelings will be given a full hearing enhance each one of the tools.

It is important that the therapist's message be rendered in a strong, assertive voice that matches or stands up against the violent mood of the client. If necessary, the violent client must also be told that the police will be called, but the point is not to rush to this outside solution, but to convey an insistence that the violent mate exercise his/her own control.

In cases where only the victim spouse comes to the therapist's office, the goal should be to invite the participation of the missing spouse. To the extent that the violent spouse shows no readiness to cooperate with the therapy and is not prepared to resolve not to be violent again, it is essential that the victim spouse develop a conviction that under no circumstances will s/he allow further violences. The "simplest" way is for the victim spouse to draw a line which says that if there is any further violence, the police will be called immediately. However, I have seen a strong and well-educated woman quaking with fear that she could not say something like this to the man—he wasn't even her husband—who was threatening to kill her if she didn't continue to live with him.

Therapists need to be aware that there are people who succumb to severe states of bondage where they feel unable to invoke any defense against being victimized and will strongly resist the therapist's counsel to call in the police. When I do encounter a spouse who shows an unyielding masochistic attitude, I respond that I will not be able to go on with treatment without indications of his/her own ability to exercise power to stop being a victim. I intend this move as a final attempt at therapeutic leverage that may get the patient to fight back against his/her helplessness, as well as an ethical statement of the limits of my professional skills.

Sometimes the threat of continuing preparations for violence becomes transformed into a transference issue in the therapy and provides a powerful opportunity for the therapist's interventions.

They were both attractive people in their 30s. He was a man whose movements bespoke a powerful aggressiveness as if he were saying that nothing and no one will stop him from getting whatever he wants. She carried herself with the grace of a beautiful woman, but her body subtly conveyed a kind of limpness and readiness to give up under pressure. Both were capable, practicing professionals in their own fields. He had been violent to her any number of times. This is what caused her to insist on therapy; thus, the threat of his further violences against her in the future was naturally in the forefront of the sessions. He acknowledged grudgingly that he might consider trying to reduce his violence, but he wasn't about to make any promises. Her attitude was a subtle, nonverbal cuing that although she said he would have to stop hitting her, she would never really get him to stop.

In the session which brought the issue to a peak, the therapist was engaging the husband in an extended, almost investigative dialogue about the kinds of feelings he had when he hit his wife and his reactions afterwards. Slowly but surely, the man's rage built towards the therapist who was daring to convey to him that he was going to have to stop doing something he wanted to do; obviously, he felt that to be violent to his wife was his inalienable right. The air became electric with the tension of an imminent assault by the husband on the therapist, at which point the therapist stopped all questioning and instead said powerfully that one violent move by the husband and the police would be called! To this the husband responded that if that happened the therapist would soon be dead! The therapist replied to this remark even more insistently, and now genuinely angrily, that another threat like that and the police would be called because the husband also had no right to threaten anyone's life! Who in hell gave him the right to beat or threaten people?! To underscore the last interchange, the therapist moved up to the client as if to put his face into the client's face and dare him to back up his words with actions so that he would see that the policy of calling the police was a real one. Dramatically, the electricity of impending violence that had filled the room disappeared. For the wife it was a very clear modeling of how to take a stand, which she was subsequently able to continue for herself.

Patronizing and Emotional Enslavement

It may appear somewhat anticlimactic now to go on to look at patronizing and other forms of emotional enslavement as forms of destructive communication which need to be treated in marital therapy, but these less dramatically negative types of messages between spouses are also immensely damaging to the human personality and to marital growth.

The purpose of a patronizing style is to establish an overriding superiority towards the other. Patronizing is delivered not in noxious bossing or insulting forms, but in seemingly considerate remarks which can be full of practical and emotional counsel. To an outsider, it can look very attractive; in fact, it is deceptive and seductive for the person who is the object of the patronizing. The "hook" is in the message that the one person is the source of giving to the other and does not need or expect to receive in kind. One is the capable one, the other the incapable; one is the granter, the other a subject in the royal kingdom who owes the benefactor everything.

Couples who settle into this kind of mode do not usually come for marital therapy as such, but they do arrive in connection with problems of the children. Some of the children may mimic almost to an extreme the underlying impotence and non-identity of the parent who is agreeing to be enslaved in an "ideal world." Others may mimic the emotional bullying of the patronizing parent. It is not easy for a therapist to open up these marital issues. In principle, when the couple come because of a child, the therapy must be devoted to working on the couple's relationship to one another as parents of children and not on the marriage per se. Premature work on the marriage as such almost inevitably leads to termination of therapy and no one gets helped. On the other hand, many of these couples do have sincere feelings toward their children. If they are given reason to hope the child can be helped, they will stick out some period of therapy during which it may be possible to show how the emotionally enslaving relationship of the parents is affecting the child.

Once an enslaving style takes hold, the patronizing mate will feel sufficiently entrenched in his/her kingdom to also engage in other symbolic and actual infidelities for anything and everything is their right. The patronized mate will often choose to remain "unaware" of the infidelity just as he/she makes him/herself unaware of all the other enslaving insults. Therapists are rarely asked to do something in these situations until they get entirely out of hand. Even when the disloyalty has become too severe to be denied and the injured spouse requires the help of a therapist, the overriding intention of the enslaved spouse may be to seek relief without challenging the mate. The seeming request for professional help may be terminated after one or a few sessions and master and slave will go back home to their reconstituted style. A number of these situations end in divorce not because the victim leaves, but when the enslaving, hubris-filled "royal" one is driven by boredom to other pastures. I have also seen situations where the slave becomes emotionally incompetent and even mentally ill, and nobody seems to know why. However, if the authority and patronizing power of the enslaver is challenged in some major way, a full-blown crisis can very well ensue for the seemingly powerful one.

> They were in their 60s, a successful couple whose children had married. She became convinced that he was having one affair after another. He was a proud man who was accustomed to being in charge everywhere in his life and to being admired, but under the pressure of her relentless questioning and accusations, he became depressed and there were indications of his possible suicide.
>
> Surprisingly, in the scrutiny of therapy, it appeared highly unlikely that he had ever had any actual affairs. However, it emerged that he had treated his wife—a successful manager of a large service organization—with disdain for many years. She had never learned to drive. He took her everywhere. He had fed the babies. To this day he continued to do the laundry. All of these he did graciously and gallantly, but with the obvious outcome that she became less and less significant. The diagnosis was indeed long-standing infidelity, but to the dignity of the wife.

REMOVING OBSTACLES TO PROCESSING CONFLICTS

Despite the fact that conflict and anger in marriage are inevitable, there are still large numbers of couples who do not accept conflict as a natural and necessary part of their marital experience. Couples need to know that differences and conflicts are inevitable, anxieties will mount, and tempers will flare, but also realize that conflicts are opportunities for arriving at new growth. Such knowledge and a positive philosophy about "troubles" arm couples with a constructive perspective that can enhance their lives.

SHE *(after a big fight that morning):* You know, even when we are fighting, I have the feeling that we are somewhere chuckling at ourselves and winking to each other.
HE: Yes. What I know is that I trust you and us that we won't hurt each other in an unfair way. I always love you—even when I'm really mad like I was today.

Healthy couples need to guard against reciprocal escalation of intensities and regressive ways of fighting. If a couple is subject to fights that "get away from them," the therapist should teach them how to put a series of "stops" into their fight process. The simplest "stop" is to be prepared to limit mechanically the length of time and style of intensity of a fight. I instruct couples who go too far—such as arguing into the small hours of the morning, following one another from room to room in the house, or yelling humiliating insults—to stop these behaviors. I give clear instructions and then insist on their rehearsing how they will carry out my instructions when the time comes.

Another "stop" is to learn to redefine insults and threats rendered in a marital fight as emotional exaggerations and not as actual policy positions which deserve a response in kind. Breaking the likely escalatory sequence needs to be practiced in exercises where the therapist assigns each mate powerful provocative attacks to make on the other (the closer these come in the therapy office to hitting the real vulnerable issues, the better). The attacked mate is to learn to respond without "raising the ante" or advancing the escalation. When couples are able to practice these simulations in therapy, the therapy work is often punctuated by bursts of a new kind of humor as the couple themselves sense that they are strengthening their immunity against the worst effects of marital fights.

The Justification of Self-Defense

The most convincing justification for hitting back at one's spouse is the experience of being so deeply hurt that one *must* respond in self-defense. Self-defense, after all, is a basic right; you have to be a fool not to defend yourself. The inner experience of the justness of self-defense is so overwhelming that it seems unquestionable. Yet we often misread the intentions of others and believe they are out to harm us when they are not. Sometimes, the attacking spouse is responding to his/her own distressing anxiety and doesn't mean "half" of what is said. Or else something entirely different is meant than what we thought. In fact, there are countless instances where one spouse actually is reaching out for greater contact and loving, but the other spouse experiences this as an attack. I often hear in therapy people using metaphors that reveal that they are suffering from an underlying claustrophobic fear of closeness and intimacy dating back to early childhood experiences of covert rejection and/or invasive parenting. This is why they have to push their mates away. They don't mean to be rejecting, but they can't help it; then the mate responds strongly in self-defense.

Even in the many instances when the experience of being attacked and in danger is entirely accurate, there is a danger of mutual escalation carrying the couple to levels of unmanageable conflict. The runaway quality of escalation is based on the ever-increasing "certainty" in each partner's experience that s/he is acting in justified self-defense. The sheer repetition of events of attack and counterattack in itself contributes to the escalation; more and more of the couple's life registers memories of hurt and recrimination. In addition, there is a natural tendency by each party to hurt the other person "as much as I've been hurt," or to "teach a lesson that won't be forgotten." It is an important corrective and preventive experience in therapy for couples to learn to check the press of their experience of wanting to react in self-defense (see Charny, 1982 for a more detailed discussion of self-defense).

Elicitation of Hurt and Attack

Expectations of being abandoned, insulted, overpowered, exploited, unloved, disregarded, sacrificed, and more can be so intensely programmed into the unconscious mind of a person from childhood experiences that s/he cannot help but seek repetition of these experiences in the marriage. This seeking of the feared experience can even take place in the context of the spouse doing everything to ensure that the events will *not* occur again; the constant looking for or guarding against the danger becomes an invitation to its appearance. There are also many spouses who directly elicit what they fear, so they provoke, anger, and reject until they "succeed" and get themselves pushed away and abandoned.

Therapeutic exploration of how a person contributes to bringing on the very troubles s/he most feared is very important. The therapist can even ask directly, "How do you help bring about this kind of situation?" In many cases, retracing the roots of the original insult-pattern in childhood will be necessary. The therapist will want to show each spouse how s/he goes about "asking for," agreeing to or even celebrating what is most feared and hated.

> She loved him so much. He was the answer to her terrible childhood. Her father had left her mother and her as a little girl, and she took on responsibility for taking care of her mother and her brother along with bringing up her own orphaned self. Now at long last she would be taken care of. But would he love her as she loved him? Would he ever leave her? Of course not, she told herself consciously. One day she discovered he was having an affair. She was inconsolable and demanded that he leave her house. When he tried to reach her to talk about things and to tell her that he had been very selfish-minded, she refused any contact. He wanted to make amends and save what had been a good marriage, but she would hear nothing. It was over. It was all she had known in her heart would happen someday.

Processing Conflicts

One basic concept for teaching couples how to process conflicts is that couples need to seek joint solutions to problems. Given a will to process conflicts, couples do best adopting a *we*-philosophy and structure, which means they treat problems as mutual problems, remove the possibility of blaming each other, and above all develop a method for searching for *joint solutions* (Craig & Craig, 1973; Lasswell & Lobsenz, 1972).

The concept of a joint solution is often distorted by couples to represent a variation on a *compromise*—a concept or model for marital peace that is widely accepted, even by many marriage counselors. The idea of compromise is that one or the other mate must yield to the need of the spouse and graciously and lovingly go along with what the other needs—move to a city one doesn't want to move to because the spouse "must" accept a job promotion there, send one's children to a religious school one doesn't believe in because it is important to the spouse, or have sex in the middle of the night because the spouse craves it even though one doesn't want to.

A *we*-concept is very different. It means that given a situation where there are diametrically opposed differences, although no solution is in sight, the couple must put their creative minds and hearts together to search until they come up with a solution that feels right to *both* of them. At first, the logic of the situation is such that there is no such solution, but then it develops that the intention to seek a mutually acceptable solution begins to produce entirely new alternatives that were never seen before.

This type of solution-seeking has been called a "no-lose" method of conflict resolution because the intention is that neither spouse is to lose. Throughout the process of searching for a solution, there is a feeling of mutuality. There is acceptance of the fact that any solution that is unacceptable to one of the spouses, even if strongly desired by the other, cannot be considered. The intention is not for one spouse to yield to the other's position, but to resubmit the issue to a joint process of searching for a solution that will be acceptable to both.

The Observing Couple Ego

The concept of an "observing couple ego" was introduced earlier to describe the capacity of a couple to learn to see themselves and how they play out their characteristic dynamics (Wile, 1979, 1981). This corresponds to the psychoanalytic concept of the self-observing ego which refers to the fact that even at heights of immaturity and disturbance, an individual can become conscious of the ways in which s/he is behaving and can draw on this knowledge to learn how to develop more healthily and maturely.

Many divorced people report years later that they are able in hindsight to see that they *could have* seen what was happening in their ill-fated marriage much more clearly and much earlier than they did. They sensed, almost knew, and almost told themselves, but stopped short of seeing the whole truth. In a troubled marriage, the spouses are busy defending themselves against disappointment, hurt, and rage, and too little energy is available to be brave about seeing the full story of how the marital system really is constructed.

In a healthy marriage, there is a continuous dialogue in which the spouses call to each other's attention the shadows, manipulations, lies, and other characteristics of each one's style and personality while sharing their inner feelings towards each other, such as how genuinely each loves the other. Each spouse is given a chance to learn both by listening to the other and by developing the courage to encounter and hear the truth from inside of him/herself. The feedback that is received from one another is thus enhanced by an ever-deepening clarity of self-observation. Together, as a result of many honest discussions in which both give and receive feedback and grow in ability to acknowledge to themselves their weaknesses, the couple progressively strengthen their bonds. They develop a "culture" in which both can trust and feel safe.

Inwardly, couples are capable of knowing when they are creating a satisfying world that is genuine versus one that is a pretense that holds them together, perhaps even comfortably, but which does not enable emotional growth. In couples therapy, the therapist seeks to tap the awareness/wisdom awaiting in the "observing couple ego" about the degree of genuine integrity of their relationship, helping them recognize their individual contributions to the good and bad of the marriage.

Wile (1979) has argued that the way to disentangle chronic marital interaction patterns is for the couple to first learn to recognize their repeated dance. He has highlighted three patterns of such repeated entanglements:

1. Mutual withdrawal
2. Mutual accusation
3. Demanding-withdrawing (one spouse pursues the other, who withdraws the more)

Martin (1976) identified other characteristic pathological marriage patterns:

1. The love-sick wife and cold-sick husband
2. The in-search-of-a-mother marriage

3. A mutual parasitic marriage where both mates are dependent or hysterical in their demands
4. A paranoid marriage

Obviously, simply knowing about one's pattern will not turn back the tides and change a habitual way of life, but the idea of helping disturbed couples step back and see themselves in a more honest way is an important clinical tool. For couples whose goal in marital therapy is genuine growth, facilitating self-observation by each spouse and for the two of them together to see how they "dance" well and poorly is an important way to immediate progress in therapy, as well as to the development of a lifelong ability to monitor themselves authentically.

Enhancing Positive Communication

Programs for teaching couples to communicate better with one another have been available for many years. Some come packaged as instructional materials for groups taking courses such as the *Minnesota Couples Communication Program* (Miller, 1975), which is taught in a wide variety of settings, including continuing education programs at universities, community centers, and church groups. Within the framework of marriage encounter groups there is the Marriage Enrichment program created by the Maces (1974, 1979). There are packages available for couples to work at home by themselves, some with workbooks, audio cassettes, and even computer-assisted materials.

Many couples who study and apply any of these programs will benefit from them. Nonetheless, other couples may react initially with pleasure at rediscovering one another, but then a powerful backlash of distancing may ensue. I have seen couples who knew but did not want to admit that they were living in a poor marriage make the "mistake" of trying to improve their marital communication in workshops and self-help courses, only to discover that they were protecting the continuity of their marriage but really didn't like or care for one another.

I have also seen enormous upset explode between couples who were very satisfied with their marital life style because they did not know that it was based on powerful defenses against knowing more about one another and about their relationship. There are, after all, countless marriages where there are longstanding infidelities of the spirit and/or body, while a cover-up construction of routine marital interaction is erected. There are also couples who maintain a distance from warmth, closeness, and pleasure with one another, which they accept and conceal in a "properly functioning" routine of their lives. It is not necessarily in their interest to attempt to get closer to each other. In all of these cases, marital communication programs, if accepted by the couple, at best will do nothing and at worst will blow up the defensive structure that has been holding the couple together.

Another broader psychoeducational approach to marital experience which teaches not only positive communication skills but also explores relatively authentically the nature of the couple's negative feelings and anger toward one another is the PAIRS program (Practical Application of Intimate Relationship Skills) created by Lori Gordon (in press). Here the couple is led step by step through experiences that involve not only positive, idealizing feelings but also encounters with their disappointments, hurt, and anger towards each other. In effect, PAIRS parallels the tradition of psychotherapy for individuals where hurt, rejection, and anger are treated first, and then, as the person is released from the bondage of negative emotions, positive skill-training follows. This program approaches more of a psychotherapeutic orientation, hence its limitation is that couples need to be more willing to undergo a more uncovering experience. One nice thing is that some couples who didn't know they would be able to learn together about themselves can be helped by the authenticity of a PAIRS program in which they enroll as a course and not as psychotherapy.

Communication skills training can give couples who are ready a huge boost towards enhancing their relationship. The key techniques to be taught are wholehearted listening to one another, recognition or reflection of feelings and messages, and shaping of communication toward mutual pleasure, growth and joint decisions. Many couples do not really listen to one another. Their "hearing" is graceless and routinized, in effect built on preformed responses to what the other one is saying even before the message is completed; and the spouse speaking feels and knows it. Wholehearted listening is a way of paying attention genuinely both to the words and to the inner music or spirit, turning conversations into real meetings of one another's personalities, feelings and ideas. There need *not* be agreement between spouses for a conversation to be a good one. Many conversations which do lead ostensibly to full agreement on what to do nonetheless leave the couple feeling bad because the solution was imposed on a base of compromise that left one party a loser, or as a result of bullying that left one spouse insulted. Genuine positive communication is not in saying nice words, nor in reaching agreements, but in really listening, saying what one feels, and appreciating the opportunity to be in a dialogue with one's spouse even when tensions of differences remain to be resolved.

Reflecting feelings refers to letting one's mate know you have heard him/her. The mechanical aspect of reflecting messages received from another person has been parodied many times since Carl Rogers first taught reflection of feelings in nondirective therapy. The point is not to parrot back "You feel . . ." statements with an insincerity that even becomes subtly mocking. Real acknowledgement of the messages of another person is far more than a mechanical experience; it involves caring and being moved to joy or to tears, to sympathy or to anger. Advanced "courses" in reflecting feelings need to teach authentic use of one's emotions and thoughts in response to what one is hearing and not simply a mechanical assurance that one has heard the words of the other. In couples therapy, the goal is to help each spouse let the other know that s/he is being heard and appreciated and to share the feelings that are being stimulated.

Shaping

Less known as a goal of marital therapy is the concept of teaching the spouses how to "shape" their marriage. The goal of shaping is that instead of being carried along uncontrollably by the events in one's marriage, each spouse learns to adopt a leadership role of moving events towards the outcomes s/he really wants for the couple. Shaping means making each day and week alive with mutual presence and pleasure—the fun of talking, doing, going places, experiencing sexual pleasures, social pleasures, surprises, and vacations. Shaping also means generally protecting the marital environment from upsets by invasive others such as children with excessive demands or in-laws encroaching on the proper boundaries of the couple. It is inner and outer *activity* on behalf of the marriage. It is the opposite of passivity, emotional sloppiness, and taking one's spouse or one's marriage for granted.

> She loved him very much, but her love had changed to a motherly or sisterly kind of caring for him over the 15 years of their marriage since they were high school sweethearts. He was sweet and loving, but slowly and surely growing fat and uninteresting. He wanted more sex with her than she was interested in having, but he hardly spoke with her. Their lives were a humdrum of routine—work, meals, TV, and bed—with little or no discovery and variety. She was seriously thinking of leaving him.
>
> In therapy, he was able to surmise sadly that he had allowed himself to become a "couch potato," but even with this knowledge he was not sure he would be able to make an effort to contribute to and shape their life together to make it more vital. She conveyed to him that he might be able to hold on to her if he learned to create conversations and plan activities that would bring them pleasure in being together, but she would leave him if he were not able to reshape their marriage to be more exciting.

FRIENDSHIP

Happily married couples are friends—in fact, best friends. The significance of friendship in human experience goes back to the earliest childhood years. Children who are in trouble are unable to play with other children. Children who are loners in childhood are usually miserable and often show a wide variety of other symptoms of failure to develop and of emotional disturbance extending into adult life. Young adults who are unable to create and maintain friendships when they move to new communities are doomed to a paralyzing loneliness. The structure of marriage provides the finest possible opportunity for the most satisfying and enduring friendship. Unhappily, many people choose to be married as if to assure the guaranteed presence of the spouse to fill the need for friendship, but without any desire to develop a close friendship with the spouse. Others do begin as friends, although they may not be aware of that experience submerged within the excitement of their romance and sexual seduction, but then fail to nurture and develop the friendship.

As reported in an earlier chapter, sociologists Robert and Jeanette Lauer (1986) studied 351 couples who were married at least 15 years and found that friendship was the single most important characteristic of successful, enduring marriages. "Successful couples regard their spouses as friends, the kind of person they would want to have as a friend even if they weren't married to them" (p. 181). The Lauers also analyzed the process through which friendship develops and is maintained and came to the conclusion that a great deal of attention and "work" goes into these friendships. Successful long-term couples do not take each other for granted. They are committed to cultivating and enhancing their friendship.

Thus, a couple who are not yet friends but want to be will do well to pay attention to their manners and habits around listening attentively to one another. A display of interest and a generous readiness to put aside one's other affairs and concerns to listen to one's mate create a climate of appreciation, pleasure in speaking further, pleasure in being a source of the other's pleasure, mutual trade-offs of readiness on the part of the spouse who is now being heard to be a good listener, and altogether a spiral of fun and eagerness to be in continuous touch with one another. It is a process that can be begun even somewhat mechanically as the kind of basic good manners that marrieds should extend to one another; many couples report that the discipline of maintaining good manners eventually leads to surprisingly good emotional experiences of friendship.

Friendship means more than listening. It includes a certain basic loyalty to the other even when s/he has erred in some way. It includes fairness. It also includes "telling it straight," which means taking risks about the continuation of friendship when one has to offer criticism or feedback that is painful and may not be acceptable to the other. Real friendship means a policy decision to say what one really thinks, without any compromise for purposes of flattery or playing it safe. In the long run, if the policy is held to by both parties and they learn to survive hurt feelings, there develops a lifelong trust that one can deal with the most difficult matters with one's real friend. This kind of integrity necessarily creates difficult moments in the marriage and is quite different from popular psychological advice that couples should always be kind to one another, which is generally taken to mean that they should suppress any comments that will hurt or upset one another. In the framework we are describing, the test of kindness is in the manner in which painful subjects are spoken about, but it does not override being authentic.

If couples radiate a basic affection and respect for one another, even if dulled and unexpressed for some time under the pressure of their difficulties, the marriage has a far better prognosis than is the case for couples who come for treatment without indications of a basic friendship bond. These qualities of affection and respect are all the more impressive in couples who are also in conflict. However, if there are strong indications of a basic rejection of one's mate and refusal to cultivate friendship and intimacy, it can even be dangerous to introduce therapeutic exercises for the practice of positive communication and interaction before the basic rejection pattern has been softened and removed. It is important to complete a thorough assessment before undertaking to treat a couple to help them be closer. Without a base of simple friendship and good will, it is unlikely that there can be successful treatment of the destructive structures and emotions that have taken over the marriage. In many cases, the couple's original failure to pay attention to the development of friendship between them could very well be what allowed dysphoric and damaging patterns of negativity to take hold of their marriage and these will not be resolved now without the couple showing that they are more interested in becoming friends.

Liking

The idea that one can prescribe or instruct people to like someone they don't like doesn't make sense. However, one can encourage people to like and even instruct them in how to like someone they really do or could like if they cultivated an art of communicating good feelings to the other person rather than taking them for granted. Many couples settle into their easy chairs of a staid marital routine and do nothing about liking and enjoying one another. Like many functions, liking needs active attention or it withers from disuse.

For those couples who can tolerate active counseling about their liking one another, the following inquiries by the therapist can help set a frame for the possible development of greater liking:

- I am going to ask such a simple-sounding question that you may be surprised. On the other hand, for some couples it is really a very difficult question, and it can be offending and alarming because it can bring home to a couple what they *don't* have. The question is: Do you like one another?
- What was it you liked most about each other when you first met?
- How long did these feelings continue?
- Did you get to feel more or less liking for one another after you were married?
- When do you remember a change for the worse beginning to take place?
- Do you think you would be able to like her/him again?

Commitment

For some years, many mental health professionals along with other liberal intellectuals tended to dismiss the concept of *commitment* of a couple to one another. The most important thing in the mental health catechism was an all-encompassing dimension of the quality of the *relationship*. Couples either loved each other (most important of all), or respected one another (less important, but it still counted) and maintained open and full communication (a necessity), in which case they were and undoubtedly would continue to be devoted to one another; if they did not love one another, they should not be committed to each other. In other words, the concept of commitment was a derivative of a state of love without independent meanings of its own. In fact, the concept of commitment was treated as a relic from a stodgy theological past of old-timer conservatives and opponents of the mental health revolution.

Spurred especially by the overwhelming epidemic of divorce and by the profound suffering both of the children of divorce and of the grown-ups themselves, a new respect has developed for the concept of commitment. Even following divorce, the mental health field now recognizes the overriding importance of commitment with respect to continued co-parenting of the children. Commitments to remain an active parent to the children, cooperate with one's ex-spouse in parenting, and remove divorce battles from the arena of parenting as much as possible are now considered the minimum that parents should strive to give their children when they end their marriages.

Beyond the issue of children of divorce, today there is also a new accept-ance of the importance of couples being committed to one another in their marriages as such. Heralding this change in American culture was a *Newsweek* feature, "How to Stay Married" (Kantrowitz et al., 1987) which had this caption: "The age of the disposable marriage is over. Instead of divorcing when times get tough, couples are working hard at keeping their unions intact. And they are often finding that the rewards of matrimony are worth the effort."

The old-fashioned meaning of commitment was burdensome. Commitment was understood essentially as a theologically-mandated con-cept of obligation. Marriage was the assumption of a lifelong obligation to take care of and remain loyal to a spouse, whether or not the spouse deserved it. Accompanying this conception of marriage were inflexible divorce laws which served as the coercive arm of the prevailing norms of the time.

The modern concept of commitment does not derive from any concept of obligation. It calls for genuine steadfastness and loyalty that are not bur-densome or punishing psychologically. It is intended to spur cycles of pos-itive behavior in both mates based on the fact that when people know that they enjoy a basically unconditional love, they are freer to rise to their better selves and as a result to give far more to their marriage. However, any strong feelings of burden or obligation should be taken as a sign that the apparent commitment is being forced and is not genuine. The new concept of com-mitment calls on people to give more of themselves to their marriage, but it does not order them to suffer impossible situations indefinitely (Charny, 1986c). The commitment is to the process and work that are called for by everyone in a good marriage. By no means does the new concept of com-mitment preclude separation or divorce. If despite one's best efforts a mar-riage is deeply dissatisfying and there are no indications that it can be corrected, divorce is accepted as a positive solution.

Responsibility

The modern-day concept of *responsibility* takes up some aspects of the original traditions of obligation that seem to be worth saving. There are many situations in life where, like it or not, individuals must continue to do their share in contributing to a common welfare with others. Responsibility refers to certain life conditions where a person of integrity is expected to stay with difficult and unrewarding tasks. Examples would be taking care of a mate who is ill; responding to the special needs of chil-dren despite personal discomfort and cost; accepting certain work condi-tions or other life arrangements because of the needs of one's spouse and family, such as giving up an opportunity for a fellowship overseas that is irreconcilable with a spouse's work situation or the academic and social needs of a child who shouldn't move at this time in his/her life.

There is a basic dialectical tension between the concepts of *responsibility* and *freedom*. Some are wont to accept the concept of responsibility as meaningful only so long as it does not curtail a person's basic freedom. Where to draw the line is often not clear to any of us. The kind of responsibility we are discussing does not refer to staying at all costs with an abusive spouse one hates just because the spouse is ill. However, it does refer to staying with one's friend-spouse after s/he has gotten into a bad way and even though the marriage is no longer pleasurable. Such a commitment gives both spouses a quiet security through their healthy years. They know they can count on one another if ever a serious blow falls and each spouse also enjoys a quiet pride in knowing that s/he is the kind of friend that can be counted on.

The Rivalry in Every Friendship

An existential/dialectical understanding of friendship also has to include an acknowledgement that even best-friend couples are subject to underlying, unconscious competition that derives from and expresses the universal principle of survival of the fittest. At our base, all of us are engaged in a primitive battle to live and take the spoils of life even at the expense of one another. The inchoate archetypal images of such rivalry, antagonistic emotions, and indifference to another's plight are embedded in the silent minds of all people. Loving attachments to others, such as between parents and children and to our spouses, overrule the rivalrous substrate but do not eliminate it. In order to be genuinely loyal, couples need also to feel a basic freedom to entertain and register competitive and hostile fantasies towards one another.

The psychodynamics of the human mind as revealed in depth psychotherapy are based on a linking of positive emotions and positions of liking and commitment with the presence of some measure of their contradictory counterparts (Assagioli, 1973, 1975; Charny, 1982; Neumann, 1969). Experiences of negative emotions and intentions are considered to be inevitable and necessary accompanists of positive emotions and choices. People who are in tune with their right to choose between their "good" and "bad" parts are able to sustain greater degrees of stress such as bursts of ambivalence, rage, and seductions of narcissistic interests, whereas not to know that one is capable of bad feelings towards one's spouse is to be more vulnerable to these bad feelings when, inevitably, they make their appearance. Under the older tradition of obligation, the only way to handle dysphoric feelings was to censor them out of existence and force one's pro-marriage behaviors into a rigidly correct stance. However, these obligations deprived many a person of pleasure and grace in marriage, however much the tradition of obligation may have protected the external institutional trappings of marriage.

Timing the Therapy Work on Friendship

Therapeutic work on the couple's friendship should not be introduced too early in therapy when there are gaping wounds and broken hearts around presenting problems that have first call on the therapy time. However, the issue of friendship also should not be introduced so late in the therapy that the possible healing and help that the couple could enjoy from improving their friendship does not have a chance to contribute to the therapy.

Again I would caution that premature work on bringing couples together to be friends, laugh with each other, say nice things to one another, and so on can force a couple apart if intrinsically either one has already consolidated a significant degree of rejection of the other. The easiest situations to spot in this regard are those where there is already evidence or strong hints of a major alternative relationship filling the basic emotional needs of one of the spouses.

A couple in their 30s with four children sought marital therapy seemingly in a positive and optimistic way. They both seemed to enjoy their early sessions and spoke warmly of their original history of falling in love and marrying. Seemingly, nothing could be elicited in regard to the marriage that connected with the fact that for some time now the wife had been depressed. For some months now, she had taken to spending most of her days in bed doing nothing. He was worried about her as befit a good husband. Although somewhat annoyed that she was doing nothing, he wasn't really angry at her.

The therapist was rather pleased with the positive and even smiling mood of the sessions. It did not strike her that the fact that she was not eliciting any dysphoric material from the couple was ominous. Actually, the husband had long since tired of the marriage, while the wife for some time had been feeling she had nothing to live for. In an effort to move the wife away from spending her days in bed, the therapist worked with the couple towards planning new joint activities and more active expression of positive emotions to one another. Following a particularly happy session, the wife made a serious suicide attempt that not only left her physically damaged but brought psychotic depressive feelings to the surface to a point where she was hospitalized. At that point, the therapist also learned that the husband had been involved with a girlfriend for some time.

BEING ONESELF

Married people also need to be themselves and live for themselves as individuals. Being for oneself does not have to conflict with being devoted to one's spouse as well. So long as one holds to seeing self/collective dialectically, one can avoid many of the common errors which derive from a failure to integrate the legitimate narcissistic interests of each spouse and their jointly shared interests (see Weeks, 1986; L'Abate, 1976). Older traditional prescriptions of marriage emphasized mainly the collective, not in the sense of enabling an expansion of the couple's spirits but rather with an emphasis on the obligation of mates to act selflessly for one another, their marriage, and family. Ironically, the heaviness of obligations in this tradition played a large role in creating the insistence on individual rights and needs which has characterized American life in recent years, to the point of what many people feel is an extreme of narcissism and overemphasis on individualism.

While many moderns easily reject obvious coercive demands imposed by parents, community, and even a demanding spouse, there are married people who do not know how to fight off their *own* enslavement of themselves through self-imposed obligations on their functioning. They wear themselves out serving their spouse's needs and not their own. There are marital counselors, especially those trained in a religious context such as pastoral therapists, and also those whose training in marital counseling has been limited to a simple-minded paradigm that mature couples do more for one another than for their own selves, who fall into the trap of accepting at face value statements such as the following: " I work hard for my wife and children. I accept this responsibility, and I put in long hours for them."

Even if it were true that this man worked *for* his wife and children, the statement represents a serious distortion and a probable cause of difficulties for him and for his marriage. Characteristically, such remarks are accompanied by complaints that after having given so much of oneself, there is no reward or appreciation forthcoming from one spouse who may even be described as complaining and demanding that their spouse "produce" more.

Working for someone else intrinsically saps a person's energies. A spouse who works "for" the mate all day may be quite sincere in wanting to do more for the spouse at night, but is already going to be in a deficit-position. Today, it is clear that women have suffered in many cultures being assigned a role of having to serve their men. But too many men also speak of making decisions about their jobs, promotions, and transfers on the basis of their obligation to produce for their family rather than on the basis of their own judgment as to what they really want to do in their careers and lives. In my experience, men who work for the satisfaction of someone other than for their own selves are especially vulnerable to some kind of personal loss of power such as stress illnesses, burnout, and even actual failure in their work or business. There is a great deal more capacity to bear stress when one is working for one's own satisfaction and is enjoying personal satisfaction and meaning in one's work. When one is working burdensomely, there is a burgeoning resentment and anger at being obligated, used, overworked—dangerous ingredients in a stress cocktail. As usual, in the area of sexual functioning we find a particularly sensitive mechanism mirroring such distortions; sexual functioning can become dysfunctional when there is a feeling that one must perform for the other rather than for oneself.

Many spouses try so hard to be pleasing to their partner that they give up not only existing aspects of their personality or activities and interests they love, but the very process of developing themselves further. Mates who married at an especially young age may not even know about talents and interests awaiting inside of them and, if they become too devoted to their spouse and marriage, do not leave enough of their energy for self-discovery. As noted, women in particular have a tradition of making their man's interests and identifications their own. On the surface, these marriages may seem to reward the denial of self by appearing far more settled and "happier" than other marriages where differences between the mates are creating tensions. Yet, couples who are too pleasing are especially vulnerable to problems of boredom with one another and a kind of depressive "routinism" in their family life. There may then develop a search for alternative sources of meaning and stimulation by at least one of the partners in overinvolvement in other friendships, activities, community causes, or affairs.

My husband and I always get along so well. We never disagree. We always enjoy ourselves together. But I don't understand Bill, because in the last six or seven years he insists on going off on long trips around the world without me. I say to him that I want to come with him—we used to travel a lot together and he still lets me come with him some of the time—but he insists that I have to understand that he likes to be with himself and that he also has fun going out with the boys in the different places he travels to. He says some men do it by going fishing and he loves to go traveling, and that I have to let him do this.

DEFINING THE APPROPRIATE GOAL OF TOGETHERNESS FOR EACH MARRIAGE

To conclude this chapter, it seems appropriate to return to some cautions. Although genuine friendship is the ultimate essence of the marital experience, and the goal of therapy wherever possible is to direct and help people to move toward friendship, there are couples for whom such a goal is not possible. Not all of these couples need or should separate. On the contrary, there are many couples for whom being together as such and the continuity of their marriage and family protect from aloneness and insecurity. There is no justification for mental health professionals to promote change here. I have no doubt that many couples have broken up because they could not stand up to the test of the new standards of communication and intimacy that our mental health professions have been promoting to the culture at large, but I believe that unless there are indications of severe disturbance, such couples' systems of safety in routine marriages should be respected.

Teaching positive communication skills can be helpful for a broad range of couples, but should be avoided with couples who are actively rejecting one another, whether overtly or in covertly guarded ways, where they maintain a phony marital structure that conceals serious dislike, deep needs to avoid closeness, and/or chronic infidelity. There are many couples for whom the pattern in their marriage has become so noxious and destructive that therapy is called for to attempt to eliminate as much as possible the most destructive aspects of the marital style such as overt violence or open insults. However, given an assessment by the therapist that the couples are limited in their potential for positive feelings and emotions, care should be taken not to confuse the goal of eliminating the destructive style with a goal of increasing positive emotion and intimacy. Often, work towards these lovely experiences should *not* be attempted in marital therapy.

For couples who have a basis for loving deeply and well, the opportunity in couple therapy to learn to improve their ability to share themselves genuinely with one another is a rewarding and enjoyable experience for them as well as for the therapist.

11

Marital Sexuality

Joyful and Loving Sexuality Versus "Good Marriages" with No Sex and "Bad Marriages" with Good Sex

This chapter is based on the happy prejudice that sex is fun and desirable for people *just because*—let alone that it is both physically and mentally healthy. Sexuality is an unequaled source of sensual pleasure. It is a way to release accumulated tensions not only of sexual desire but of tiredness, aloneness, disappointment, and upsets in the existential "travelogue" of all of us. It is invigorating and enabling of new energies for tackling life tasks and challenges. In the context of friendship, it is a way both of expressing and receiving warmth, appreciation, and acceptance. In the context of a committed long-term relationship, it is an ever-repeating confirmation of fealty, belongingness and trust.

Sexual responsiveness is based on highly sensitive mechanisms, so that vigorous human beings respond to sexual stimulation with a remarkable immediacy and excitement. On the other hand, there are relatively frequent disturbances in sexual responsiveness for people who are upset or whose inner balance is shaky at the time. The most common disorders of sexual functioning are chronic premature ejaculation in the male, impotence in the male, and orgastic dysfunction in the female (Kaplan, 1974). In addition, disorders of desire or lack of sexual passion are common (Kaplan, 1979). There are also many couples who virtually or actually give up sexual functioning altogether; surprisingly enough, many of these sexually inactive couples are in their 30s.

There was little study of actual human sexual functioning in the normative training of medical and mental health professionals as late as the end of the 1950s. In the training of psychotherapists, the prevailing message was that a person's basic or underlying psychological problems need to be identified and that sexual difficulties were to be understood as a consequence of these basic problems. Treatment, in effect, was to focus on the underlying psychodynamic problems, with the expectation and hope that the sexual problems would go away in the process. In my own doctoral training in clinical psychology in the 1950s, the notion that the healthy human personality strove towards sexual freedom and pleasure was certainly in evidence both in the formal and informal contexts of training. As far as *actual* instruction was concerned, however, all disorders of sexual functioning were seen as outgrowths of whatever mental and personality problems a person had and there was no direct instruction on the subject.

Sexual dysfunction can be described on at least four levels: (1) description of the symptom; (2) the known psychodynamics of such symptoms; (3) the specific couple's handling of their sexual difficulty; and (4) the couple's other basic relationship problems, if any.

The statement of the symptom is generally descriptively clear-cut— premature ejaculation, impotence, and so on—although clinicians must learn to differentiate between normal developmental lags and actual problems. The problem with traditional concepts of psychodynamics about overall personality organization such as overdependent personality, hostile personality, narcissistic disorder, and so on is that they are generally observations of the person as a whole and not attached with that much specificity to the different sexual dysfunctions. These descriptions of personality can be very important pieces of information in the treatment of sexual dysfunctions, but since they are on a different level of description they generally do not yield specific methods of treating any given sexual dysfunction. In effect, they are templates of information that are superimposed on the statement by the person or couple of the specific sexual problem. Thus, as referred to earlier, pioneer psychoanalyst Karl Abraham (1957) described early in the century the common psychodynamic pattern in the male who suffers from premature ejaculation, including passivity, narcissism, and hostility to the female. If clinical observation of a given man confirms this paradigm, such psychodynamic information gives a rich picture of information and guidance for treatment of the man's overall personality, but it does not approach the dysfunction directly.

Family therapy concepts add two further dimensions of information about what is going on in the relationship between the two partners who are living with a dysfunction. The first is that, given a dysfunction in either mate, there obviously develops in some real way a problem for the couple as a twosome as well. Clinical observations of how the couple cope with their problem is needed: In some cases, the couple may be very upset and the marriage is threatened; in others, there may be no stress and there is a collusive acceptance of the dysfunction.

The second dimension is that clinical observation of the dynamics of the couple's characteristic interaction with one another enables us to describe the relationship pattern and any difficulties they suffer. For example, the couple may be described as creating a couple system that is childish, overly kind, and nonconfrontational. Altogether, the assembled information from several levels of individual and couple dynamics begins to constitute a diagnostic statement of what, how, and why the problem is being maintained, leading us towards identifying possible foci of treatment.

The great contribution of Masters and Johnson (1970) to the understanding and treatment of sexual dysfunctions is that they mapped in detail the territory of the dysfunction itself and its possible treatment on a behavioral level, meaning instruction and practice in the performance of the function itself. Among other things, they created for the first time the possibility of treating some sexual dysfunctions directly and briefly. Insofar as a faucet can be repaired without redoing the plumbing lines to a bathroom, let alone the plumbing of the entire house, it is ridiculous to do anything but fix the faucet. There are some sexual problems which do not require work on the personality of the individual who carries the primary dysfunction or on the relationship between the husband and wife. Moreover, even in the many cases where psychotherapy of the person and of the couple are needed, Masters and Johnson provided new techniques for therapy which shorten treatment considerably by focusing work around the actual sexual functions and adding techniques for therapists to teach couples the "how to" of doing sex. The simplicity and directness of the sexual behavior tasks created by Masters and Johnson are a brilliant contribution to the treatment of countless sexual dysfunctions that are based primarily on immaturity, habit, or developmental blocks, as well as many cases of personality disorder and relationship problem which respond with improvement in their dynamics when a constructive experience of being helped by a therapist with the specifics of sexual functioning takes place.

Because the Masters and Johnson concepts cut through to the direct issues about which psychodynamicists had little to say for so many years, they constituted a resounding "slap" at psychodynamic and even relationship therapies which had been involved in the complexity of the woods as a whole and had missed the trees in the woods. However, the new knowledge also fostered a grave error of dismissing as unnecessary and irrelevant all psychodynamic and relationship concepts. To this day, a large number of clinics for sexual dysfunctions are based *only* on reconstructing the sexual learning sequence and do not pay attention to emotional and characterological difficulties in either partner or to major relationship difficulties between the couple. An exception to the latter is that insofar as the couple are too contentious and are unable to cooperate in undertaking sexual behavior tasks in their treatment, the judgment will be made that they need help for their bickering and squabbling through another kind of therapy. But the many couples who cooperate only too well in sexual treatment based on overaccommodation to one another or on a collusion to achieve sexual competence without dealing with other personality issues, such as feeling old or passive and unexciting, are not helped with their personality problems when the only criterion is whether they can get along sufficiently well to do the prescribed sexual tasks together.

Unfortunately, many cases do not respond to sexual behavior tasks as such, and many who do respond with dramatic improvement in sexual functioning at the time of treatment soon lose their gains or experience even more serious difficulties in their relationship *because* of the gains they made in their sexual functioning. Levay and Kagle (1977a) described a follow-up study of couples who were originally seen by them in classical two-week Masters and Johnson type of therapy. Out of 45 original cases, 10 had failed to show improvement or had deteriorated, while 35 had shown improvement. Of these, 19 (54%) had returned on their own initiative for additional treatment. Of the 19, 8 responded to additional short-term sex therapy, while 11 failed to respond and then were seen in traditional psychotherapy—either in individual psychoanalytic therapy or in conjoint treatment for "an extended period." In other words, out of the original 45 couples, a minimum of 10 couples and then 11 additional couples were not successfully treated by sexual behavior therapy, a total of 47%. No follow-up information is available on an additional 16 (36%) of the original cases.

Following Masters and Johnson, probably the most influential therapist of sexual disorders of the last two decades has been Helen Singer Kaplan (1974, 1979). Her work builds on the seminal contribution of Masters and Johnson, but returns our attention to the broad panorama of psychodynamic and relationship considerations with regard to the man and woman who come for treatment of sexual dysfunction. She proposes that in many cases treatment must first address outstanding relationship issues. Under circumstances where the relationship is intrinsically shattered or secretly eroded by distinct disloyalty, hatred, and emotional sabotage, *no treatment of the sexual dysfunction itself should be undertaken*. This means that not only must a couple demonstrate the Masters and Johnson requirements of a readiness to cooperate in the completion of sexual behavior tasks, but the couple relationship must "pass a test" of an examination of its integrity, commitment, willingness to deal with conflicts, and an absence of basic rejection, repugnance, or desire to do harm to one's mate.

Soon after Masters and Johnson had published their work on the use of sexual behavior tasks in the treatment of couples, a therapist brought the following case to consultation: The couple were in their late 30s and had three children. They lived on a kibbutz in Israel. Some four or five years earlier, the wife had taken up with a boyfriend and had moved out of the "family room" to live with her boyfriend. In the unraveling that followed, the husband moved into a room with a girlfriend. No divorce took place (as is often the case on kibbutzim), and the children in any case lived in the collective children's homes from which base they were able to visit regularly with each of their parents. In that sense, the overall family structure was maintained.

The couple came to see the therapist some years later after the wife's lover left her. She was very distraught over her boyfriend's leaving, and in her deep upset over being alone she turned back to her husband and proposed that they move back together and try to make a new go of their marriage. He agreed and gave up his girlfriend to move in with his wife.

One thing was clear to both of them. Their sex together had been very poor, but since each had enjoyed an excellent sexual relationship with their lovers, it proved that there was nothing basically "wrong" with either of them. The therapist proposed to the couple that they retrace their steps as a sexual couple by following the sequence of the Masters and Johnson sexual behavior tasks, which he proceeded to begin to teach them. At the time of the consultation, the couple had completed a period of several weeks of such exercises, specifically the "sensate focus" exercise in which the couple take turns being caressed by one another while concentrating on learning how to deepen enjoyment of being caressed. Initially, this caressing is directed to all parts of the body other than sexually erogenous zones. Each mate was reporting enjoyment at being touched and caressed; in the last week the therapist had extended the instructions to include touching sexual organs and zones as well.

The therapist described in detail the ways in which he had induced the couple to cooperate and had instructed them in the exercises. It was obvious that the therapist was a skillful mentor. However, although the consultant expressed admiration for the therapist's skill, he also indicated that he had grave reservations about fostering a sexual reconnection before much more therapy work was done on the dynamics which had led to their separation for some years, the meaning of that separation for each of them, and the meaning of each one's connection to another lover.

The consultant's recommendation was to suspend instruction in the sexual tasks until more work was done on the couple's relationship. The therapist never had the chance to carry out the recommendation because a few days later the husband committed suicide. Although it is not possible to state with certainty what the cause of suicide was, the information available suggested the possibility that bringing the couple together led to a re-experience of an underlying rejection reaction that was more devastating than the actuality of having separated and living apart with other partners.

The sexual behavior tasks constitute enormously powerful tools of treatment which make it possible in many cases today to offer effective treatment of a sexual dysfunction in a relatively short period of time. There is no longer any justification for treating sexual problems of married couples only through the psychodynamics of the one partner who is the bearer of the dysfunction, nor for treating the couple over long periods of time for relationship issues in the hopes that the sexual blockage or difficulty will be released without direct retraining of the sexual function itself. But it is also unjustified to treat only through behavior tasks. In each case, there must be an assessment of what might be the optimal sequence and timing for treatment work in each area of the self (individual dynamics of one or both mates), the couple relationship, and actual retraining of sexual functioning.

THE DIALECTICS OF SEXUALITY

In this chapter, a new way of thinking about sexual dysfunction will be introduced that is based on the same existential/dialectical framework that is being applied to other aspects of marriage in this book. The purpose of this way of thinking is to see in the sexual experience and behavior of each mate how basic existential needs are or are not given necessary expression alongside of and in juxtaposition with their no-less-natural antagonists or dialectical counterparts. As in all other matters, the conception guiding us here is that sexuality is organized and transacted through dimensions of contrast and contradiction.

An easily recognizable way of understanding the basic structure of such a conception of sexuality is to refer to Jung's presentation of the male *and* female that are present in every human being: the male who allows himself contact with and acceptance of the tenderness, gentleness, and receptivity of the female parts in himself along with his predominant and decisive masculinity; the female who allows herself contact with and acceptance of the aggressive, penetrating, dominant male in her along with her prevailing femininity. Both are going to be sexually complete and uninhibited, whereas people who out of fear, disdain, or rejection deny their own gender identity or the opposite-sex parts of themselves will be plagued by various forms of sexual distress.

A wide range of personal and interpersonal experiences are profoundly involved at the core of human sexuality above and beyond an "orgasm count." The proposal that will be made here is that any splitting of the complementary dimensions of these experiences will lead to polarization of the predominant side of the experience chosen *versus* the neglected or denied aspect. It is this splitting that explains a good deal about many sexual dysfunctions.

The following complementarities in sexual experience will be presented:

1. Relationship and desire
2. Tenderness and aggression
3. Commitment and freedom from obligation
4. Taking and giving
5. Filling and emptying
6. Individuality and togetherness
7. Satisfaction and disappointment

Relationship and Desire

As indicated earlier, many married couples do not continue with their sexuality after their first few years as couples. When one looks at the real degree of passion which these couples originally brought to their first years together, we will find one group of couples who were excited at the thought of being grown up and marrying, but who did not experience profound excitement in the sexuality itself. Theirs was a kind of role playing or doing what one is expected to do when one becomes an adult, but not an undeniable excitement in fondling, discovering, penetrating, and concluding in an orgastic finale. There is also a second group of couples who were explosively and crazily sexual with one another, but who did not really love one another in their hearts. Admittedly, these couples began by delighting in their sexual feelings, but before too many years passed they "burned out" and succumbed to a frightening indifference and sense of having "used up" their excitement for one another.

Many people in the first group actually are suffering from disorders of desire, a lack of passion which we now conceptualize diagnostically as different from sexual dysfunctions which intrude on people who do have normal sexual desire but then cannot function satisfactorily (Kaplan, 1979). The prevailing professional opinion is that most disorders of desire are difficult to treat with the skills we have available to us today, whereas sexual dysfunctions have a high rate of treatability. Some of the persons suffering the second type of problem will be familiar to us from what has been called in psychiatry for many years Don Juanism, or the pursuit of other people as sexual objects to be used in a psychology of triumph and power rather than with affection and love.

Both groups tend to suffer from dysfunctions such as impotence and orgastic dysfunction. What they have in common is the absence of the synergistic power that grows from the combination of being sexually turned on and emotionally excited by a sexual partner who is at once appreciated and desired. It is this power that leads to passionately satisfying sex.

> They are a lovely couple who are very good friends to one another, but there is a shallowness as well as childishness about them. Their relationship seems to be on the level of a presexual friendship. Neither is excited by the other. They do not get excited at seeing one another naked; they do not seize opportunities to fondle each other joyfully; and neither approaches the sexual act (for all that they have had "successful intercourse" many times) with any wave of strong desire. Still in their 30s, they report that their sexuality has waned to a very low frequency. They have some intellectual understanding that their situation is unnatural and that something is missing, but they do not really feel any great lack.
>
> *
>
> They had been passionate lovers once and they had often enjoyed sexual delights in her student apartment. They married on the wave of their intense excitement with one another and continued in the same way for a few years. However, slowly there grew in him a kind of boredom and even distaste for her familiar body. He found himself returning to the joys of pursuit and conquest of other women whom he met in the course of his work. On her part, slowly but surely there grew a disappointment and dissatisfaction with him as a person. She suspected that he was a manipulator and perhaps even worse in the way he conducted his business. She felt a shallowness about him in the way he went about his social relationships, winning people but not really liking them. She wasn't sure that he really loved her and something began to die inside of her. Had she been too blind with sexual passion to see what he was really like?

Tenderness and Aggression

Some lovers take pride in the excellence of their sexual performance without ever succumbing to needing their mate emotionally. They experience needing the other as humbling, even humiliating. Some are capable of tenderness in appreciation of the *other's* needs, but deny any need for tender feelings for themselves. For them, the only thing that matters is to be strong, vigorously expressive, and enjoy good healthy sex. In contrast, other lovers are sweet and tender to a fault, forever grateful for attention given to them and ready to limit any excesses of passion should their mate express discomfort of any sort. They are eager to please and unashamed about wanting to be treated lovingly. But they refrain from any assertions of sexual power and do not play out any aspect of sexual conquest. They take pride in being perceived as gentle and understanding and are embarrassed by any attribution to them of passion and strength.

> She appreciated his kindness over many years; a more sensitive, sweet lover one could not ask for. Yet, unknowingly, she became increasingly bored and restive. One day, when she was particularly enjoying a conversation with her daughter's piano instructor, she agreed to accept his invitation to come to his apartment. A torrid affair ensued. She loved the way he transformed her into a frenzy of excitement and pleasure she had never known. How could she ever explain to her husband? He was so good and she was hurting him so badly. Yet she could never give up her newfound pleasure.
>
> *
>
> She had been so impressed with the man who was to become her husband from the time she first met him. He was masterful and vigorous, and that was the way he was in bed where he took her forcefully time after time. Yet, as the years went by, almost without knowing it, she began to pine for a sweetness she never found in his arms. She longed to be held and treasured tenderly and gently, not just captured and "taken" even though she enjoyed the excitement. She wished that somewhere she could find a manly man who was not afraid of sweetness.

Both types of lovers frequently report sexual difficulties or marital difficulties that are related to their ways of splitting the psychosexual experience into tenderness versus aggression rather than integrating the two into a single unity. Long-standing potency and depth of pleasure for both sexes are best nourished by a constant alternation and interpenetration of both power and gentleness: lustful taking of the other as one's sexual spoils, along with a poetry of pleasure and gratitude for the sweet beauty and tenderness of one's beloved. Stimulation grown of alternating aggression and appreciation seems to channel sexual power to both partners.

Commitment and Freedom from Obligation

There are frequent cases in marital practice of couples who discover that not long after getting married, one of them, sometimes both, becomes seriously turned off to the other. Sometimes, the complaint is of being bored; other times, strong negative feelings flood a person or a mate becomes consciously frightened of the other. In any case, what happens is that more and more the spouse thinks of pulling out of the marriage and may even feel compelled to do so.

Many of these cases are defined by therapists and in the popular literature on marriage as involving people who are "afraid of commitment." Marriage has proven "heavy" and an "obligation." One hears statements such as these: "S/he wants so much from me." "There is nothing I can do to satisfy her/him." "S/he is always bossing me." The obligation to perform for one's mate weighs so heavily that it overwhelms any sense of pleasure and enjoyment at being together. Sexual functioning is knocked for a loop by feelings of having to perform for the other.

Too much commitment can also be too much of a good thing. Blind unwavering commitment in the face of being repeatedly hurt and insulted makes a laughingstock out of a person. Some people give their all from the beginning of marriage and never tire no matter what they get in return. Even severe marital problems do not deter them from the totality of their commitment. They try again and again to repair all problems and save the marriage at all costs, including going through as many therapies as necessary. They are inspired by the religious and psychological devotional literatures to give their best. When finally their mates hurt them beyond repair, they are thoroughly confused by the injustice done them.

> He gave everything he could. It was the second marriage for each and he vowed that this one would succeed. If he had been a loyal husband the first time when his disturbed and errant wife had left him, he was now ever more tactful and devoted. He loved the children in their own right, but he also wanted to take the burden from her and care for them as often as she needed to get away to practice her profession as a physician. Obviously, this marriage would work.
>
> When she become increasingly uninvolved with him, it came as a crushing blow to him. He began to suspect that she was involved with other men and confronted her. She then proposed to him very rationally that what she wanted to do was to have the freedom to enjoy a series of relationships with other men, but also to continue with the basic framework of their marriage. She insisted that it was important for her to stay married, that she appreciated him and his kindness and

reliability, but as a modern professional woman in this age she saw no reason why she could not also enjoy excitement and novelty with other men.

He was furious and tried to argue with her, to no avail. He tried insisting that he would not agree to her demands and that if she didn't come home he would leave her, but even he sensed that these were not so much real threats but pleas for mercy. It required an intensive experience in therapy before he could muster the power to overcome being enslaved in the name of commitment and to take a genuinely powerful stand with her. This worked and she came home to him.

There are only so many erections and orgasms which can be commanded either by obligation or by blind commitment. Demand and obligations to remain in a marriage under any costs weigh heavily and make marital, let alone sexual, joy impossible.

Two senior psychotherapists who had known each other some 25 years earlier and had lost contact met at a professional conference. They were excited and pleased at the reunion, but soon it also became clear that one had a score to settle with the other. As they spoke about their respective lives and marriages—both had been divorced, the one twice and the other once—one therapist burst out bitterly to the other: "You know, you had a lot to do with the fact that I stayed so long in my two marriages and tried so hard to make them better. I believed you when you said back then that a decent person tries and tries again before one can allow oneself to divorce. I have wanted to tell you this for a long time. I think I may even have made those marriages worse by trying so hard."

In our age, there are many young people who have been frightened by the marital disasters of their parents and other adults they have seen breaking up; as a result, they have adopted (consciously or unconsciously) a self-protective strategy never to commit themselves deeply to a member of the opposite sex. Many people actually do not marry because of such an inner decision; others do marry, but cannot give of themselves to the marriage. The tempered check-and-balance of commitment and freedom enhances the validity of both positions, and it is this integration which gives power and grace to sexuality as well. No few sexual dysfunctions in both men and women can be traced to the tyranny of either extreme of an absence of commitment or an obligatory excess of commitment—which is then no longer a free person's offering but an enslaved person's ordeal.

Taking and Giving

Which is the more blessed state in sexuality, giving or taking? Many people have a clear disposition one way or the other. For some it is simply self-evident that they are in sex to take, receive, and be pleasured as much as possible; any giving they do comes essentially as a follow-through added on to their major purpose of receiving for themselves. For others, the arena of sex is one in which they take enormous pride in giving of themselves to the other, pleasuring and honoring their partner. Taking for themselves is perhaps not entirely denied, but that only follows on the first order of the day which is to give to their mate.

Couples who are composed of one follower of the "giving" group and one follower of the "taking" group may "enjoy" long periods of no complaint. Between the two of them, after all, they are seemingly managing to cover the full gamut of giving and taking; the extreme of each mate's contribution may seem to generate a complementary wholeness. However, in the long run, each mate's inability to complement or integrate taking and giving for himself/herself is likely to lead to some sexual dysfunction.

> He was a leader, respected and liked in his community, as well as by his wife who also depended on him a great deal. She had ample reason to need him and to be grateful for his leadership. Her personal life story was one of considerable confusion and sadness from childhood. Although she was a bright and positive human being, she often suffered uncontrollable periods of negative thoughts and depressed feelings. In her mid-30s these feelings got the better of her to a point where she suffered considerable depression and sought professional treatment. As was his style, her husband spared no effort to arrange the treatment constructively. He came with his wife to the initial session and was on call whenever requested to come in for couple sessions.
>
> For various reasons, the therapist's judgment was that working through the wife's childhood material would best be done in individual sessions for her; most of the therapy was organized in this way. She did well in therapy and her depression was improving. There was now time and energy to turn to an area of her life about which she had never really complained before, even to herself—the fact that she did not enjoy sex with her husband. She was glad to be available sexually to him, she enjoyed being with him and especially the experience of being held, but she did not succeed in experiencing passion or reaching a climax for herself. In this area of life, too, she was very appreciative that he did not criticize her or demand of her anything

that she was unable to give, but stood by loyally and was grateful to her for taking care of his sexual needs.

After a period of individual therapy around stimulating her sexual fantasies, masturbation, and rehearsal of sexual excitement, couple sessions devoted to sexual behavior tasks were initiated. Before long she catapulted forward to achieve orgasms, which she welcomed with a laughing pleasure that was also becoming part of her general personality. At this point, her husband went into a tailspin (as expected in such cases where there is recovery from a sexual dysfunction by one partner) and proceeded to lose his erections. He was in panic at the loss of his potency and at being driven to such a lowly position. Moreover, the fact that he was now vulnerable and himself in need of help panicked him even more. A hurried effort to recoup his position with another woman was also met with shameful failure. There was no alternative but to enter a period of treatment for himself—to learn about how it is also important to receive and not only to give.

Taking and giving need to be integrated into a symphonic unity in which the pursuit of one's own pleasure joins with the joy of giving to the pleasure of one's partner.

Filling and Emptying

He enjoyed the sexual act like any other man as far as he could tell, but once he was finished, a strange disquieting feeling would overcome him. Instead of being relaxed and pleasurably spent, he found himself agitated and ill at ease.

Feelings of disquiet in men after orgasm often go unrecognized, but they are common enough. Young people report such feelings in their "naive" discoveries of the different sides of their sexual experiences. When such feelings persist in mature people, they are indicators of a significant dysfunction. Some men report intense experiences of anxiety after ejaculation and/or feelings their penis is damaged, a condition that in its time even warranted a Latin name, *post-orgastic horror vacui*—a horror of emptiness following ejaculation (Agoston, 1953). These men unconsciously dread that they are empty shells who won't be able to replenish what they have lost after emptying their sexual vigor.

Essentially, the same condition is present among females where more commonly it is represented by feelings of depression, confusion, and even psychotic equivalents following the emptying of orgasm. Developmentally, some depressive experience is relatively common among young females when they reach their first orgasms. Most women work through such transitional experience and move on to whatever becomes their more stable level of enjoyment of orgasm. It has been suggested that some women may suffer chronic orgastic dysfunction because of their fear of experiencing the dysphoric feelings which would follow on orgasm; therefore, these women escape from achieving the orgastic experience to begin with.

There are also men and women who are happy to achieve orgasm so long as they themselves are in charge of the experience and do not have to end up by lying in the arms of their partner, emptied but grateful. To be discharged of one's energy by another person, and then to remain in his/her embrace, is too dangerous.

> She adores sex. She loves building up to a pitch of frenzy and delights in it for as long as she can until she moves over the threshold of her explosion ("it's always terrific") and release. However, she explains that no man alone can bring her the buildup she enjoys so much as when she has the extra benefit of a vibrator to help her reach orgasm. She simply couldn't understand one of her lovers who objected to having to share her with the vibrator, so she dragged him off with her to a sexologist to get an opinion. She was convinced that whatever way a woman can reach an orgasm must be accepted as valid.
>
> Her lover realized intuitively that she was depending on her vibrator more than on him and that he was being cheated of giving her any pleasure as coming from him. Using her vibrator, she was managing to stay independent of him, not needing him, and not appreciative of him; she was thus truly "her own woman." Not surprisingly, it emerged that she had a long history of bitterness with her mother about whom she said without hesitation, "That woman is interested only in herself, I learned not to depend on her for anything and she can go to hell for all I care."

The psychology of filling is a psychology of being able to take nourishment, build up a sense of fullness and pleasure, and bear intensification of excitement. The psychology of emptying is a pleasure of digesting one's "meal" and "letting go," evacuating it, and trusting that there is a cyclical process that will bring on new hunger and then new food to fill that hunger. In the natural cycling of life, feelings of emptiness alternate with feelings of fullness. In orgasm, the explosion of emptying is to be welcomed as releasing and joyful rather than feared as an experience in which one will be drained.

Individuality and Togetherness

"If I am not for myself, who will be, but if I am only for myself, what am I?" Thus spoke the ancient Jewish sage, Hillel. This famous passage is obviously full of wisdom for many aspects of life; although we don't know if Hillel had this in mind, it very much includes sexuality. I often joke with students that Hillel was perhaps the first sexologist and that he teaches us that sex must be done through a combination of proprietary self-serving and involved empathy for the other. In a way, we already looked at this issue when we saw those who emphasize giving to their partner at the expense of their own desire. The point here is even stronger, however, and involves a basic question of whether one is "into sex" first of all for one's own needs or in response to the other's needs. One can subvert any natural function by assigning its significance to another person rather than to oneself. For many years, this is what clergymen and even marital counselors preached about sexuality, especially to women who were regularly told to care more about the man than themselves. The understandable result was a limiting of the range of passion and pleasure that could be taken for one's own self.

She had been doing sex "for him" for many years. He claimed he was satisfied and that no man had a better wife than he, and he went out of his way to shower her with his thanks. Yet the fact that he was waking up at night seriously upset seemed related to a subtle marital tension. He also was nervous about his work, where he tried so hard to be pleasing to everybody, yet never seemed to reach the level of achievement and prestige that would satisfy him.

She had devoted herself to making him happy, but then became dissatisfied with him, even disenchanted, because of his constant lack of satisfaction at work, including jealousy and anger at others who were passing him by in the promotion parade. She started talking about him disparagingly to her girlfriends and then increasingly turned a bitter and accusing face to him. Finally, she found herself unable to stand being close to him. His very touch made her shudder with a kind of disgust which frightened her.

In therapy, she revealed to him that she had been "faking it" for many years. He was shocked. His illusions about his marriage were shattered. He now needed to learn to cope with realities of life both in his marriage and in business; not to attempt to be pleasing to everyone, nor to be naive about people's real attitudes to him. She in turn needed to learn to be far more honest and authentic, contrary to what her mother had taught her: that a child's obligation is to make her parents happy, that a wife's obligation is to make her husband happy, and that she did not have a right to seek "selfish" pleasure for her own self. Both needed to develop a philosophy of being true first of all towards their own selves rather than giving their all to others and seeking to create appearances of success.

Satisfaction and Disappointment

There is no way that sexuality can be pursued without a person learning that there is a great deal of natural variability from experience to experience. Some sexual experiences are magnificent peaks of pleasure and one is lost in a state of rapture, forgetting virtually everything else. Other sexual experiences are limited even though they may provide a basic physiological release. In short, sexual experiences are distributed along a continuum that ranges from terrific to terrible. If one is unable to tolerate disappointments, then one has to drop out of the sexual game, or at least minimize one's participation in this area of life, because there is no way not to be disappointed on occasion. Better than tolerating disappointments is learning even to appreciate certain degrees of disappointment as different aspects of the privileges of sexuality and its multifaceted process. In any case, there is no way that one can stay actively sexual without being able to tolerate some unhappy sexuality.

Even though sexuality brings peaks of excitement and pleasure, these experiences, too, are not so easy for people to accept. Many lovers will recall how their earliest sexual experiences led to overwhelming excitement and pleasure that terrified them. For many men and women, there were conscious associations of dying. The feeling afterwards was one of depletion, exhaustion, or collapse. One also has to learn to tolerate pleasure and some people seemingly never do. They maintain their lives on low burners of reduced activity and pleasure, or they fill their lives with complaints and sourness so that they will be safe from having to face the far greater dangers of being successful and happy. These people, in effect, "fire" themselves before they are fired by the boss (life). They disappoint themselves before they are endangered by success.

"GOOD MARRIAGES" WITH NO SEX VERSUS "BAD MARRIAGES" WITH GOOD SEX

If one asks people whether they would prefer a "good marriage" with little to no sex to a bad marriage with good or great sex, a good many would respond that they want neither, but the facts of life are that there are a great many of both. One can't find out about the number of couples who are not having an active sexual life together simply by asking couples about their "sexual satisfaction" and "dissatisfaction," because we know that many couples enter into collusive arrangements to deny that the absence of sexuality is a problem. I have seen many such couples in my practice and have been struck by a common denominator in many of them that they have given up on challenge and tension. They are conflict-avoidant couples. Some are manifestly cheerful and happy, even paragons of domestic bliss, committed to a praiseworthy family loyalty; sometimes they are also public spokesmen of the good family life in their community.

Although it is impossible for an outsider to prove the causality, I have developed the impression that these so-happy people achieve much of their appearance of success by virtue of their ruling out in their lives tensions and conflicts, including the inherent tension that we refer to as "sexual tension" between a man and a woman. Unlike other husbands and wives who must integrate their sexual tension into the fabric of a complex relationship of love and hate and struggle with one another, these couples maintain a steady state of "All is well and happy for us."

I have also seen couples who have given up on sexuality and appear chronically sad, bored, or prematurely aging and lacking in interest and enthusiasm for life. The best that can be said about some of them is that they are "nice quiet folks," or that they remind one of a brother and sister who are living comfortably with one another in their older years; the worst that can be said is that they are old before their time.

There are also couples who avoid sex because they have had such difficulty with their underlying conflicts that they do not believe that they can ever find their way towards a more satisfactory relationship, yet they are afraid of separation. The solution they adopt is to avoid the emotional excitation and stresses of fights that might lead to their breaking up. These couples don't mind complaining about being depressed and deprived so long as they can continue being the way they are. They do *not* want help to get closer to one another because they fear that experiencing more emotion will move them towards a confrontation from which there is no return. The possible breakup of the marriage for them is worse than surrendering to being chronically miserable.

There are few if any statistics for how many couples continue to maintain a reasonable frequency of sexual activity but suffer chronic problems such as the husband's premature ejaculation or the wife's failure to achieve orgasm. Traditionally, many sex therapists comment that in such situations people should enjoy whatever sexual release they have, since not everybody can achieve a full measure of sexual skill and pleasure. Therefore, whatever ways people do achieve orgasm or a degree of sexual and contact pleasure are to be honored and encouraged. From this point of view, any criticism or confrontation of the chronic sexual problem becomes an expression of a refusal to accept human beings as they are. However, I have seen many instances where the willingness to settle down into long-term chronically poor sexuality carries with it a heavy price, not only in the quality of the sexuality, but also in the quality of the marriage, as well as in the extent of people's overall joy and even their health. Still, if I feel the couple cannot do any better or will suffer irreparable damage to their self-esteem as a result of a negative judgment of their poor sexual functioning, I will not confront the subject. But if I judge that there are possibilities of bringing about positive change, I will state my real opinion which is that it is a shame to renounce sexuality or have a chronic sexual difficulty, just as it is a shame to leave uncorrected other chronic difficulties in one's functioning.

> The wife was a well-meaning but terribly sharp-tongued, commanding woman who expected total obedience. Her husband did not challenge her. On the contrary, he had transformed his personality into being an unusually congenial man. He absorbed her demands with a gracious smile. For the last 20 years or so, he had first been relatively impotent and finally totally impotent. But neither of them made a fuss about it. Unfortunately, he couldn't enlist his body to join him uncompromisingly in his "excellent adjustment" to his wife. He also suffered from a succession of physical ailments.

Would a clinician have the right or obligation to raise questions about the impotence of this man and the problematic dynamics of this couple if they were seen, say, in response to one of their children's problems? To restore sexual functioning in such a situation might also help the man's health, but one has also to be prepared for the likelihood that serious new tensions may be stirred up that are otherwise being kept down by the defense of renouncing sexuality and other aspects of vitality. Each case requires thoughtful evaluation of whether or not to open up the issues of absent sexuality. It is difficult to conceptualize how the therapist is to make the choice, but the very fact that the therapist undertakes to struggle with the choice is, to my mind, an advance over the simplistic, risk-avoiding position that therapists accept whatever attitude clients take about their sexuality, as if in psychotherapy, too, "the customer is always right."

Bad marriages with good sex are probably more familiar and plausible than good marriages without sex. However, for these couples, too, there are questions to be posed such as whether the good sex makes it worthwhile to stay in these distressing marriages, and whether the good sex does not blindfold the marital partners to their bad marriages. If sex is sublime, then it can, like any other narcotic, trick a person into being oblivious to the self-damage he/she is doing by continuing in a marriage that is intrinsically hurtful. Intensely conflicted marriages, for example, can be kept together by sexual passion for a long time until, eventually, the fighting and distrust wear the couple out.

There are couples who are so rooted on the subject of sexuality that they virtually do not involve themselves in anything else but their great lovemaking. They are the Greek gods of sexual prowess and fulfillment. Everything else so pales by comparison that they do not have any basis for reporting that they are having marital difficulties. What could be wrong if they are enjoying the ultimate turn on? Why bother to ask about any other aspect of their relationship if it is not a problem to them?

Good sex often blinds young people during the period of their original courtship. The saga of the sexual chase and triumph may override any awareness of other personality characteristics or considerations of what it will be like to live together over many years. It has always been considered proper for parents and counselors to caution young people against following their sexual urges to a blind conclusion that if you have good sex, marriage will work out just fine. Here, too, the question is how far a professional therapist should go in advising couples that they are in a false paradise? If in some marriages paradise was based on eliminating sexuality in order to lower the level of tension between the couple, here paradise is being gained through having the best sex in the world but leaving other important aspects of the marital relationship neglected or uncorrected.

On a broad cultural level, too, there are wide swings between extremely different views of sexuality. One decade in our time saw a "sexual revolution" which called for unlimited sexuality without discrimination between different types of sexuality. Following this came a new cultural trend for some which celebrated relative celibacy as the ultimate self-realization which made it possible to concentrate on "friendship" and "meaningfulness" in relationships without the distractions and distortions of sexual needs (*Newsweek*, 1980). My point of view is that both views of sexuality, either as an ultimate, overriding pleasure or as disposable and unimportant in comparison to "real" qualities of friendship, are wrong choices. The goal, in my judgment, should be a joyful and loving sexuality for as many married couples as is possible.

JOYFUL AND LOVING SEXUALITY

It sometimes seems that one of the best kept secrets of married life is that there can be joyful and loving sexuality for couples over many, many years.

Obviously, couples who achieve this great pleasure are a distinct statistical minority. That is one of the reasons why the possibility of genuinely exciting sex between a man and wife whose love for one another deepens progressively over the years is not spoken about very much; to be aware of the possibility of enjoying long-time sexual love and pleasure is to embarrass the majority of people who do not enjoy this great gift.

An authentic psychology of marriage must acknowledge that there are large numbers of long-time marrieds who are passionate, romantic and vital, and very much sexually pleasuring/pleasured by one another. It has served a defensive purpose for many who don't really enjoy long-term loving sexuality to maintain that normal couples cannot possibly preserve over the long term their curiosity, fascination, delight in seeing one another naked, breathless revelry in exploring and touching one another, and passionate delight in entering, penetrating and consuming one another for the thousandth and ten thousandth time. The word out "on the street" is that *everybody* knows that men especially get bored by the same body after so many times, and, in our age of women's liberation, there are more liberated women who have gotten into being collectors of many different men in the same vein. Part of the interest in multiple partners is rooted in a natural desire to engage in sexual pursuit and the understandable pleasures of new conquests. Part is based on a natural desire to explore and compare different partners. But the bottom line is that most people do not believe that lovers can continue to be genuinely passionate and loving of one another.

Given genuine goodwill and interest in being a couple, I am convinced that most couples can overcome the dysfunctions in their sexual functioning. I think that three different qualities (which can mistakenly be lumped together) are called for: 1) a genuine regard for the specific person to whom one is married; 2) a commitment to the institution or continuity of the marriage—out of basic loyalty to oneself, to a concept of family, and even to the extended family and community (including religious tradition) in which one's marriage is anchored; and 3) a readiness to recognize one's own basic limitations, shortcomings, and failures, and to be prepared to rise above them and become something better. I don't know a single sexual dysfunction which will not yield to some considerable extent in the face of the power of a couple who both have a full commitment to making themselves and their marriage better.

How far up the ladder to the heavens of poetic love a given couple will reach, I never know. The mystery of deep connection between the hearts of any given man and woman has never been plumbed in psychology; it is glowingly described by many writers and poets, but I don't think they actually explain it either. I have seen couples who achieve genuinely fine, mature relationships in which they appreciate one another as friends, enjoy good sexuality and really care for each other, but do not reach a special feeling of deep love for each other. The special gem of poetic love remains a mystery—to my mind, one of the most fascinating, untouched challenges of couple psychology.

12

"Catering and Not Catering Affairs"

The Proper and Improper Pursuit of Extramarital Relationships

It is not a secret that affairs occur often in our culture. Some years back, Hunt (1969) described a variety of characteristic styles for the emergence and unfolding of the affair and its outcome. He also observed that the frequency of affairs far exceeded Kinsey's startling statistics of 50 percent of men and 25 percent of women engaging in at least one extramarital experience (Kinsey, 1948, 1953). "It does not require marital discontent and emotional deprivation to stir up disturbing and provocative fantasies of infidelity," said Hunt. "It takes only our own polygamous instincts, particularly when exacerbated by the passage of time" (p. 37).

In the everyday work of mental health practitioners, reports of affairs flow unceasingly at every level of society. Is it all good sport? For those who are not restrained by an absolute religious or other proscriptive requirement of total fidelity and who are prepared to appreciate that there are many attractive people in this world whom we might enjoy, it could be a delicious story of *Boccaccio* pleasures. But we must also ask the critical question whether affairs serve constructive purposes for renewal and strengthening of our marriages. In the long run, it is the strengthening of our marriages that many people want more than anything else.

A happy side of the answer is that many (but hardly all) affairs are born of deep wishes to stimulate and support further growth in one's marriage— plus, of course, the tonic and pleasure of attractive variety. Some affairs do bring a new zest back to the marital process. Unfortunately, many affairs hardly contribute to marital growth.

220

The existential truth is that there always have been extramarital affairs and there always will be. During a given period of time and history, such as during an epidemic of AIDS or in the course of a strong revival of a severely religious society, the frequency may drop, but affairs certainly will not disappear. It becomes part of existential wisdom for all married people to do some serious thinking about what their "foreign policy" will be with regard to availability or unavailability to affairs under the various circumstances of life—exciting feelings towards an attractive person with whom one works, delectable opportunities of trips away from home to conferences, or Aladdin's-lamp fantasies come true of a naked beauty turning up uninvited in one's bed. It is also the better part of existential wisdom to be prepared, as best one can, for the possibility that one's mate will transgress.

A quick glance at the world of affairs reveals an obvious dialectical picture. There is something both wonderfully "good" and terribly "bad" about affairs. The affair can bring tremendous pleasure, but it can also set the stage for enormous difficulties, if not actual tragedy, as was seen in the popular movie, *Fatal Attraction*, which stirred and frightened millions of viewers.

The mental health literature separates largely into three kinds of treatments of the subject:

There are statements which call for the preservation of fidelity in marriage because of the tremendous damage that infidelity brings. The work by Saul (1967) is an example in point. He stressed that the requirements of integrity and loyalty overrode succumbing to passion and its narcissism.

A second group of publications, largely during the decade of the "sexual revolution," spoke to the legitimacy of affairs and other arrangements for sexual variety, such as "open marriage" (O'Neill & O'Neill, 1972) characterized by agreements between couples where each can have certain sexual experiences with others or by exchanges of partners in swinging arrangements or group sex, as described by Constantine and Constantine (1973) and Neubeck (1969). (Note, however, that neither of these books calls for these modes of sexual freedom; in fact, Neubeck presented some of the first empirical data on how swinging and wife-swapping led to increased marital breakdown.) The only caveat was that no sexual arrangement should be *forced* on one's mate. Some of the mental health literature during this period treated with disdain those professionals who remained "reactionaries" in their insistence on traditional forms of marriage and loyalty of spouses to one another.

A third school moves back and forth between appreciating the naturalness of affairs, with some leading to improvement in marriages, and emphasizing the considerable emotional hurt and damage to marriages wreaked by others. This point of view does justice to the dialectic—that affairs can be good, bad, and both good and bad. But most of these publications do not organize their observations about affairs into any kind of coherent model that professional readers can retain as a guide for work with clients. They are largely anecdotal and describe some affairs which were good, some which were bad, and some which were both, but how one goes about understanding the dynamics which define these outcomes remains unclear.

One partial exception has been the voice of rational-emotive therapy innovator Albert Ellis (1969), who was convinced that some affairs are wise, and some unwise. He offered some criteria for differentiating between healthy and unhealthy adultery:

1. The healthy adulterer is non-demanding and non-compulsive. He prefers but does not need extramarital affairs.
2. The undisturbed adulterer usually manages to carry on his extramarital affairs without unduly disturbing his marriage and family relationships, nor his general existence.
3. He fully accepts his own extramarital desires and acts and never excuses or punishes himself because of them, even though he may sometimes decide that they are unwise and may make specific attempts to bring them to a halt.
4. He faces up to specific problems with his spouse and family, as well as his general life difficulties, and does not use his adulterous relationships as a means of avoiding any of his serious problems.
5. He is minimally hostile when his spouse and family members behave in a less than desirable manner. He does not drive himself to adultery because of self-deprecation, self-pity, or hostility to others.
6. He is sexually adequate with his spouse as well as with others and therefore has extramarital affairs out of sex interest rather than for therapeutic gains.

The problem with Ellis' presentation, which is clearly tilted towards the acceptance of adultery, is that while it is true to the natural desires of some human beings to enjoy a variety of sexual partners, it does not treat with equal sensitivity the hurt, confusion, demoralization, and long-term damage to marriage that are so often seen, even when the adulterous mate pursued affair(s) in the supposedly healthy ways defined by Ellis.

In my judgment, affairs impact for many people on aspects of feelings that have to do with their basic sense of *trust* and *belonging*. It is the violation of both these deep feelings that leaves many people shattered by the affairs of their spouses.

Initially, one can understand the guilt of the person carrying on the affair either as doing something wrong that is prohibited by one's religious or moral code, or as running a danger of "being caught" by an angry and vengeful spouse, with all the complications that can follow. But I have become convinced that there is also a profound intuition that being with another partner constitutes a painful and powerful attack on one's mate's inherent sense of belonging and on his/her capacity to trust.

For the individual who learns about the spouse's affair, the shattering of trust can be horrendous. Alvarez (1983) observes, "I do not believe any marriage, however liberated, is immune to jealousy . . ." (p. 209). It is seemingly sufficient to describe the breakdown of trust simply as a response to the sexual betrayal—the terrible feeling that many people report when they learn their mate has been with somebody else is that they will no longer be able to trust their mate's sexual loyalty and exclusivity. But powerful and significant as issues of sexual trust are, in most cases the sexual betrayal triggers even deeper feelings of lack of trust on much more sensitive, inchoate levels of emotional experience.

Erikson (1963) taught that establishing basic trust is a profound developmental task of early infancy. Every clinician knows that there are countless people who have seemingly made it through this earliest level of experience and gone on to master subsequent levels of development, so that ostensibly they are fully functioning adults, but who really were left deeply damaged by serious incompleteness on the earlier level of basic trust. This lack haunts them all their lives. They are often defined as emotionally borderline. Not believing Mother can be counted on when needed weakens something crucial in the foundation of a personality—such as a person's ability to love genuinely. In my judgment, it is this zone of experience that is reactivated by affairs. For the many people who are vulnerable because of long-standing damage to their ability to trust, the trauma of sexual disloyalty can shatter the shaky adjustment they have built around their weak structures of trust.

> They came for therapy after she had caught him with his secretary. To all appearances, this was a routine marital problem of a brief affair for a man in his mid-forties with one of his employees. The marriage and family appeared quite solid, both historically and in its current status. The husband and wife were devoted to one another, sincerely respectful of one another, and although it was the last thing in the world that the wife would admit to at this point in her inconsolable rage, obviously loved one another. In only one respect were they an unusual couple—they had 10 children. Neither of them knew exactly why they had had such a large family, but both reported that their family was a source of considerable satisfaction.
>
> She was distraught. The fact that he had always been faithful didn't change anything for her. This was a brief dalliance of a middle-aged man seeking to get some excitement before he was too old. He was

genuinely sorry for the pain he had caused her. He was prepared to commit himself to not having further affairs. But none of this mattered to her one bit. Her anger had a powerful, even ominous, quality about it that was truly frightening.

Nothing seemed to work in the therapy. She did not allow herself to yield at all and was obviously blocking the natural cycling that one sees in most people following an emotional trauma. No processing of her emotions, no amount of support, explanation, or guidance seemed to help; on the contrary, the intensity of her anger was growing and there was a danger that she would soon become captive of a process that would be much more than the original natural burst of hating feelings she had suffered on discovering herself betrayed.

Under the circumstances, the therapist decided to change the method of treatment to a psychoanalytic approach, including the use of therapist silence, an invitation to free associate and make contact with inner feelings and fantasies from more "irrational" and free-flowing parts of the mind, and encouragement of dream work. Within a few sessions, she entered into a remarkable, never-to-be-forgotten encounter with lifelong fears of aloneness, abandonment, and nothingness. An embarrassing revelation was that this was one of her main reasons for having the 10 children. Like many women who solve neurotic fears of aloneness through pregnancy, when they feel no longer empty, she thoroughly enjoyed her pregnancies and was aware that only when she was pregnant did she not suffer the feelings of profound nothingness that were now welling up in her.

For many victims of affairs, the shock and pain of becoming aware of their spouse's sexual connection with another person are experienced in feelings that resemble a sense of being killed. Time and other meanings of life seem to come to a dead stop. Nothing else seems important. The victim feels violated to the core of his/her existence. Many question if they will be "able to go on"; in effect, they fear that they may have been dealt a blow from which they will never recover. These phenomena of experiencing virtual death could be understood in terms of fears of the end of one's marriage, if not in actuality then in the sense that the marriage may never be the same again. However, these fears of death can also be understood in terms of feelings that trust has been killed and that one cannot live without trust.

The other profound security feelings which come under attack when one's mate has an affair are feelings of belonging. People need very much to have a sense that they belong along a continuum of levels of connection. They need to be able to internalize the presence of their parents, family, community, and larger tribal, ethnic, and national identities. The psychological experience of one's mate sharing his/her intimate self with another person is a strong assault on personal feelings of belonging. An invisible boundary around the couple is penetrated. For many people, the blow to their hopes of belonging is overwhelming, and they never recover from the shattering of their basic experience of connection. Some couples manage to put the marriage back together again; in that sense, "nothing terrible happened," but they will tell you that in their hearts, "It is never the same again." I believe that what they are saying is that their basic system of psychological safety has been penetrated beyond their ability to heal it.

LIVING WITH ONE'S CHOICES

A basic tenet of existential philosophy is that along with the fact that so much of life is determined for us and we have no choice but to live out our destiny, there is also a wide range of choices for each of us in how we shape our lives. I have no glib answer to the question of whether or not one should have affairs, and I can no longer subscribe (as I did when I was younger and decidedly unhappy in a marriage that has since terminated) to Ellis' position that we should have some affairs on a healthy basis. Even the "healthy" basis Ellis describes can set off powerful problematic effects in both mates and initiate processes that will undermine the quality, if not the actual existence, of the marriage. Affairs are dangerous intrusions into the territory of marriage. What is evident is that each person and each couple make their choices, unknowingly or knowingly, and then have to be responsible for living with the consequences and new sets of choices that are created in the dynamics of the unfolding situation.

As therapists, our role is to support couples in regaining a sense of continuity and positive direction for their lives even through the pain and crisis of an affair. The therapeutic work involves a combination of reclarifying the potential of the marriage for providing a "good home" for each of the partners, and strengthening both mates' inner machinery of security as individuals who know they belong, deserve to belong, and can trust one another and be trustworthy.

This way of thinking implies that there is a definite limit as to how much affairs can be tolerated by any couple. Some couples—for good and bad reasons—can tolerate no affairs whatsoever without paying a terrible price. Others can tolerate a good deal, but they, too, will have their limit beyond which their ability to trust on the more inchoate levels of security feelings will be damaged beyond repair. Even couples who have agreements which permit open marriages and group sex from the outset have a tacit limit as to how much of this they can live with. Already in the earlier heyday of spouse swapping, experience showed that a great number of couples ended up regretting the arrangement and had to make a distinct about-face in order for their marriages to survive (Beltz, 1969).

Much couple therapy has been a stab in the dark, trying to see if a couple who are in crisis about extramarital events can reconstitute themselves. If they do, fine, and if they do not, how sad, but there has been relatively little conceptualization to help guide the therapist in understanding the meanings of different affairs and how they impact on the marriage. For example, how do different responses of the betrayed mate impact on the erring spouse and on the marriage, and how do the two mates create different systems around the affair? The following section describes some emergent thinking and research which aim at a better understanding of the individual and system meanings of different types of affairs.

AN INDIVIDUAL AND SYSTEMS ANALYSIS OF AFFAIRS

The following effort at a classification began with an attempt to create a range of concepts for describing the major motivation or dynamic thrust of the affair for the "affair-*er*," following which a parallel classification of the dynamics of the "affair-*ee*" was developed.* By choosing the appropriate classification for each partner, one can identify the major motivations of each and create a description of an interacting *system* of the couple: how their different motivations are at play and affect one another in the extramarital behaviors.

The classification that follows aims to create a *single* set of concepts applicable to the dynamics of both the affair-*er* and affair-*ee*. The immediate purpose was to create categories which are directly comparable, so that the same pool of descriptive dynamic concepts is available for the understanding of each partner's contribution to the system-picture of the couple together. Since the original conception focused on the dynamics of the affair-*er*, it may be that some of the concepts may force us into unwarranted corners and meanings when applied to the affair-*ee*. In the long run, it may prove better to use different categories for the two positions; at the moment, the ideas presented here are based on an effort at a single unified language for the spouse having the affair and the spouse who is on the receiving end.

Figure 5 presents a continuum of concepts which are to be applied separately to the affair-*er* and to the affair-*ee*. The purpose of this classification

---

*The schema was developed by me and presented in many workshops over the years. Its most recent development has been in collaboration with Sivan Parnass, a graduate student at the Bob Shapell School of Social Work at Tel Aviv University.

is to create a series of reasonably different categories so that each represents a discernible and logical step beyond the preceding category. Altogether, the continuum includes 18 conceptualizations; these are subclassified in three smaller bands or groupings of dynamics (01–06, 07–12, 13–18).

The first band (01–06) refers to emotions and attitudes that bespeak considerable lack of commitment—sexual infidelity plus infidelity to the marriage in a larger sense in that there is a disavowal of intimacy and meaningfulness. In religious terms, there is an avoidance of any goal of "sacredness." The marriage is not celebrated and honored as a unique and special relationship. ("She's my wife and I can always replace her," said one husband matter-of-factly when his wife insisted he give up going out every night, in this case not with another woman but to another activity which he chose over being with her.) What characterizes the dynamics in this group is an overall exploitative or manipulative psychology, where the partner spouse is treated with psychological indifference, a thing-object to fit into one's needs and to be used.

The *third* band (13–18) also bespeaks a lack of commitment to the sacredness or specialness of the marriage, but here the direction of the energy is towards hedonism or seeking unlimited pleasure as one's prime motivation and value. There is a distinct inability, even a lack of interest, in learning how to tolerate tension, resulting in an avoidance of the dramatic subtleties of the interactive process between the couple. Thus, the tensions that build up naturally between a couple in the course of their relationship can never be processed directly. Having a good time, having fun, being sensual, enjoying the good things of life, relaxing, "not being hassled," "playing it cool" are the purposes not only of affairs but of married life in general.

Note the difference from the previous group where the lack of commitment is a function of manipulative and exploitative intentions to use the other spouse for one's ends; this is not the case here. The end result of the hedonistic orientation may also be manipulative and exploitative of the other, but that is not the primary motivation so much as getting one's way and pleasure.

If we look at the continuum of categories and observe the movement from one end to the other, we can see that the process comes around full circle to meet up with variations on different types of inability to make a commitment to one's partner and marriage.

The *second* band (07–12) is based on a commitment to the marriage. Here the organizing concepts describing the affair tell of efforts to respond to and resolve problems in the marriage through the affair, in many cases to save or improve the marriage. There is no indifference to the mate here. Even if the affair was intended to hurt the mate deeply, there was no overriding intention of using the mate for one's own selfish needs and desires;

FIGURE 5

AN INDIVIDUAL AND SYSTEMS ANALYSIS OF EXTRAMARITAL BEHAVIORS

AFFAIR-EE __ Husband __ Wife		Instructions: Identify each spouse's role and check off the category which is most explanatory of that role	AFFAIR-ER __ Husband __ Wife
01 ☐	**LACK OF COMMITMENT ALONG WITH EXPLOITATIVE, MANIPULATIVE INDIFFERENCE TO OBJECT**	01 CORRUPTION, INCLUDING SADISM/MASOCHISM	01 ☐
02 ☐		02 SUPERFICIALITY AND APATHY	02 ☐
03 ☐		03 ESCAPISM	03 ☐
04 ☐		04 "A MATTER OF NO IMPORTANCE"	04 ☐
05 ☐		05 "SEARCH COMMITTEE": FALLING IN LOVE TO FIND A REPLACEMENT SPOUSE	05 ☐
06 ☐		06 FALLING IN LOVE TO THREATEN SPOUSE: IF THERE IS NO CHANGE, WE SEPARATE	06 ☐
07 ☐	**COMMITMENT TO THE MARRIAGE, BUT NEED FOR A MISSING OR FURTHER EXPERIENCE**	07 FALLING IN LOVE TO COMPLETE MISSING QUALITIES IN ONESELF	07 ☐
08 ☐		08 ENABLES CONTINUATION OF THE MARRIAGE, INCLUDING "SETTLING THE SCORE" FOR THE OTHER'S INFIDELITY	08 ☐

LACK OF COMMITMENT ALONG WITH HEDONISTIC PLEASURE-SEEKING AND FAILURE TO TOLERATE PROCESS TENSIONS

09 ☐ CHALLENGE TO IMPROVEMENT AND RE-CREATION OF THE MARRIAGE ☐ 09

10 ☐ RENEWAL OF EXCITEMENT AND ADVENTURE ☐ 10

11 ☐ DESIRE—DARING—SURVIVAL: A TEST OF COURAGE AND POWER ☐ 11

12 ☐ SEXUAL EXCITEMENT PLUS "SAFE" OPPORTUNITY ☐ 12

13 ☐ FUN AND VARIETY, ANTI-BOREDOM, SOCIAL CONTAGION ☐ 13

14 ☐ RELEASE OF NONMARITAL TENSIONS ☐ 14

15 ☐ HOPE AT DIFFICULT MOMENTS ☐ 15

16 ☐ FREEDOM AND INDEPENDENCE ☐ 16

17 ☐ OPEN MARRIAGE ☐ 17

18 ☐ HEDONISM—AN INSISTENCE ON THE PLEASURE PRINCIPLE ☐ 18

on the contrary, the purpose of the affair is to go on somehow to complete missing aspects of one's marriage so that life will be better with one's mate and for both partners.

More detailed descriptions of the dynamic concepts now follow.

01–06. Lack of Commitment Along with Exploitative, Manipulative Indifference to Object

01. Corruption, Including Sadism/Masochism

Affair-*er*: The affair serves narcissistic needs of the affair-*er*. There is no consideration of the spouse's feelings and no respect for the spouse. Thus, the affair can take place in the most insulting and abusive time and circumstances, as when a wife is giving birth or involving giving away what should be family resources, such as large sums of money. This category also includes open brutality and sadism.

Affair-*ee*: The affair-*ee* allows the affair-*er* to do what s/he wants so that the marriage can be preserved, thus avoiding any danger of being alone, while also possibly exploiting the marriage on a monetary or property level. This category also includes willingness to be the masochistic recipient of open brutality and sadism.

02. Superficiality and Apathy

Affair-*er*: Affairs are repetitive, usually without much emotional involvement. The affair is a continuation of an inability to create a strong emotional connection in the marriage, so that the affair itself generally represents a sexual experience without much feeling for the partner. The affair is characterized as unimportant and simply "fun."

Affair-*ee*: Even though the affairs are numerous, they are treated as totally unimportant and without significance for the spouse or the marriage. In general, the affair-*ee* has difficulty in relating to the significance of the marital "relationship" or to the spouse as a person. The characteristic response of the affair-*ee* is, "It doesn't bother me at all." There is a good deal of apathy—whether as a defense against being hurt or as a characterological lifestyle.

03. Escapism

Affair-*er*: The affair is a means of dissipating tensions and pressures in the marriage and a way of overcoming difficulties without facing them for what they are. The affair takes place as a means of escape from the pressures in the marriage—for example, flight from a domineering spouse without confronting the mate's controlling.

Affair-*ee*: The prevailing policy of the affair-*ee* is not to process difficulties and conflicts with the spouse. The tensions that are present in the marriage are ignored, as is one's own role in producing the tensions. Any sense of possible infidelity by one's spouse is dismissed as not being likely or viewed as a statement by the partner about the marriage that is of little consequence.

04. "A Matter of No Importance"

Affair-*er*: The affair takes place for "the heck of it" because it is opportune and satisfies sexual desires; sometimes it is a short, passing experience, but it may also be part of a way of life of repeated affairs. Quite simply, the affair-*er* wants to have more sexual pleasure.

Affair-*ee*: The spouse ignores the affair as "a matter of no importance," a non-event of no significance. There is no emotional involvement in knowing whether there is extramarital behavior or in seeking the symbolic meanings of an affair by one's spouse. Sexuality is treated as a physiological need that needs satisfying; it doesn't matter how, where, or with whom.

05. "Search Committee": Falling in Love to Find a Replacement Spouse

Affair-*er*: The affair is intended to fill needs that are definitely not being fulfilled by one's mate. Even if unconsciously, it constitutes a "search committee" which is out to find a person with whom to fall in love in order to be able to divorce one's spouse, who will be replaced by the newly selected partner.

Affair-*ee*: The affair-*ee* allows and enables the affair to take place in order to pave the way for the spouse to find a replacement that will enable him/her to end the marriage. The affair-*ee* has given up on the marriage and waives all intentions of working to save it. In some situations, there is covert prodding or instigation of the affair-*er* to get on with it so that the marriage can be brought to an end.

06. Falling in Love to Threaten Spouse: If There Is No Change, We Separate

Affair-*er*: The purpose of the affair is to force a change in one's mate. If the mate will not change, the purpose then becomes to go on towards marital separation. The affair represents a movement between two poles: a desire to change the marriage and a desire to separate if it does not change.

Affair-*ee*: The affair-*ee* allows the affair and even legitimizes it out of a desire for a major crisis which will either force changes in the marriage that the affair-*ee* has been unable to bring about or hasten a conclusion that a separation is inevitable and necessary.

07–12. Commitment to the Marriage, But Need for a Missing or Further Experience

07. Falling in Love to Complete Missing Qualities in Oneself

Affair-*er*: The affair is intended to fill in "missing parts" in the affair-*er* thanks to personality qualities of the lover that are not present in the spouse. With the lover, the affair-*er* becomes a whole person that s/he has not been. This category includes needs to prove one's masculinity/femininity.

Affair-*ee*: The affair-*ee* allows the affair to take place owing to feelings (conscious or unconscious) of lack of confidence and a recognition that s/he is unable to fulfill the missing qualities/needs of the spouse. The affair is "given" as a kind of compensation for the fact that the affair-*ee* is unable to provide what the spouse needs, such as confirmation of the other's masculinity/femininity.

08. Enables Continuation of the Marriage, Including "Settling the Score" for the Other's Infidelity

Affair-*er*: The affair-*er* seeks through the affair to be able to continue to preserve the marriage. The affair is a compensation for what is missing and the affair-*er* consciously announces, to his/her own self and to the lover, that s/he has no intention of allowing the marriage to be damaged. The affair may be an effort to "even the score" or revenge a past or present infidelity of the spouse, so that the marriage may continue on the basis of an essential equality.

Affair-*ee*: The affair-*ee* allows the affair to take place, based on an assessment that the affair will help preserve the marriage. If the spouse is responding vengefully to knowledge of the affair-*ee's* infidelity, the need for such revenge and re-equalization of the couple's status is tacitly accepted.

09. Challenge to Improvement and Recreation of the Marriage

Affair-*er*: The affair is intended to create a major crisis so that positive changes which will improve and recreate the marriage will take place. This category includes protests against being taken for granted.

Affair-*ee*: The affair-*ee* enables the affair to take place out of agreement that a crisis is needed which will trigger significant improvement and growth in the marriage. Sometimes, the affair-*ee* even realizes he/she has been taking the other for granted and needs a shock to wake up to the other's needs.

10. Renewal of Excitement and Adventure

Affair-*er*: The affair is intended to renew the excitement and adventure which have been withering in the marriage. It arouses emotions and passions for which the affair-*er* has yearned. Often the affair is a brief adventure, although it also can be part of a lifestyle of seeking new adventures periodically so as to "bring home" the excitement needed in the marriage.

Affair-*ee*: Indirectly, the affair-*ee* allows the spouse's affair out of identification with the possibility that the "new blood" or sense of adventure will introduce new excitement into the marriage. Or the affair-*ee* may experience emotional-sexual excitement at the thought of a third party with the spouse.

11. Desire-Daring-Survival: A Test of Courage and Power

Affair-*er*: The affair-*er* tests his/her ability to act with passionate desire and survive it. The affair is an "ordeal of courage" for a person who is not sure that s/he can dare to "sin" and survive. Or it can be a test of one's ability to become more "powerful." Following "success," there may be a continuation of further affairs, or the one test of one's courage may suffice.

Affair-*ee*: The affair-*ee* invites the affair with the intention of examining his/her own reactions and ability to survive the experience of being betrayed and hurt. It is a self-challenge of facing a feared experience in order to see if one can contend with it. The affair-*ee* may have an active part in pushing the mate towards an affair in order to prove his/her own self. There may be an attempt to become more "powerful" through being a victim.

12. Sexual Excitement Plus "Safe" Opportunity

Affair-*er*: The affair is an expression of sexual passion under conditions which facilitate the conduct of the affair without apparent risk. A meeting of surging lust and opportune conditions enables the affair. The affair takes place in situations which seemingly guarantee the marriage will not be damaged, such as a convention away from home.

Affair-*ee*: The affair-*ee* understands the irresistible passion of the spouse and accepts it as a force that cannot be held back. The affair-*ee* is willing for an affair to take place under circumstances that s/he "doesn't know" about and assumes there will be no loss in the quality of family life as a consequence.

13–18. Lack of Commitment Along with Hedonistic Pleasure-Seeking and Failure to Tolerate Process Tensions

13. Fun and Variety, Anti-Boredom, Social Contagion

Affair-*er*: The affair-*er* is convinced that affairs are necessary in order to introduce sufficient variety into life. The relationship with the spouse is generally routine and boring. The affair-*er* rarely makes any efforts to enliven and renew the marriage and is convinced that boredom is inevitable in a long-term marriage. The affair may take place in the context of a "contagious" social surroundings—where "Everybody's doing it."

Affair-*ee*: The affair-*ee* provides legitimation for the spouse to have the affair out of a feeling that s/he cannot provide sufficient variety and fun to overcome the boredom of their marriage. If the social surroundings are such that many other people are involved in affairs, the affair-*ee* will not believe that s/he has a right to stand against the prevailing norm, nor be able to have the influence and personal attractiveness to do so.

14. Release of Nonmarital Tensions

Affair-*er*: The affair-*er* feels a need for an affair as a way of releasing severe tensions that are not connected to the marriage, such as serious problems at work. There is no effort to seek or expect significant help with these tensions from one's mate. The affair is a form of flight from coping with problems and from difficulties in getting help from the spouse through an easier alternative route to an experience with someone else.

Affair-*ee*: The affair-*ee* allows the mate to utilize an affair in order to reduce personal tensions because s/he does not feel able to help the spouse.

15. Hope at Difficult Moments

Affair-*er*: In a moment of severe pressure, often when there is heightened life/death awareness such as in time of war or in the context of a hospital, there develops an unquenchable thirst for an affair, to feel alive and in close contact with another human being, and to experience the respite of sexual release. The intention is not to hurt the marriage. If the spouse is available, the meaning of the affair is that the affair-*er* does not expect to find solace and closeness with their spouse.

Affair-*ee*: The affair-*ee* recognizes the spouse's need for an affair as irresistible under the special circumstances surrounding life/death vulnerability. The affair-*ee* generally does not feel able to provide the mate with the powerful intimacy that is needed in order to handle life's difficult situations, and therefore does not feel bitter about the mate turning elsewhere at a critical time.

16. Freedom and Independence

Affair-*er*: Marriage is perceived as a constricting structure which severely limits personal freedom. The affair is a way of overcoming the restrictions of marriage. Intimacy is generally experienced as trapping and choking.

Affair-*ee*: The affair-*ee* also fears intimacy and understands the mate's need to enjoy greater independence and freedom than is possible in marriage. There is agreement that the essential nature of marriage is constricting.

17. Open Marriage

Affair-*er*: The affair is based on an understanding that legitimates a certain number of outside relationships for either or both spouses. The number, frequency, and nature of the affairs vary according to the terms and conditions agreed upon.

Affair-*ee*: The affair-*ee* is a party to a contract allowing for certain conditions of other sexual relationships for the partner and/or themselves. The agreement may be explicit, but it also is often tacit and implicit.

18. Hedonism—An Insistence on the Pleasure Principle

Affair-*er*: The affair-*er* subscribes to hedonism as a basic guiding value. Affairs are a type of self-pleasuring among the variety of pleasures to which one is entitled. The affair is not intended to harm anyone, but by the same token, to be denied the right to have affairs is seen as intolerable pressure.

Affair-*ee*: The affair-*ee* subscribes to a hedonistic philosophy of life and sees the spouse's affair as a form of gratification which is justified.

AFFAIRS WHICH TRADE IN REPLACING MISSING PERSONALITY FUNCTIONS

As indicated above, there are affairs that are characteristic of people who are committed to their marriage, but need something more than they think it gives them. Their affairs often turn out to be repeating the worst problems of the marriage. Not that they start out that way. On the contrary, people start their affairs seeking to break away from whatever it is that is most blocking and unfulfilling in their marriages. Many affairs are an effort to escape from those aspects of the marriage which are locked against the possibilities of further growth.

For example, in a possessive marriage, the affair is an effort to break away from being possessed. Similarly in a dependent marriage, the affair announces a new independence, while in the too-good marriage, the affair expresses the joy of being really bad. In a marriage where one partner plays the role of the competent one who guides and provides for the incompetent mate, the supposedly incompetent spouse proves new-found competence, at least to win a lover. In a marriage where there is denial of tenderness, the affair is a wonderful new well of comfort. When the marriage is one of complacency, the affair makes life exciting and unpredictable again. In an angry and punishing marriage, the affair provides solace and affection.

> Ah, there you are, beautiful other human being. You are so attractive. So exciting. And so understanding. I feel good when I see you, no longer crazy with my fury towards my spouse, nor with despair. I'm alive again. And romantic. It's like days of old. I feel great with hope. And anticipation. Yes, yes, let's . . . !

It all could make for a perfectly exciting correction or compensation for what is missing in the marriage. Unfortunately, the affair often ends up repeating, of all things, the worst that is going on in the marriage! Although the partner chosen for the affair is in many ways an immediately more satisfying person than the spouse—so much more receiving, warm, giving, powerful, smart, humorous, or whatever spice it is that's so sorely lacking in the legal spouse—nonetheless, the person with whom one is having the affair often repeats in subtle if not grotesque forms the very weaknesses one is protesting in one's spouse!

The reason for this, by virtue of the strange and incompletely understood "psychogeometry" of male-female partner selection, is that the person with whom one is having the affair often is a continuation of *the same central weakness* in oneself that contributed to the selection of one's marriage-mate and to the resulting problematic marriage. The most serious trouble in a marriage generally builds around a central inner limitation that is shared by both spouses, even though outwardly the two mates appear very different. When a spouse has an affair with a third party who is apparently the "opposite" of one's mate and more like one's own personality or what one would like to be, there is a good chance that the lover will have a similar inner emotional weakness.

As a result, too many otherwise luscious opportunities for affairs seem more like invitations to personality surgery, rather than to simple pleasure and fun: "Protect me from my anxiety. From my incompleteness. My fears. My sense of doom. Ah, come, love, it will be so great. I will get everything from you I could not find in my spouse—or in myself—and give you *everything* you need."

Few people know how to have sex with an attractive person just for the fun of it, without intensely complicated personality intrigues. The affair which seeks to make up for something missing in the marriage is an attempt at another marriage, with all the complexities and pain therein. Lovely as the other is, invitations to affairs which are to replace missing emotional experiences are likely to lead to demands and requirements of emotional transfusions that go far beyond a dalliance in the Garden of Eden, and hence lead to serious "complications."

It is not hard to spot these affairs in the making. They are characterized by *too much asked* and *too much given*. Both are equally ominous. They are orchestrated in tones of seriousness and the as-if of a love that would have been had the lovers actually wedded. Behind their fun-laugh, such affairs are laden with a drama and seriousness that are quite different from the gaiety, foolishness, and lightheartedness that ought to be in an emotional vacation. It is not an easy message to get across to clients, but in many cases therapists need to try to help men and women consider turning down oh, so-lovely propositions for delectable affairs on the basis that the invitation card reads, "Come and rescue me."

The other common problem with affairs which begin with an intention to preserve one's marriage is that quite often the falling in love gets out of control and becomes an overwhelming force that cannot be managed. At the simplest level, if one wants to maintain one's marriage and one falls in love with another person, the experience of guilt can be considerable. At more complex levels, falling in love is a powerful state, whether the equivalent of an obsessional state, in Freud's language, or an altered state of consciousness, in contemporary terms. It has a gripping, narcotic power that mounts and pulls a person with it towards intensities, changes and implications they may not have wanted. Of course, the endings to the stories vary from happy to unhappy, from desirable to undesirable, with no seeming rhyme or reason.

There are countless people who have divorced who are able to look back and say it was the best thing they ever did for themselves, and there are others divorced of their own volition who look back and say that their life has been worse ever since and they regret the choice they made (see reference to Willi's [1984] report earlier in Chapter 4). The warning note that has to be sounded is that falling in love with another person, or "just" having a good carnal time frequently set off tremors and upheavals of quake-like potential.

Nonetheless, it is in this zone of affairs in which people are looking for something they are not finding in their marriages, and especially if the affair is within a context of strong conscious intentions to preserve one's union, that therapists report the best treatment results of extramarital crises. The real challenge for the maturing of our work as marital therapists is to learn to think differentially as to when and under what conditions affairs are likely to be destructive, and under what conditions they may be generative or at least leave the marriage salvageable.

In a pilot study by the author and Sivan Parnass, 27 practicing therapists were asked to describe in detail an affair about which they had extensive knowledge. The therapists were asked to rate the extent to which both husband and wife cared about the continuation of their marriage, as well as to report on the impact of the affair and the outcome for the marriage. Altogether, 26 cases were reported. In 21 cases, the husbands were described as caring very much about the continuation of the marriage, while in 24 cases the wives were described as caring strongly about the continuation of their marriages. Yet, at the time of the study, 10 of the marriages were reported as having ended in divorce, 4 were described as under intense pressure, and the remaining 12 distributed themselves along a continuum of categories that included reports of continuing upset and further infidelity that was being denied. In only a few cases was significant improvement reported in the marriage following the infidelity.

"KNOWLEDGE OF THE AFFAIR": DOES THE SPOUSE "KNOW" THE MATE IS HAVING AN AFFAIR EVEN WHEN HE/SHE "DOESN'T KNOW?"

The next and eternally fascinating question is to what extent spouses choose whether or not to "know" of their partners' affairs when they "don't know" about them in the conscious factual sense. There is a time-honored exercise that teachers of philosophy have introduced to generations of students: *If a tree falls in the forest and there is no one there to hear it, does it make a sound?* Thus, if an affair takes place and the mate really does not consciously know of it, does that mate nonetheless experience intuitively the emotional reverberations of the hidden affair taking place in the marital forest? I believe in most cases, *yes*.

Even if the affair-*ee* does not say so, s/he *knows* and/or agrees and/or allows and maybe even instigates the spouse's affair. The underlying assumption in virtually all cases is that whether or not the affair-*ee* knows of the affair in the sense of conscious, open knowledge, on a dynamic level this spouse is an active participant in an emotional-symbolic process with their mate through which permission is given for an affair and it is facilitated or allowed after the fact.

Note that these processes may be taking place only at an unconscious level—just as the dynamics that are at play in the affair-*er* may be unfolding on an unconscious level. No doubt, many readers will challenge the assumption that the affair-*ee* is always involved. However, I believe that even when a spouse "really" doesn't know about the mate's fling at a conference or a weekend of "fatal attraction" when the mate was traveling, the groundwork has been laid in the marriage through many cues, conversations, and non-conversations—meaning failure to talk about the danger—which "opened the door" to the possibilities of an extramarital relationship. I also believe there is intuitive knowledge of a mate's betrayal after the fact, even if s/he is the greatest liar on the level of conscious communication.

An important question that follows is whether the above definition applies to situations where the affair-*ee* fights back on learning of an affair. In many situations, the choreography of the infidelity begins with complicity and collusion between the affair-*er* and the affair-*ee* in enabling the extramarital behavior in any of the ways described. However, once there is a dramatic unfolding which brings the information of the affair out into the open, the affair-*ee* may move on to another level of response and fight back against the affair s/he helped create. Sometimes, this fight is disingenuous, such as when the affair-*ee* is now hell-bent on taking revenge for the affair s/he had facilitated in order to have an opportunity to take revenge! Other times, the fight against the affair is genuine; although there was a wish for or allowance of the mate's affair beforehand, once it becomes a reality, a new, sincere concern to reclaim the mate for oneself arises.

We often see retroactively how there was a period of time when the betrayed spouse made an unconscious effort to deny the information of the mate's straying elsewhere before the information became too explicit to be denied. Often, messages were being received all along, but the affair-*ee chose* not to act on them.

> In the case of a very nice religious family, the wife experienced terrible pangs of jealousy of her husband. She suspected he was having affairs with other women, but nonetheless she decided (chose) to consider her agonizing jealousy as a symptom of her own problem of being too possessive. Actually, the insistent refrain of the jealousy in her mind reflected the truth. For some time, her husband, a professional person, had been driven by seriously disturbing unconscious feelings into uncontrolled acting out. He had been involved in a sordid sequence of perverted affairs that in his case were a warning of the deeper unconscious perversity of his serious hatred of

women. Ultimately, the husband exploded in a knife-wielding assault on a woman that led to criminal proceedings and a prison sentence.

However, prior to going to jail, he had an opportunity to undergo intensive psychotherapy that included sessions for his wife and for the couple. The treatment was successful and the therapist and two other consulting clinicians were able to appear on behalf of the man at his trial. In the therapy, it became clear that the wife's unconscious failure to act on her intuition of her husband's infidelity was in the service of her deep neurotic conviction that she could not hope to hold on to love; therefore, she did not deserve to fight its loss. Had she trusted her inner messages and acted on them earlier, the odds are she might have been able to avert the deadly serious problems that followed for her husband and their entire family.

In the course of treatment, it is important to understand at what point the news of the unknown affair becomes known. Many times the affair-*er* does a good deal to convey the news of the affair to the spouse! Perhaps there is a bit of the scoundrel in the affair-*er* in such instances. Or a boast. Other times, there is honesty. In any event, the significant issue is to what extent the affair-*er* seeks to convey the knowledge to the spouse in order to generate a process of clarification of the destiny of the marriage. Also important is how and when the affair-*ee* claims the right to gain knowledge of the affair and to steer that knowledge towards reclarification of the meaning and future of the marriage.

The Couple's Policy Positions Towards Affairs and How Much They Care About Their Marriage

Some people believe they cannot live without extramarital experiences and even have a clear frame of reference about the frequency and intensity of the affairs they *must* have. Virtually nothing that the spouse will say will change their position, so that theirs becomes a "take me or leave me" position. There are others who have no doubt that there can be no continuation of the marriage if there are affairs, or even a single violation by their mate, regardless of the circumstances. In ancient biblical and other traditions, knowledge of a wife's single adulterous act was sufficient to set loose the demons of vengeful retaliation. Some therapists will argue that if a spouse ends a marriage because of one affair, more than likely there were motivations to end the marriage all along and the affair provided the excuse. This may not always be the case, and I am inclined to believe that the "political philosophy" of each spouse regarding affairs has to be treated as a dimension of personality style in its own right that can have its own serious consequences.

It is the therapist's responsibility to help people to face their own and their spouses' policies regarding affairs, to be aware of the implications of these policies, and to know what empirical knowledge we have about the consequences of various policies. Thus, I convey to my patients my understanding of the literature on arrangements for open marriages, mate swapping, and group sex, and my observations through the years teach me that the great majority of extramarital arrangements lead to breakdowns of the marriage and cannot be carried on indefinitely. At best, these arrangements lead to a powerful crisis in the marriage where the spouses then agree to redefine their mutual policy as one of fidelity, thus saving the marriage.

There are many cases where a therapist learns of an affair before either spouse has made the choice to get the story fully out in the open. The therapist is then charged with responsibility as to whether or not to push the marital system towards exposing the story. It is a complex decision for which nobody has yet written the definitive rules of professional practice. I believe it is the marital therapist's responsibility to respect the privacy of an individual's secrets; many, but not all, therapists abide by the dictum that they will not themselves tell the other spouse of an affair that they have learned about. However, even with this constraint, there is a good deal that marital therapists can do to suggest disclosure and even push the affair-*er* to tell the other. They might even raise questions in the mind of the affair-*ee* and prod his/her nonfunctioning machinery for knowing what s/he knows.

For those couples whose mutual system is to allow one or both to go on with regular affairs, the question is what are the long-term effects? In most cases, a price is paid which is serious enough to warrant careful consideration of whether such affairs are in people's best interests. Sometimes the price paid is a decline of the overall quality of the marriage, which becomes lackluster, boring, dutiful. Or the mental or physical health of the cuckolded spouse is affected, for in the final analysis affairs are a serious blow to the dignity of the affair-*ee* and the sense of belonging and safety in the marriage.

There are some couples who tell us that they have carried on "open marriage" for many years, or that one spouse has indulged in affairs "in moderation" all during their marriage, and it has been good for them. My own concern is that in one way or another the couple are likely to be paying some kind of "price" even if it is unknown to them. It is difficult to accept that the deepest feelings of security and trust are not hurt. But I am not aware of any studies which have plumbed these hard-to-observe meanings and implications.

Along with the policy position of each spouse about affairs, the clinician needs to evaluate the full past history of affairs of both mates. Therapists do not always know for sure; they often have to surmise the truth and act on their hunches without having been told by a spouse.

Sometimes, it may even be advisable to accept and even encourage the affair-*ee* to have his/her own extramarital experiences in order to "even the score," in the sense of overcoming having been pushed into a cuckolded position. Some aggrieved spouses will never be able to rest unless they thus restate their power not to be victimized and "prove" they also can have an affair. The "retaliatory affair" serves to help the affair-*ee* regain a sense of equality. However, the question now becomes whether the marriage will be able to survive the sequence of both the original injury and the inevitable follow-up injury by the affair-*ee*, for all that the latter is designed to put the couple back on an even footing. Regardless of justification, an affair in all cases is a provocative act that adds fuel to the fires of the couple's relationship. Unless what ensues is a process of healing and growth of genuine mutual trust and commitment, the attempt to even the score can become another marker on the couple's road to marital breakdown.

One of the common errors of marital therapists is to resolve a crisis of an affair by placing on the affair-*ee* too much of the responsibility for the spouse's infidelity.

> He had been in analytic therapy when he learned that his wife was having an affair. The information came to him in a tortured series of dreams and feelings which gave him no rest despite her denials when questioned, until finally he learned about it from an outside source. They went for emergency help to his therapist who listened to the tale and then "ruled" that the husband—the affair-*ee*—must take responsibility for having allowed his wife to prove the vulnerability he had always anticipated. He was told, in effect, that he had allowed her to act out his neurotic script and was therefore not justified in remaining enraged at her.
>
> Properly chastised by this judgment, he made his peace with her and the two went on to 10 years more of marriage, many additional affairs by her, and a series of corresponding affairs by him until slowly but surely the glue of hope and respect dried out and they were divorced. A more thorough look at the extent and meaning of the affair at the time of the original crisis might have led to the intensification of that crisis and either a satisfactory resolution leading to a better marriage or a much earlier divorce. In either case, there could have been opportunities for a better life years earlier.

Invariably, the marital therapist needs to evaluate the extent to which each spouse cares about the continuation of the marriage. In the last case presented, there were indications from the beginning of the marriage that the wife did not care about its long-term survival and harbored a self-fulfilling prophecy that the marriage would end in divorce.

Knowing how spouses really feel about continuing their marriage is a major piece of information from which a therapist works in guiding a crisis around extramarital affairs to its outcome. There are spouses who care very much about the continuation of their marriage, but the main focus of their caring is for the continuation of their marriage as an institution, not that they care about being married to their specific spouse. Marriages which do not involve a real interest in living with one's spouse as a person who is loved and desired for who and what he/she is have far less "immune capacity" to withstand the damages and tremendous stress that extramarital affairs place on them.

WHEN YES AND WHEN NO?

What then should be a prudent person's philosophy about affairs, given the information available to us today? What are the implications for wise counsel by therapists?

In a sense, I not only do not know the answer, but believe that I will probably never know. It seems that we must first yield to the relative inescapability and naturalness of the fact that many of us want to be with other sexual partners, and that at some point in their lives many people do need to act on this wish. It is not by chance that one of only 10 original Commandments at the dawn of Judeo-Christian civilization was devoted to the prohibition of coveting a neighbor's wife. On the other hand, it is evident that in the majority of cases affairs cause significant damage to marriages, structurally and/or psychologically. Ultimately, we are struggling here with one of the insoluble existential dilemmas of life for which there is no absolute answer.

One could make an argument in favor of a period of experimentation with different partners for young people, under sufficient safeguards, before committing to a single relationship, and even for occasional affairs for partners who find it difficult to be faithful but want to continue, and perhaps challenge, their marriage.

However, in general, it has to be concluded, that the business of marriage does call for commitment to the exclusive sexuality of the marital relationship, and that the majority of would-be affairs should not be "catered" for they serve up "too much to digest." Overall, I believe that fidelity is the best prescription for wholesome and long-standing marriages.

The proper pursuit of affairs at best is a "sometimes venture." Perhaps one or so times as a declaration of independence that neither spouse is the possessor or the possessed one. Perhaps an affair as a major unconscious ploy to foment a crisis of deep stock-taking in the marriage to decide whether to renew or deepen one's commitment. Perhaps occasional times in the sheer natural fun-flow of it all with attractive others. The final paradox is that the more emotionally grown up people are, the more they will be in a better position to set up occasional fun affairs that are not the entrapping efforts at "personality transfusions," but the same grown up people will generally be quite busy with their spouses, and more often than not they will decide that it is not in their interest to overschedule themselves or to risk damaging the heartfelt security needs of the mate they love. In time, the knowledge that both spouses choose over and over again to stay with each other, get really good at having sex with each other, and are genuinely faithful friends is much more warming and reassuring either than affairs, fun though they may be, or than stable unexciting marriages, safe though they be.

A majority of couples do better when they come to a basic fidelity of commitment to their marriages—not for self-righteous, prudish or mirthless reasons, but because they want to concentrate on successful catering to their own marriage affairs as a continuing orgy of growth.

13

Helping Couples with Complexity and Inevitability

Becoming as Much as One Can and Reconciling with What One Cannot

It is hardly news that even a relatively large number of couples who stay married are not happy. Add these to the huge number of couples who do divorce and the conclusion is overwhelming that the great majority of marriages are failures and/or unhappy. Nonetheless, there are the many marriages that are psychologically and spiritually successful, proving an important point—that it can be done.

Enter marriage counseling, education, psychology, sociology, theology, and marriage-watchers of all kinds and our hopes grow that some day new understanding and new models of marriage will emerge that will make it possible for more people to enjoy the security and pleasure that good marriage makes possible. I identify with this hope entirely and am prepared to speculate that some kind of shakedown is currently taking place towards the evolution of new models of marriage, learning how to choose good partners, and developing methods of correcting and overcoming marital problems. However, we are not yet there. It is certainly understandable why so many people today are terrified of marriage as a losing proposition. They have seen the overwhelming price that so many have paid in peace of mind, health, ability to work, and other losses from bad marriages, and have decided not to marry as a result. There are also many people who marry hoping for the best, but who prepare themselves in advance for the difficulties they know will arise by removing their emotional investment, which means their real selves, from the experience. Their plan is to let the marital structure go on for whatever it is and can give them and their children without their being involved enough to experience hurt and upset. The choice not to risk too much in marriage is understandable after all that is known of how people suffer intensely because of marital problems. Yet, not to be deeply involved emotionally with one's spouse is obviously never to have a chance at the happiness that many couples do achieve; more than likely, it is also to give up on any possibility of living even a quietly good "average marriage."

I think it is important for marital therapists to keep their sights on the poetry of genuinely happy marriages even though the majority of treatment situations in which we are involved call for helping people to make an effective accommodation to their marriages, a fair number require us to help couples to divorce, and only in a smaller number of cases are we able to help people to move towards fuller marital joy. Nonetheless, it is important to know what can be. Those couples who have the courage and hope to risk trying for the rewards of a full marriage need to know that their therapists appreciate that wonderful marriages are possible.

MARITAL ENTROPY

Like all life, marriages move towards some kind of staleness, loss of magic, irritability, aging and ailing, and superficiality. Such entropy has been described as getting so used to a man or a woman that there is no longer any sense of discovery or triumph in the relationship. I don't like this kind of explanation. Although it obviously describes validly the experience of many people, it also implies that *no* couple ever can retain their excitement for one another and overcome entropy. It denies the continuous rediscovery of one another that many loving couples describe. Nonetheless, just as there is inevitable entropy built into the life cycle in general, over the long haul of a marriage there is some kind of habituation to repeated stylized encounters with one's mate and taking him/her for granted. There is also growing awareness of the personal limitations and weaknesses of character in one's spouse.

The life cycle of a couple together, as it is for each individual, is marked by an inevitability of changing functions and meanings. Attraction and romance are at the forefront of the early story of the marriage. Then follow the calls of life tasks in work, child rearing, and relationships to one's family and community, all of which compete with lovers' availability to one another and now reveal each of them at times as worried, unsure, perhaps driving too hard, perhaps unfair. If worries of parenthood are not enough to expose the weak and unattractive in a person, then the combination of needing to struggle both in work and in parenthood certainly unravels many adults to some degree. Tragedies of parenthood are frequent with children who are seriously ill or who have special developmental needs. Thus, many marriages come under severe attack because parents lose faith and pride in themselves in view of the difficulties of their child. Even with healthy and robust children, the going is rough as each generation of children is the product of a changing society and generally threatens parents with the culture shock of redefinitions of the values that were the cornerstones of the education of the parents.

The marital process is also affected by many inevitabilities which go beyond the human life cycle and its built-in mortality. There are a tragic number of premature deaths as a result of natural ecological disasters. Men are taken off to war and no small number fail to return. Families are separated in Holocaust and other events of genocide, and by countless other historical events.

When I work with couples who are coming out of a period of tragedy and loss, I prescribe a good deal of mourning together for whoever and whatever have been lost. I try to ritualize and structure the mourning for the couple in ways that are appropriate for them, be it in a park that is attractive and restful to them, in a traditional religious setting, or quite simply at home. I also use stretches of the therapy time unashamedly to philosophize about the fates that befall all of us, how difficult it is to stand up to these fates, and how easy it is to give up the belief in life and love. I often share with couples the data we have about the greater mortality of marriages following tragedies in the lives of a couple and family, calling their attention to the fact that they and their marriage are naturally at risk.

WHY DO SO MANY COUPLES CHOOSE TO LIVE WITH SEVERE CHRONIC PROBLEMS?

Alongside the fact that many couples break up when they have suffered a loss is the fact that many other couples do *not* break up even though their lives together are miserable in obvious ways.

Their homes are cold. They don't speak to one another. One may actively hate the other. There is no end to accusations and recriminations. Touch and intimacy, let alone sexuality and love are missing. Yet so many couples in situations like this continue to live together without thought of separation or divorce. A number of them do turn to therapists for help when the misery becomes too overwhelming, but if the therapist brings up the possibility of their separating, they become upset and often break off the therapy.

> In a workshop at one major mental health center, the staff were asked to list the treatment problems that concerned them the most. The most common was the question of what to do with couples who live in chronic bitterness and hatred and do not want to consider any major change in their lives. The feeling was that these couples are very limited in their potential response to treatment, among other things because they cannot entertain any possibility of leaving one another if there is no improvement.

The fact that so many couples insist on staying together even though they are "dying" in their marriages might be thought of as another aspect of *inevitability*. These are people who feel they have no choice and must live out whatever their unhappy destiny ordains.

Why do so many couples agree to live this way? Some of the common dynamics of couples who stay in chronically bad marriages are described below.

1. Couples Who Have No Choice

In many situations there is a constellation of events that leave people feeling they have no choice. One mate may be ill. Or a child in the family may be ill and require long-term care which a decent human being cannot decline to give even though there is no possibility of satisfaction in the marriage. (Depending on the circumstances, I believe that therapists can often be helpful in some of these situations to free a person to supplement some aspects of friendship and relationship with others outside of their marriage.)

2. Fears of Aloneness

Probably the greatest single reason why couples stay together even in mutual dislike is that they fear terribly being alone. To feel alone, "lost" and terrified is overwhelming. For some people, the prospects of being separated are worse than death and they are more than willing to stay in dead marriages to protect themselves from being alone. Erich Fromm (1956) has suggested that people whose personal lives have protected them from any period of being alone themselves *arrange* to be away from their loved ones, preferably in an environment in which they engage in no other activities, in order to practice aloneness, a state of being with oneself that realistically we must all prepare for.

3. Fears of Failure

Marriage is a major undertaking in our lives and for many people the possibility of a breakup of the marriage represents an unbearable "failure." They will do anything in the world to avoid it—even live together with someone they can't bear. There are also many people who after the failure of their marriage do not believe they have a chance to succeed at a new marriage.

4. Avoiding Uncertainty

Ending a marriage means entering into a period of serious uncertainty in one's life. The whole structure of management of one's daily existence is thrown wide open; to many people, this seems totally overwhelming and impossible.

5. Continuing the Familiar

Misery becomes a familiar way of life for people. Although the great majority of miserable people do not say that they are happy to continue in their misery, like most of us they are nonetheless "happy" to continue a life style that is familiar, since familiarity is intrinsically reassuring.

6. The Necessity of Family Continuity

Some people or couples cannot possibly consider destroying the continuity of their marriage and family. For many the issue is one of religious or moral tradition. For others it is a matter of obligation to one's parents. Social shame often plays a large role. Divorce simply cannot be tolerated.

7. Fear of Good Feelings

Surprisingly, many people are afraid to enjoy good experiences or to feel good. In their inner psychology, good is bad, sinful, distressing, perhaps dangerously inviting of punishment or worse things to come (Reich's [1949] classic on *Character Analysis* dealt with success and pleasure as unwanted feelings; see also Levay & Kagle, 1977b, 1983). Some people are literally afraid to have or to try for a happy marriage. They may "say" to themselves statements like these: "My parents were not happy in their marriage, and I won't be happy either"; or "I don't deserve to succeed in making a good marriage"; or, "If by some mistake I found myself in a happy relationship, something would happen to take it away, so better that I should reconcile myself to whatever I have since I know how to be satisfied with an unsat-isfactory marriage" (see also Ellis, 1962; Ellis & Harper, 1968).

8. Misery Is What I Deserve

There is no shortage of cases where people sentence themselves to the punishment of a poor marriage and an unhappy life. The *why* is compli-cated, but traceable in most instances (although not necessarily successfully treatable). An example would be a woman who feels very guilty over the fate of her alcoholic brother, who was the black sheep alongside of her lily-white successes in childhood. As a result, she punishes herself in a mar-riage to a man who abuses her.

Couples Who Are "Happy" to Stay Together Miserable

Over time, the choreography of a miserable marriage even becomes trea-sured by some couples. It is like a bad joke—she would be seriously insulted if he didn't beat her on the appointed day each week! Some spouses create an illusion that the insults they garner from their mates are really disguised messages of love and that the day will come when the mate will reveal his/her fullest loving sentiments. Thus say some wives of philan-dering husbands, alcoholics, and so on. Similarly, some husbands of ruth-less, abusive women who are busy pummeling them with scorn and rejection share this illusion.

When there is chronic acquiescence and surrender to suffering in the mar-riage, the marital therapist has both a clinical and ethical responsibility to make an assessment as to whether or not the couple are capable of breaking out of the pattern. If the answer is no, as it frequently is, I believe the ther-apist must undertake to support the marriage and accept the couple's sur-render to misery while trying to offer *some* help towards reducing the degree of suffering. This is especially true with regard to older couples when emotional and/or realistic life resources are on the wane. When one gets into old age, maintaining a long-term marriage in itself offers impor-tant support and gratification to people based on the objective security of continuity and the comfort of familiarity. Only if a couple are strong enough to undertake new lives can therapists responsibly consider supporting their breakup. We know, too, that the breakups of older parents often have a pow-erful disturbing impact on their children, even those who are already into their own married lives. It is also the province of the marital therapist to consider the larger ecology of the welfare of the extended family unit as well, let alone that what happens to the children rebounds on the emotional well-being of the parents.

She had recently completed psychotherapy for a mild depression, to all intents and purposes successfully. The therapy had included couple sessions for herself and her husband. The marriage seemed solid. They were a nice couple in their early 30s, devoted to their several young children. The therapy had been formally terminated in the spring, but during summer vacation the patient heard from her parents that they were going to be divorced forthwith. Her parents had led a traditional, religiously-oriented family life. They had never argued and there had been no warning of a possible break between them, so that the news came as a total shock to their daughter. A few weeks later she plunged into a deeply agitated depression and made a very serious suicide attempt.

Even with younger couples, the therapist may come to the same assessment that starting anew will be too hard for both mates, since there are few prospects for changing deeply rooted personality problems in a new marriage. The couple themselves make it clear, directly or indirectly, that although they are unhappy in their marriage, and even think about divorce, in fact they do not want to split up. Under these circumstances, the therapist should act as a friendly counselor, offering concrete ways for improving the quality of the couple's lives without attempting to tamper with their basic defense system.

He is a jolly, colorful personality, while she is a reclusive, obsessional type. He is always dissatisfied with what he gets from her—sexually, emotionally, socially. Unconsciously, her dessicated, nervous qualities replicate a core of rejection that he suffered at his mother's hands but had denied to himself. He and his mother had appeared close and had actually joined in a collusion of superiority over his inept father and into collusive approval of the acting out for which he had been tossed out of several schools. However, despite their seeming closeness in their alliance, his mother had given him very little warmth and emotional closeness.

His wife had seen him as a possible ray of life in her dull universe. To her he was a colorful relief to the boring, empty manners of her childhood home. Yet he also repeated her childhood experience of not being held and loved; despite his ebullient manner he did not approach her with tenderness and rarely touched her. She had grown up in a "perfect family" where everything spontaneous and demonstrative was suppressed, so that she had known a "correct" routine of life, but with little closeness.

She spoke bitterly of their marriage, but at the same time even more fearfully of striking out on her own. He spoke with bravado about leaving the marriage, but took no steps towards doing so. Among other things, a few years earlier he had been struck with a serious disease which he would need to monitor for the rest of his life. Although he certainly wished he could change to another wife, indications were that he did not trust himself to make a move.

The therapist's judgment was that both mates needed help to reduce the toll of their chronic tension rather than to attempt to make a break. The couple were told that they should not expect to be happy in their marriage, since neither was emotionally prepared to experience close and warm feelings to others, but that it was clear that they wanted to stay together. It was suggested that they should make a point of scheduling a certain amount of sexual contact, say every two or three weeks, in order to keep up this mode of experience and tension-release. They should also plan to go out twice a week to whatever activities were enjoyable to both of them and then go to a restaurant and talk about their experience over cake and coffee so that they would develop a pattern of pleasure from their companionship, but without expecting to find love and intimacy.

I do not agree with those who argue that it is only the couples themselves who make up their minds in therapy as to whether or not they will stay together. I have seen many couples who made impulsive decisions to break up and paid a terrible price for it. I believe the therapist needs to participate in shaping the couple's decision-making process based on the therapist's judgment of the dynamics, ego strengths and potentials of the couple.

BECOMING AND RECONCILING

For all married couples, even those who do enjoy the happiness of loving and growing together, there are boundary lines which limit the extent of their possibilities. As in all other aspects of life, there are disappointments and limitations to what couples can reach in their marriage. In the human heart, there are always dreams of wholeness that are progressively battered and shattered by the realities of limitations, aging, illness, and fate. (Ellis [1987] has formulated a summary statement that when all is said and done, consistently good mental health cannot be achieved in the human condition.) The sorrows of these limitations are an important theme in everyone's life.

There are those who do not yield to this sorrow and instead arm themselves with bravado and pseudo-invincibility. There are also many who sing songs of sorrow and wail their way through life unattractively. The pseudo-invincible ones bluster their way through life at considerable expense to others who are associated with them; often they suffer serious declines when they can no longer strut on the stage of life. Even during the years of their "successes," they are not likely to enjoy closeness and intimacy with others. On the other hand, the sufferers and mourners can "enjoy" being miserable, but don't savor the pleasure of happiness. They, too, are unlikely to enjoy closeness and intimacy.

There is a wonderful paradox in life that if one is prepared to admit to the impossibility of total success and to acknowledge some number of fail-ures, the possibilities of pleasure and fulfillment are likely to be enhanced because the senses are then sharpened to accept and enjoy the ordinary gifts of life and experience. This is especially true when the yielding to lim-itations and fate is accompanied simultaneously—dialectically—by striving for achievement and improvement of one's situation as much as possible. Becoming what one can become and reconciling to what one cannot pro-duces greater strength than unavailing efforts to be only strong and suc-cessful or ascetic, self-renouncing postures of humility before the fates. This is what the Zen masters as well as wise men of several other philosophies teach us: Surrendering to what we cannot master and cannot be, together with efforts to try to change and become the most that we can become, sets the stage for discoveries of newfound strengths and deeper pleasures in life. (See Hoffman [1975] for an introduction to Zen and its remarkable teaching koans or questions; the dialectical concept leads also to the liter-ature of paradoxical psychotherapy such as Fisher, Anderson & Jones [1981], Weeks & L'Abate [1982], and Weeks [1985].)

The effort to become what we can is a maddening one, beset by painful limitations. It sets off considerable anxiety for all of us. Yet, if one stays with the anxiety and does not fear it, there come points of transcendence, calm, and pleasure in knowing that one is doing the best with the privilege of life.

He forever worried. He complained about illness, problems at work, fears of the future, the safety of the children, and everything that could possibly trigger fearfulness in a sensitive soul. She understood many of his fears and even appreciated the sensitivity of his feelings for life and for the people who were close to him, but she also let him know that he was overdoing this sensitivity and weakening himself. She also told him that beyond a certain point she did not enjoy hearing his worries, that eventually we all have to die after encountering many insoluble problems along the way, but that one cannot sacrifice one's basic optimism and attractiveness as a person to inordinate worry.

Spurred by her helpful criticism, he learned to reduce the amount of worry he experienced.

Formulating A Realistic Treatment Goal For Couples in "Terrible Shape"

It is important to differentiate between different types of requests for marital therapy, especially as regards the couples who come to therapy not because they are asking for help to improve the marriage, but because the marriage has become so problematic or painful that *something* has to be done. That something often carries with it a demand by one mate that the therapy whip the other partner "into shape" to behave in certain ways. The therapy may also be sought, knowingly or unknowingly, to reach a divorce that is now inevitable. Many of the cases where therapy is to facilitate a divorce involve situations where one of the mates is already committed to another potential or actual "replacement partner," but needs a professional's help to finalize his/her own decision and/or to communicate the decision to the spouse. Sometimes the spouse who has decided to leave wants a therapist to help the mate endure the burden of being left and may not be conscious that this is a primary reason for coming to "therapy."

Willi (1984) has written extensively about contraindications to marital therapy. He sees situations where one mate isn't really interested in the other as contraindicated for marital therapy; the therapist is really being asked to bestow a blessing or provide a kind of alibi for a divorce. He also includes among the contraindications the many situations where one partner comes for therapy only under the pressure of the other. He also calls our attention to the efforts of some spouses to use marital therapy in order to dig out secrets they have been unable to uncover at home. Willi sees marital therapy as not useful when the clinical picture is one of a couple who intend to hold on to their mutual dependency and are not willing to tolerate anything that involves independent growth. Interestingly enough, he says that if one or both mates claim that they no longer have any feeling for the partner, he does not necessarily treat this as a contraindication, because he does not accept at face value such protestations. "Often one partner tries to defend himself against unfulfillable demands by asserting that his love for the other partner is dead" (p. 23).

My own feeling is that all of the above situations, which differ from the ideal one of a couple sincerely and openly asking for help to correct their marriage and improve it, are nonetheless legitimate cases for marital therapy so long as the therapist is (a) diagnostically alert to differentiate between well-motivated couples and those whose use of therapy is in connection with the tactics of their fight or attempts to dissolve their marriages, and

(b) the therapist accepts as an important and legitimate professional role work with couples who *cannot* be helped to love and live well to help them towards a healthier stabilization and reorganization—the best that is possible for them. The goal of therapy may be to help the couple live together in a framework of a constructive agreement, even though without love and intimacy, or it may be to help the couple arrive at a decision to separate and divorce.

Couples who are in any kind of "bad shape" are very much part of the population we marital therapists are supposed to accept for evaluation and whatever kind of treatment is appropriate. The important thing is not to approach cases which are in a really bad way or which are marked by an irreparable ugliness of spirit or abusiveness with idealistic hopes of "treating" the couple to love and appreciate each other. The treatment techniques the therapist will employ need to be appropriate to the situation. Thus, a marriage where a great deal of acting out is taking place calls for the therapist's firmness and directive clarification and restructuring of the reality that is going on in the marriage rather than efforts to bring the couple closer to experience kindness to each other.

Judgments of the effectiveness of marital therapy for many years were based on whether the couple stayed married (*success*) or divorced (*failure*), which today we should understand is inherently an incorrect way to evaluate couples therapy. Even if we judge the success and failure of couple therapy according to the quality of relationship and the quality of life a couple achieve following therapy, we will still be incorrect. The judgment of each therapy's effectiveness and ineffectiveness has to be placed in a diagnostic context of what was possible and what was desirable. Couple therapy should seek the highest level of functioning and fulfillment possible for each couple given the total picture of their possibilities and their limitations. There is always so much more that we can become, but there is also so much more we can never be. Marital therapy and healthy living are based on the wisdom of a dialectical synthesis of becoming much more and accepting much less than we would have hoped for.

References

Abend, S. M. (1986). Countertransference, empathy, and the analytic ideal: The impact of life stresses on analytic capability. *Psychoanalytic Quarterly, 55* (4), 563–575.

Ables, B. S., & Brandsma, J. M. (1977). *Therapy for Couples: A Clinician's Guide for Effective Treatment.* San Francisco: Jossey-Bass.

Abraham, K. (1957). Ejaculatio praecox (1917). In *Selected Papers of Karl Abraham.* New York: Basic Books, pp. 280–298.

Achterberg, J., & Lawlis, G. F. (1978). *Imagery of Cancer.* Champaign, IL: Institute for Personality and Ability Testing.

Agoston, T. (1953). Post-orgastic emptiness, fear of. In E. Podolsky, (Ed.), *Encyclopedia of Aberrations.* New York: Philosophical Library, pp. 418–428.

Ahrons, C. R., & Rodgers, R. H. (1987). *Divorced Families: A Multidisciplinary Developmental View.* New York: W. W. Norton.

Alexander, F. (1950). *Psychosomatic Medicine.* New York: Norton.

Alvarez, A. (1983). *Life after Marriage: Love in an Age of Divorce.* New York: Bantam.

Anthony, E. J., & Benedeck, T. (1970). *Parenthood: Its Psychology and Psychopathology.* Boston: Little Brown.

Arnon, Y. (1984). A tool for the assessment of the marital relationship. Master's Thesis, School of Social Work, Tel Aviv University. (Hebrew)

Ashkam, J. (1984). *Identity and Stability in Marriage.* Cambridge, England: Cambridge University Press.

Assagioli, R. (1973). *The Act of Will.* Baltimore: Penguin.

Assagioli, R. (1975). *Psychosynthesis: A Manual of Principles and Techniques.* London: Turnstone Books.

Asianeli, S. (in press). Development of A Computerized Questionnaire for Couples to Assess Marital Functioning and Interaction Based on an Existential/Dialectical Model. Master's Thesis, Bob Shapell School of Social Work, Tel Aviv University. (Hebrew)

Bach, G. R., & Wyden, P. (1969). *The Intimate Enemy: How to Fight Fair in Love and Marriage.* New York: Morrow.

Bader, E., & Pearson, P. T. (1988). *In Quest of the Mythical Mate: A Developmental Approach to Diagnosis and Treatment in Couples Therapy.* New York: Brunner/Mazel.

Barker, R. L. (1984). *Treating Couples in Crisis: Fundamentals and Practice in Marital Therapy.* New York: Free Press.

Bates, C. M., & Brodsky, A. M. (1988). *Sex in the Therapy Hour: A Case of Professional Incest.* New York: Guilford.

Beach, S. R. H., & O'Leary, K. D. (1985). Current status of outcome research in marital therapy. In L. L'Abate (Ed.), *The Handbook of Family Psychology and Therapy.* Vol. 2. Homewood, IL: Dorsey Professional Books, pp. 1035–1072.

Beck, A. T. (1988). *Love Is Never Enough: How Couples Can Overcome Misunderstandings, Resolve Conflicts and Solve Relationship Problems through Cognitive Therapy.* New York: Harper & Row.

Bell, N. W., & Vogel, E. F. (Eds.) (1960). *A Modern Introduction to the Family.* Glencoe, IL: Free Press.

Beltz, S. E. (1969). Five-year effects of altered marital contracts: A behavioral analysis of couples. In G. Neubeck (Ed.), *Extramarital Relations.* Englewood Cliffs, NJ: Prentice-Hall, pp. 162–189.

Berglas, S. (1986). *The Success Syndrome.* New York: Plenum.

Bockus, F. (1980). *Couple Therapy.* New York: Jason Aronson.

Bohannan, P. (Ed.) (1971). *Divorce and After: An Analysis of the Emotional and Social Problems of Divorce.* Garden City, NY: Doubleday.

Bohannan, P. (1973). The six stations of divorce. In M. E. Lasswell & T. E. Lasswell (Eds.), *Love, Marriage and Family: A Developmental Approach.* Glenview, IL: Scott, Foresman, pp. 475–489.

Bornstein, P. H., & Bornstein, M. T. (1986). *Marital Therapy: A Behavioral Communications Approach.* London & New York: Pergamon.

Boszormenyi-Nagy, I., & Spark, G. N. (1973). *Invisible Loyalties.* Hagerstown, MD: Harper & Row.

Bowen, M. (1969). The use of family theory in clinical practice. In B. N. Ard, Jr. & C. C. Ard (Eds.), *Handbook of Marriage Counseling.* Palo Alto, CA: Science and Behavior Books, pp. 139–168. (Originally published in *Comprehensive Psychiatry,* 1966, *7,* 345–374)

Bowen, M. (1978). *Family Therapy in Clinical Practice.* New York: Jason Aronson.

Brody, J. E. (November 11, 1980). Success and failure in sex therapy: Case histories. *New York Times.*

Byng-Hall, J. (1985). Resolving distance conflicts. In A. S. Gurman (Ed.), *Casebook of Marital Therapy.* New York: Guilford, pp. 1–20.

Carter, E. A., & McGoldrick, M. (Eds.) (1980). *The Family Life Cycle: A Framework for Family Therapy.* New York: Gardner.

Cashdan, S. (1988). *Object Relations Therapy: Using the Relationship.* New York: Norton.

Casriel, D. Video of workshop presentation. Courtesy of Lori Heyman Gordon, PAIRS, Family Relations Institute, Falls Church, VA.

Catherall, D. R., & Pinsof, W. M. (1987). The impact of the therapist's personal family life on the ability to establish viable therapeutic alliances in family and marital therapy. *Journal of Psychotherapy & the Family,* 3 (2), 135–157.

Charny, I. W. (1966). Integrated individual and family psychotherapy. *Family Process,* 5, 179–198.

Charny, I. W. (1967). The psychotherapist as teacher of an ethic of nonviolence. *Voices: The Art and Science of Psychotherapy,* 3, 57–66.

Charny, I. W. (1969a). Marital love and hate. *Family Process,* 8, 1–24.

Charny, I. W. (1969b). *Individual and Family Developmental Review*. Los Angeles: Western Psychological Services. Manual, Folders of History forms. I. Counseling Objectives. II. Family Developmental History. III. Personal Developmental History. IV. Child Developmental History.

Charny, I. W. (1972a). Injustice and betrayal as natural experiences in family life. *Psychotherapy: Theory, Research & Practice, 9*, 86–91.

Charny, I. W. (1972b). *Marital Love and Hate*. New York: Macmillan. Original paper: Charny, I. W. (1969). Marital love and hate. *Family Process, 8*, 1–24.

Charny, I. W. (1972c). Parental intervention with one another on behalf of their child: A breaking-through tool for preventing emotional disturbance. *Journal of Contemporary Psychotherapy, 5*, 19–29.

Charny, I. W. (1973). And Abraham went to slay Isaac: A parable of killer, victim and bystander in the family of man. *Journal of Ecumenical Studies, 4*, (3), 304–318.

Charny, I. W. (1974). The new psychotherapies and encounters of the seventies: Progress or fads? *The Humanist*, (two-part series: May-June, July-August).

Charny, I. W. (1980a). Recovery of two (largely) autistic children through renunciation of maternal destructiveness in integrated individual and family therapy. In L. R. Wolberg & M. L. Aronson (Eds.), *Group and Family Therapy 1980*. New York: Brunner/Mazel, pp. 250–281.

Charny, I. W. (1980b). Why are so many (if not really all) people and families disturbed? *Journal of Marriage & Family Therapy, 6* (1), 37–47.

Charny, I. W. (1982). *How Can We Commit the Unthinkable?: Genocide, the Human Cancer*. In collaboration with Chanan Rapaport. Boulder, CO: Westview Press.

Charny, I. W. (1983a). Structuralism, paradoxical intervention and existentialism: The current philosophy and politics of family therapy. In L. R. Wolberg & M. L. Aronson (Eds.), *Group and Family Therapy 1982*. New York: Brunner/Mazel, pp. 200–215.

Charny, I. W. (1983b). The personal and family mental health of the family therapist. In F. Kaslow (Ed.), *The International Book of Family Therapy*. New York: Brunner/Mazel, pp. 41–55.

Charny, I. W. (1985a). Videotape: *A Profile of Marital Functioning and Interaction*. A training film. Produced at United States International University, San Diego, CA.

Charny, I. W. (1985b). Videotape: *Marital Evaluation: A Healthy Couple Who Keeps Problems Under Control . . . (But Whose?)*. A training film based on a live interview with a couple. Produced at United States International University, San Diego, CA.

Charny, I. W. (1985c). Videotape: *Marital Therapy: Who Is Listening?* A training film based on role playing of a full-length couple session. Produced at United States International University, San Diego, CA.

Charny, I. W. (1985d). Videotape: *Live Therapy-Consultation to a Couple and their Therapist in the "Master Therapist Series."* Produced and distributed by the American Association of Marriage and Family Therapy.

Charny, I. W. (1986a). Genocide and mass destruction: Doing harm to others as a missing dimension in psychopathology. *Psychiatry, 49* (2), 144–157.

Charny, I. W. (1986b). What do therapists worry about: A tool for experiential supervision. In F. Kaslow (Ed.), *Models, Supervision and Training: Dilemmas and Challenges*. New York: Haworth Press, pp. 17–28.

Charny, I. W. (1986c). An existential-dialectical model for analyzing marital interaction. *Family Process, 25* (4), 571–590.

Charny, I. W. (1987). "Marital trap analysis"—Incompetence, complementarity and success traps: Identifying potential future dysfunctions based on a couple's current collusive agreements. *Contemporary Family Therapy, 9* (3), 163–180.

Chessick, R. D. (1971). *Why Psychotherapists Fail.* New York: Science House.

Constantine, L., & Constantine, J. (1973). *Group Marriage: A Study of Contemporary Multilateral Marriage.* New York: Macmillan.

Craig, J. H., & Craig, M. (1973). *Synergic Power: Beyond Domination and Permissiveness.* Berkeley, CA: Proactive Press.

Cuber, J. (1948). *Marriage Counseling Practice.* New York: Appleton-Century-Crofts.

Davidson, S. (1980). The clinical effects of massive psychic trauma in families of Holocaust survivors. *Journal of Marital and Family Therapy, 6* (1), 11–21.

Davidson, S. (in press). *Holding On to Humanity—The Message of Holocaust Survivors: The Shamai Davidson Papers.* Edited by Israel W. Charny. New York: New York University Press.

Dell, P. F. (1980). The Hopi family therapist and the Aristotelian parents. *Journal of Marital & Family Therapy, 6,* 123–130.

Deutsch, F., & Murphy, W. M. (1955). *The Clinical Interview.* Volumes 1 & 2. New York: International Universities Press.

Dicks, H. V. (1967). *Marital Tensions: Clinical Studies Towards a Theory of Interaction.* New York: Basic Books.

Dinkmeyer, D., & Carlson, J. (1984). *Time for a Better Marriage.* Circle Pines, MN: American Guidance Service.

Dreikurs, R. (1964). *The Challenge of Marriage.* New York: Duell, Sloan & Pearce.

Eisenstein, V. W. (Ed.) (1956). *Neurotic Interactions in Marriage.* New York: Basic Books.

Ellis, A. (1962). *Reason and Emotion in Psychotherapy.* New York: Lyle Stuart.

Ellis, A. (1969). Healthy and disturbed reasons for having extramarital relations. In G. Neubeck (Ed.), *Extra-marital Relations.* Englewood Cliffs, NJ: Prentice-Hall, pp. 146–152.

Ellis, A. E. (1978). Techniques for handling anger in marriage. *Journal of Marriage & Family Counseling, 2* (4), 43–50.

Ellis, A. (1987). The impossibility of achieving consistently good mental health. *American Psychologist, 42,* 4, 364–375.

Ellis, A., & Harper, R. A. (1968). *A Guide to Successful Marriage.* Hollywood, CA: Wilshire.

Encyclopedia of World Problems and Human Potential (1986). 2nd edition. Munchen: K. G. Saur.

Epstein, N. B., Baldwin, L. M., & Bishop, D. S. (1983). The McMaster Family Assessment Device. *Journal of Marital & Family Therapy, 9,* 171–180.

Epstein, N., Schlesinger, S. E., & Dryden, W. (1988). *Cognitive-Behavioral Therapy with Families.* New York: Brunner/Mazel.

Erel, D. (1990). Marital Interaction of Children of Holocaust Survivors: The Intergenerational Transmission of Post-Traumatic Impacts on Marital Functioning. Master's Thesis, Bob Shapell School of Social Work, Tel Aviv University. (Hebrew)

Erikson, E. H. (1963). *Childhood and Society.* New York: Norton.

Erikson, E. H. (1964). *Insight and Responsibility.* New York: Norton.

Everett, C. A. (Ed.) (1987). *The Divorce Process: A Handbook for Clinicians.* New York: Haworth.

Everett, C., Halperin, S., Volgy, S., & Wissler, A. (1989). *Treating the Borderline Family: A Systemic Approach.* Saddlebrook, NJ: Psychological Corp.

Falicov, C. J. (Ed.) (1988). *Family Transitions: Continuity and Change over the Life Cycle.* New York: Guilford.

Feiffer, J. (1962). *Feiffer's Marriage Manual.* New York: Random House.

Fields, N. S. (1986). *The Well-seasoned Marriage.* New York: Gardner Press.

Fisher, L., Anderson, A., & Jones, J. E. (1981). Types of paradoxical intervention and indications/contra-indications for use in clinical practice. *Family Process, 20,* 25–35.

Framo, J. L. (1976). Family of origin as a therapeutic resource for adults in marital and family therapy: You can and should go home again. *Family Process, 15* (3), 193–210.

Framo, J. (1979). A personal viewpoint on training in marital and family therapy. *Professional Psychology, 10,* 868–875.

Framo, J. L. (1981). The integration of marital therapy with sessions with family of origin. In A. S. Gurman, & D. P. Kniskern (Eds.), *Handbook of Family Therapy.* New York: Brunner/Mazel, pp. 133–158.

Framo, J. L. (1982). *Explorations in Marital and Family Therapy: Selected Papers of James L. Framo.* New York: Springer.

Framo, J. L. (1992). *Family of Origin Therapy: An Intergenerational Approach.* New York: Brunner/Mazel.

Fromm, E. (1956). *The Art of Loving.* New York: Harper.

Gabbard, G. O., & Menninger, R. W. (1988). *Medical Marriages.* Washington, D.C.: American Psychiatric Press.

Gelles, R. J. (1972). *The Violent Home: A Study of Physical Aggression between Husbands and Wives.* Beverly Hills: Sage.

Giovacchini, P. L. (1965). Treatment of marital disharmonies: The classical approach. In B. L. Greene (Ed.), *The Psychotherapies of Marital Disharmony.* New York: Free Press, pp. 39–82.

Givon, D. (1974). Diagnosis and treatment through joint interview of married couples. *Saad, 18* (6), 19–26. (Hebrew)

Golan, N. (1981). *Passing through Transitions.* New York: Free Press.

Gordon, L. H. (1990). *Love Knots: How to Untangle Those Everyday Frustrations that Keep You from Being with the One You Love.* New York: Dell.

Gordon, L. H. (in press). *PAIRS—Practical Application of Intimate Relationship Skills.* New York: Simon & Schuster.

Gordon, T. (1970). *Parent Effectiveness Training: The "No Lose" Program for Raising Responsible Children.* New York: Peter Wyden.

Gottman, J. M. (1991). Predicting the longitudinal course of marriages. *Journal of Marital and Family Therapy, 17* (1), 3–7.

Green, Robert, Jay (1989). "Learning to learn" and the family system: New perspectives on underachievement and learning disorders. *Journal of Marital and Family Therapy, 15* (2), 187–203.

Greenberg, L., & Johnson, S. (1985). *Emotionally Focused Couples Therapy.* New York: Guilford.

Greene, B. L. (Ed.) (1965). *The Psychotherapies of Marital Disharmony.* New York: Free Press.

Greene, B. L. (1970). *A Clinical Approach to Marital Problems.* Springfield, IL: Charles C. Thomas.

Greene, B. L., Lee, R. R., & Lustig, N. (1973). Transient structured distance as a maneuver in marital therapy. *Family Coordinator, 22,* 15–22.

Greene, B., & Solomon, A. (1963). Marital disharmony: Concurrent psychoanalytic therapy of husband and wife by the same psychiatrist. *American Journal of Psychiatry, 17,* 443–450.

Gross, S. J., Turner, M. C., & Roseann, F. U. (1979). *Crisis in the Family: Three Approaches.* New York: Gardner.

Grotjahn, M. (1960). *Psychoanalysis and the Family Neurosis.* New York: Norton.

Guerin, P. J. Jr., Fay, L. F., Burden, S., & Kautto, J. G. (1982). *The Evaluation and Treatment of Marital Conflict. A Four-Stage Approach.* New York: Basic Books.

Guerin, P. J., & Hubbard, I. (1987). Impact of therapist's personal family system on clinical work. *Journal of Psychotherapy & The Family, 3* (2), 47–59.

Gurman, A. S. (Ed.) (1985). *Casebook of Marital Therapy.* New York: Guilford.

Gurman, A. S. (1986). *Clinical Handbook of Marital Therapy.* New York: Guilford.

Gurman, A. S., & Kniskern, D. P. (1978). Deterioration in marital and family therapy: Empirical, clinical and conceptual issues. *Family Process, 17,* 3–20.

Gurman, A. S., & Kniskern, D. P. (Eds.) (1981a). *Handbook of Family Therapy.* New York: Brunner/Mazel.

Gurman, A., & Kniskern, D. (1981b). Family therapy outcome research. In A. S. Gurman & D. P. Kniskern (Eds.), *Handbook of Family Therapy.* New York: Brunner/Mazel, pp. 742–775.

Gurman, A. S., & Rice, D. G. (Eds.) (1975). *Couples in Conflict: New Directions in Marital Therapy.* New York: Jason Aronson.

Haley, J. (1980). How to be a marriage therapist without knowing practically anything. *Journal of Marital & Family Therapy, 6* (4), 385–391.

Hamburg, S. R. (1988). The possible and the plausible: The current state of marital therapy. *Journal of Family Psychology, 1* (4), 459–468.

Harrison, J. (1978). Warning: The male sex role may be dangerous to your health. *Journal Social Issues,* (1), 65–86.

Heiman, J., LoPiccolo, L., & LoPiccolo, J. (1976). *Becoming Orgasmic: A Sexual Growth Program for Women.* Englewood Cliffs, NJ: Prentice Hall.

Herrigel, E. (1953). *Zen in the Art of Archery.* New York: Pantheon.

Hoffmann, J. (1975). *The Sound of One Hand: 281 Zen Koans with Answers.* New York: Basic Books.

Huber, C. H., & Baruth, L. G. (1987). *Ethical, Legal and Professional Issues in the Practice of Marriage and Family Therapy.* Columbus, OH: Merrill.

Humphrey, F. G. (1983a). *Marital Therapy.* Englewood Cliffs, NJ: Prentice-Hall.

Humphrey, F. G. (1983b). Extramarital relationships. In F. G. Humphrey (Ed.), *Marital Therapy.* Englewood Cliffs, NJ: Prentice-Hall, pp. 47–66.

Humphrey, F. G. (1987). Treating extramarital sexual relationships in sex and couples therapy. In G. R. Weeks, & L. Hof (Eds.), *Integrating Sex and Marital Therapy: A Clinical Guide.* New York: Brunner/Mazel, pp. 149–170.

Hunt, M. (1969). *The Affair: A Portrait of Extramarital Love in Contemporary America.* New York: World Publishing.

Imber-Black, E. (1988). *Families in Larger Systems: A Therapist's Guide through the Labyrinth*. New York: Guilford.

Isaacs, M. B., Montalvo, B., & Abelsohn, D. (1986). *The Difficult Divorce: Therapy for Children and Families*. New York: Basic Books.

Israelstram, K. (1988). Contrasting four major family therapy paradigms: Implications for family therapy training. *Journal of Family Therapy, 10*, 179–196.

Jackson, D. D. (1969). The question of family homeostasis. In D. D. Jackson (Ed.), *Communication, Family, and Marriage: Human Communications*. Volume 1. Palo Alto: Science & Behavior Books, pp. 1–11. (Original publication 1957)

Jackson, D. D. (1972). Family rules: Marital quid pro quo. In G. D. Erikson & T. P. Hogan (Eds.), *Family Therapy: An Introduction to Theory and Technique*. Monterey, CA: Brooks/Cole. (Originally published in *Archives General Psychiatry, 1965, 12*, 589–594.)

Jacobson, N. S., & Gurman, A. S. (Eds.) (1986). *Clinical Handbook of Marital Therapy*. New York: Guilford.

Jacobson, N. S., Waldron, H., & Moore, D. (1980). Toward a behavioral profile of marital distress. *Journal of Consulting and Clinical Psychology, 48*, 696–703.

Johnston, J. R., & Campbell, L. E. G. (1988). *Impasses of Divorce: The Dynamics and Resolution of Family Contact*. New York: Free Press/Macmillan.

Jourard, S. M. (1963). *The Transparent Self*. Princeton, NJ: Van Nostrand.

Jourard, S. M. (1975). Marriage is for life. *Journal of Marriage and Family Counseling, 5* (1), 199–208.

Kantrowitz, B., et al. (1987). "How to stay married." *Newsweek*, August 24, 52–58.

Kaplan, H. S. (1974). *The New Sex Therapy: Active Treatment of Sexual Dysfunctions*. New York: Brunner/Mazel.

Kaplan, H. S. (1979). *Disorders of Sexual Desire*. New York: Brunner/Mazel.

Kaslow, F. W. (1979/80). States of divorce: A psychological perspective. *Villanova Law Review, 25*, pp. 718–751.

Kaslow, F. W. (1981a). A dialectic approach to family therapy and practice: Selectivity and synthesis. *Journal of Marital & Family Therapy, 7* (3), 345–351.

Kaslow, F. W. (1981b). Divorce and divorce therapy. In A. S. Gurman & D. P. Kniskern (Eds.), *Handbook of Family Therapy*. New York: Brunner/Mazel, pp. 662–696.

Kaslow, F. W. (Ed.) (1982). *The International Book of Family Therapy*. New York: Brunner/Mazel.

Kaslow, F. W. (1984). Treatment of marital and family therapists. In F. W. Kaslow (Ed.), *Psychotherapy with Psychotherapists*. New York: Haworth, pp. 79–100.

Kaslow, F. W. (1988). *The Family Life of Psychotherapists: Clinical Implications*. New York: Haworth.

Kaslow, F. W., & Schwartz, L. L. (1987). *The Dynamics of Divorce: A Life Cycle Perspective*. New York: Brunner/Mazel.

Kempler, W. (1981). *Experiential Psychotherapy within Families*. New York: Brunner/Mazel.

Kerr, M. E. (1981). Family systems theory and therapy. In A. S. Gurman, & D. P. Kniskern (Eds.), *Handbook of Family Therapy*. New York: Brunner/Mazel, pp. 226–264.

Kerr, M. E., & Bowen, M. (1988). *Family Evaluation: An Approach Based on Bowen Theory*. New York: Norton.

Kessler, S. (1975). *The American Way of Divorce: Prescription for Change*. Chicago: Nelson Hall.

Kinsey, A. C., et al. (1948). *Sexual Behavior in the Human Male*. Philadelphia: W. B. Saunders.

Kinsey, A. C., et al. (1953). *Sexual Behavior in the Human Female*. Philadelphia: W. B. Saunders.

Kirschner, D. A., & Kirschner, S. (1986). *Comprehensive Family Therapy: An Integration of Systemic and Psychodynamic Treatment Models*. New York: Brunner/Mazel.

Kirschner, P. (1988). *Changes in Marital Functioning and Interaction Following Treatment of Couples in Mid-Life Crisis*. Master's Thesis, Bob Shapell School of Social Work, Tel Aviv University. (Hebrew)

Klagsbrun, F. (1985). *Married People: Staying Married in the Age of Divorce*. New York: Bantam Books.

Klimek, D. (1979). *Beneath Mate Selection and Marriage: The Unconscious Motives in Human Pairing*. New York: Van Nostrand Reinhold.

Knox, D. (1971). *Marriage Happiness: A Behavioral Approach to Counseling*. Champaign, IL: Research Press.

Koestenbaum, P. (1974). *Existential Sexuality: Choosing to Love*. Englewood Cliffs, NJ: Prentice Hall.

Kressel, K., & Dutsch, M. (1977). Divorce therapy: An in-depth survey of therapeutic views. *Family Process, 16* (4), 413–443.

Kuhn, T. S. (1962). *The Structure of Scientific Revolution*. Chicago: University of Chicago Press.

L'Abate, L. (1976). *Understanding and Helping the Individual in the Family*. New York: Grune & Stratton.

L'Abate, L. (1986). *Systematic Family Therapy*. New York: Brunner/Mazel.

L'Abate, L., Ganahl, G., & Hansen, J. C. (1986). *Methods of Family Therapy*. Englewood Cliffs, NJ: Prentice-Hall.

L'Abate, L., & McHenry, S. (1983). *Methods of Marital Intervention*. New York: Grune & Stratton.

Laing, R. D. (1970). *Knots*. New York: Random House.

Laing, R. D. (1971). *The Politics of the Family*. New York: Pantheon.

Lang, M. (1982). Bad therapy—a way of learning. In F. Kaslow (Ed.), *The International Book of Family Therapy*. New York: Brunner/Mazel, pp. 447–462.

Lansky, M. R. (1981). Treatment of the narcissistically vulnerable marriage. In M. R. Lansky (Ed.), *Family Therapy and Major Psychopathology*. New York: Grune & Stratton, pp. 163–182.

Lasswell, M., & Lobsenz, N. (1972). *No-fault Marriage: The New Techniques of Self-Counseling and what It can Help You Do*. Garden City, NY: Doubleday.

Lauer, J. C., & Lauer, R. H. (1986). *Til Death Do Us Part: How Couples Stay Together*. New York: Haworth.

Layton, M. (1989). Letter to the editor [in re article that follows]. *Family Therapy Networker, 13* (3–4), 11.

Layton, M., & Kirschner, D. A. (1988). When three makes two. *Family Therapy Networker, 12* (6), 42–47.

Lederer, W. J., & Jackson, D. D. (1968). *The Mirages of Marriage*. New York: W. W. Norton.

Levant, R. F. (Ed.) (1986). *Psychoeducational Approaches to Family Therapy and Counseling*. New York: Springer.

Levay, A. N., & Kagle, A. (1977a). A study of treatment needs following sex therapy. *American Journal of Psychiatry, 134* (9), 970–973.

Levay, A. N., & Kagle, A. (1977b). Ego deficiencies in the areas of pleasure, intimacy and cooperation: Guidelines in the diagnosis and treatment of sexual dysfunctions. *Journal of Sex & Marital Therapy, 3*, 10–18.

Levay, A. N., & Kagle, A. (1983). Interminable sex therapy: A report on ten cases of therapeutic gridlock. *Journal of Marital & Family Therapy, 9* (1), 1–9, 15–17.

Levinson, D. J. (1978). *The Seasons of a Man's Life*. New York: Knopf.

Libby, R. W., & Whitehurst, R. N. (Eds.) (1977). *Marriage and Alternatives Exploring Intimate Relationships*. Glenview, IL: Scott, Foresman.

Lindemann, E. (1944). Symptomatology and management of acute grief. *American Journal of Psychiatry, 101* (9), 141–148.

London, P. (1969). *The Modes and Morals of Psychotherapy*. New York: Holt, Rinehart & Winston.

LoPiccolo, L. (1980). Low sexual desire. In S. R. Leiblum & L. A. Pervin (Eds.), *Principles and Practice of Sex Therapy*. New York: Guilford, pp. 29–64.

Mace, D., & Mace, V. (1974). *We Can Have Better Marriages*. Nashville, TN: Abingdon Press.

Mace, D. (1979). Marriage and family enrichment—a new field. *Family Coordinator, 28*, 409–419.

Machlin, R. (1988). Changes in Marital Functioning and Interaction of Couples Following Stroke in Younger Patients Who Have Been Active in the Work Force and as Parents of Dependent Children. Master's Thesis, Bob Shapell School of Social Work, Tel Aviv University. (Hebrew)

Margolin, G. (1982). Ethical and legal considerations in marital and family therapy. *American Psychologist, 37* (7), 788–801.

Martin, P. A. (1976). *A Marital Therapy Manual*. New York: Brunner/Mazel.

Maslow, A. (1981). *The Journals of A. Maslow*. Edited by Richard J. Lowry. Vol. 2. Monterey, CA: Brooks/Cole.

Masters, W. H., & Johnson, V. C. (1970). *Human Sexual Inadequacy*. Boston: Little Brown.

May, R. (1977). *The Meaning of Anxiety*. New York: Norton. (Published in 1950 by Ronald Press)

McDougall, J. (1984). *Theaters of the Body: A Psychoanalytic Approach to Psychosomatic Illness*. New York: Norton.

McGoldrick, M., Pearce, J. R., & Giordano, J. (Eds.) (1982). *Ethnicity and Family Therapy*. New York: Guilford.

Menninger, K. (1958). *Theory of Psychoanalytic Technique*. New York: Basic Books.

Messer, S. B. (1986). Behavioral and psychoanalytic perspectives at therapeutic choice points. *American Psychologist, 41* (11), 1261–1272.

Messer, S. B., & Vinokur, M. (1980). Some limits to the integration of psychoanalytic and behavior therapy. *American Psychologist, 35* (9), 818–827.

Middlefort, C. F. (1982). Use of family in the treatment of schizophrenic and psychopathic patients. *Journal of Marital & Family Therapy, 8* (2), 1–11. (Originally presented May 1952)

Miller, A. (1981). *Prisoners of Childhood: The Drama of the Gifted Child and the Search for the True Self.* New York: Basic Books.

Miller, A. (Ed.) (1989). *Depressive Disorders and Immunity.* Washington, D.C.: American Psychiatric Press.

Miller, S. (Ed.) (1975). *Marriage & Families: Enrichment through Communication.* Beverly Hills, CA: Sage.

Mills, S., & Weisser, M. (1987). *The Odd Couple Syndrome: Resolving the Neat/Sloppy Dilemma.* Great Neck, NY: Jameison Publishing.

Minuchin, S. (1974). *Families and Family Therapy.* Cambridge, MA: Harvard University Press.

Minuchin, S., Rosman, B. L., & Baker, L. (1978). *Psychosomatic Families: Anorexia Nervosa in Context.* Cambridge, MA: Harvard University Press.

Minuchin, S., & Fishman, H. C. (1981). *Family Therapy Techniques.* Cambridge, MA: Harvard University Press.

Mitscherlich, A., & Mitscherlich, M. (1975). *The Inability to Mourn: Principles of Collective Behavior.* New York: Grove.

Mittleman, B. (1948). Concurrent analysis of married couples. *Psychoanalytic Quarterly, 17,* 182–197.

Napier, A. Y. (1988). *The Fragile Bond: In Search of an Equal, Intimate, and Enduring Marriage.* New York: Harper & Row.

Napier, A. Y., & Whitaker, C. A. (1978). *The Family Crucible.* New York: Harper & Row.

Neill, J. R., & Kniskern, D. P. (1982). *From Psyche to System: The Evolving Therapy of Carl Whitaker.* New York: Guilford.

Neubeck, G. (Ed.) (1969). *Extra-marital Relations.* Englewood Cliffs, NJ: Prentice-Hall.

Neumann, E. (1969). *Depth Psychology and a New Ethic.* New York: G. P. Putnam. (Originally published in German in 1949)

Newsweek (1980). "The joy of not having sex." September, 15, 57.

Newsweek (1987). "Not tonight, dear: Lack of sexual desire is painful, complicated and surprisingly common." October 26, 46–48.

Nichols, M. P. (1984). Experiential family therapy. In M. Nichols (Ed.), *Family Therapy: Concepts and Methods.* New York: Gardner, pp. 261–294.

Nichols, M. P. (Ed.) (1984). *Family Therapy: Concepts and Methods.* New York: Gardner.

Nichols, W. C. (1987). *Systemic Family Therapy: An Integrative Approach.* New York: Guilford.

Nichols, W. C. (1988). *Marital Therapy: An Integrative Approach.* New York: Guilford.

Nugent, M. D., & Constantine, L. L. (1988). Marital paradigms: Compatibility, treatment, and outcome in marital therapy. *Journal of Marital & Family Therapy, 14* (4), 351–369.

Olson, D. H., Sprenkle, D. H., & Russell, C. S. (1979). Circumplex model of marital and family systems: I. Cohesion and adaptability dimensions, family types, and clinical applications. *Family Process, 18* (1), 3–28.

O'Neill, N., & O'Neill, G. C. (1972). *Open Marriage: A New Life Style for Couples.* New York: Evans.

Otto, H. A. (Ed.) (1970). *The Family In Search of A Future: Alternate Models for Moderns.* New York: Appleton-Century-Crofts.

Palazzoli, M. S. (1987). Towards a general model of psychotic family games. *Journal of Marital & Family Therapy, 12* (4), 339–349.

Paolino, T. J., & McGrady, B. S. (Eds.) (1978). *Marriage and Marital Therapy.* New York: Brunner/Mazel.

Parloff, M., Waskow, I., & Wolfe, B. (1978). Research on therapist variables in relation to process and outcome. In S. Garfield & A. Bergin (Eds.), *Handbook of Psychotherapy and Behavior Change* (2nd ed.). New York: Wiley, pp. 233–282.

Piercey, F. P., Sprenkle, D. H., & Associates (Eds.) (1986). *Family Therapy Sourcebook.* New York: Guilford.

Piercey, F. P., & Wetchler, J. (in press). Family-work interfaces of psychotherapists: I. A summary of the literature. II. A didactic-experiential workshop. *Journal of Psychotherapy and the Family.*

Pittman, F. S. (1987). *Turning Points: Treating Families in Transition and Crisis.* New York: W. W. Norton.

Pittman, F. (1989). *Private Lies, Infidelity and the Betrayal of Intimacy.* New York: W. W. Norton.

Rhodes, Sonya (1984). Extramarital affairs: Clinical issues in therapy. *Social Casework, 65* (9), 541–546.

Reich, W. (1949). *Character Analysis.* New York: Orgone Institute Press.

Rowan, J. (1980). Heresy-hunting in the Association for Humanistic Psychology. *Newsletter of the Association for Humanistic Psychology,* April, 4–7.

Sager, C. J. (1976). *Marriage Contracts and Couple Therapy: Hidden Forces in Intimate Relationships.* New York: Brunner/Mazel.

Sager, C. J., & Hunt, B. (1979). *Intimate Partners: Hidden Patterns in Love Relationships.* New York: McGraw-Hill.

Salin, L. (1985). We're OK. They're OK. It's time for individual and family therapists to bury the hatchet. *Family Networker, 9* (4), 31.

Sanders, C. (1984). The theory behind the traps—considerations for the practice of family therapy in a multi-frame work team. *Australian Journal of Family Therapy, 5* (1), 53–60.

Satir, V. (1965). Conjoint marital therapy. In B. L. Greene (Ed.), *The Psychotherapy of Marital Disharmony.* New York: Free Press, pp. 121–134.

Satir, V. (1967). *Conjoint Family Therapy.* Palo Alto, CA: Science & Behavior Books.

Satir, V. (1977). *Peoplemaking.* Palo Alto, CA: Science & Behavior Books.

Saul, L. J. (1967). *Fidelity and Infidelity: And What Makes or Breaks a Marriage.* Philadelphia: J. B. Lippincott.

Scarff, M. (1987). *Intimate Partners: Patterns in Love and Marriage.* London: Century.

Schiff, N. P., & Belson, R. (1988). The Gandhi technique: A new procedure for intractable problems. *Journal of Marital & Family Therapy, 14* (3), 261–266.

Schwartz, R., & Pessotta, P. (1985). Let us sell no intervention before its time. *Family Networker, 9* (4), 18.

Segraves, R. T. (1982). *Marital Therapy—A Combined Psychodynamic Behavioral Approach.* New York: Plenum.

Selvini Palazzoli, M. (1974). *Self-starvation: From the Intrapsychic to the Transpersonal Approach to Anorexia Nervosa.* London: Chaucer.

Sheehy, G. (1976). *Passages: Predictable Crises of Adult Life.* New York: E. P. Dutton.

Simon, R. (1988). "From the editor." Introduction to special feature on couples therapy. *Family Therapy Networker, 12* (6), 2.

Slattery, G. (1987). Transcultural therapy with aboriginal families: Working with the belief system. *Australian/New Zealand Journal of Family Therapy, 8* (2), 61–70.

Slipp, S. (1988). *The Technique and Practice of Object Relations Family Therapy.* Northvale, NJ: Jason Aronson.

Sprenkle, D. H. (Ed.) (1985). *Divorce Therapy.* New York: Haworth.

Sprenkle, D., & Olson, D. (1978). Circumplex model of marital systems. IV. Empirical study of clinic and non-clinic couples. *Journal of Marriage & Family Counseling, 4* (2), 59–74.

Steinzor, B. (1969). *When Parents Divorce.* New York: Pantheon.

Sternberg, R. J. (1988). *The Triangle of Love: Intimacy, Passion and Commitment.* New York: Basic Books.

Stierlin, H. (1969). *Conflict and Reconciliation.* Garden City, NY: Doubleday, Anchor.

Stream, H. S. (1985). *Resolving Marital Conflicts: A Psychodynamic Perspective.* New York: Wiley.

Strupp, H. (1974). Some observations on the fallacy of a value-free psychotherapy and the empty organism. *Journal Abnormal Psychology, 83,* 199–201.

Stuart, R. B. (1980). *Helping Couples Change: A Social Learning Approach to Marital Therapy.* New York: Guilford.

Stuart, R. B., & Jacobson, B. (1985). *Second Marriages.* New York: Norton.

Tauber, E. S., & Green, M. R. (1959). Counter-transference as subthreshhold communications. In E. S. Tauber & M. R. Green (Eds.), *Prelogical experience: An Inquiry into Dreams and Other Creative Processes.* New York: Basic Books, pp. 127–148.

Tennov, D. (1979). *Love and Limerence.* New York: Stein & Day.

Time (1984). Magazine cover: "Sex in the '80's: The revolution is over." Story: "The revolution is over: In the 80's caution and commitment are the watchwords." April 9, 48–54.

Toffler, A. (1971). *Future Shock.* New York: Bantam.

Toumin, M. K. (1975). Structured separation for couples in conflict. In A. S. Gurman & D. G. Rice (Eds.), *Couples in Conflict: New Directions in Marital Therapy.* New York: Jason Aronson, pp. 353–362.

Trotter, R. J. (1986). The three faces of love: Commitment, intimacy and passion are the active ingredients in Sternberg's three-sided theory of love. *Psychology Today, 20,* September, 46–50, 54.

Visher, E. B., & Visher, J. S. (1979). *Stepfamilies: A Guide to Working with Step-parents and Step-children.* New York: Brunner/Mazel.

Voyse, M. (1975). *A Constant Burden: The Reconstitution of Family Life.* London & Boston: Routledge & Kegan Paul.

Wachtel, E. F., & Wachtel, P. L. (1986). *Family Dynamics in Individual Psychotherapy: A Guide to Clinical Strategies.* New York: Guilford.

Watzlawick, P., Weakland, J. H., & Fisch, R. (1974). *Change: Principles of Problem Formation and Problem Resolution.* New York: Norton.

Wallerstein, J. S. (1983). Children of divorce: The psychological tasks of the child. *American Journal of Orthopsychiatry, 53,* 2, 230–243.

Wallerstein, J. S., & Blakeslee, S. (1989). *Second Chances: Men, Women, and Children a Decade after Divorce.* New York: Ticknor & Fields.

Wallerstein, J. S., & Kelly, J. B. (1980). *Surviving the Breakup: How Children and Parents Cope with Divorce.* New York: Basic Books.

Wallerstein, R. S. (1986). *Forty-two Lives in Treatment: A Study of Psychoanalysis and Psychotherapy: The Report of the Psychotherapy Research Project of the Menninger Foundation*. New York: Guilford.

Weeks, G. R. (Ed.) (1985). *Promoting Change through Paradoxical Therapy.* Homewood, IL: Dow Jones-Irwin.

Weeks, G. R. (1986). Individual-system dialectic. *American Journal of Family Therapy, 14* (1), 5–12.

Weeks, G. R. (1989). *Treating Couples: The Intersystem Model of the Marriage Council of Philadelphia*. New York: Brunner/Mazel.

Weeks, G., & L'Abate, L. (1982). *Paradoxical Psychotherapy: Theory and Practice with Individuals, Couples and Families*. New York: Brunner/Mazel.

Weingarten, H., & Leas, S. (1987). Levels of marital conflict model: A guide to assessment and intervention in troubled marriages. *American Journal of Orthopsychiatry, 57* (3), 407–417.

Weisman, R. S. (1975). Crisis theory and the process of divorce. *Social Casework, 56*, 205–212.

Weiss, R. (1976). *Marital Separation*. New York: Basic Books.

Wertheimer, D. (1980). Trial separation as a planned therapeutic intervention in marital therapy. In L. R. Wolberg & M. L. Aronson (Eds.), *Group and Family Therapy, 1980,* New York: Brunner/Mazel, 384–393.

Westfall, A. (1989). Extramarital sex: The treatment of the couple. In G. R. Weeks (Ed.), *Treating Couples: The Intersystem Model of the Marriage Council of Philadelphia*. New York: Brunner/Mazel.

Westley, W. A., & Epstein, N. B. (1970). *The Silent Majority.* San Francisco: Jossey-Bass.

Wetchler, J. L., & Piercy, F. P. (1986). The marital/family life of the family therapist: Stressors and enhancers. *American Journal of Family Therapy, 14* (2), 99–108.

Whitaker, C. A., & Bumberry, W. M. (1988). *Dancing with the Family: A Symbolic-Experiential Approach*. New York: Brunner/Mazel.

Whitaker, C. A., & Keith, D. V. (1981). Symbolic-experiential therapy. In A. S. Gurman & D. P. Kniskern (Eds.), *Handbook of Family Therapy.* New York: Brunner/Mazel, pp. 187–225.

Whitehouse, J. (1981). The role of the initial attracting quality in marriage: Virtues and vices. *Journal of Marital and Family Therapy, 7* (1), 61–68.

Wile, D. B. (1979). An insight approach to marital therapy. *Journal of Marital & Family Therapy, 5* (4), 43–52.

Wile, D. B. (1981). *Couples Therapy: A Nontraditional Approach*. New York: Wiley.

Wile, D. B. (1988). *After the Honeymoon: How Conflict Can Improve Your Relationship*. New York: Wiley.

Willi, J. (1982). *Couples in Collusion*. New York: Jason Aronson.

Willi, J. (1984). *Dynamics of Couples Therapy: The Uses of the Concept of Collusion and Its Application to the Therapeutic Triangle*. New York: Jason Aronson (Originally published in London in 1978.)

Winnicott, D. W. (1965). Hate in the countertransference. *Voices: The Art and Science of Psychotherapy, 1* (2), 102–109. (Originally presented in 1947 and published in *International Journal of Psychoanalysis* in 1949.)

Wolman, B. B. (Ed.) (1972). *Success and Failure in Psychoanalysis and Psychotherapy.* New York: Macmillan.

Wylie, M. S. (1988). Marriage triumphant: Outlasting the demons of marital discord. *Family Therapy Networker, 12* (2), 71.

Wylie, M. S. (1989). Looking for the fenceposts. *Family Therapy Networker, 13* (2), 22.

Wynne, L. C., Ryckoff, I. M., Day, J., & Hirsch, S. I. (1958). Pseudomutality in the family relations of schizophrenics. *Psychiatry, 21*, 205–220. Reprinted in N. Bell and E. F. Vogel (Eds.), (1987), *A Modern Introduction to the Family.* New York: Free Press, pp. 628–649.

Yalom, I. D. (1980). *Existential Psychotherapy.* New York: Basic Books.

Yalom, I. D. (1989). *Love's Executioner And Other Tales of Psychotherapy.* New York: Basic Books.

Zaman, R. M. (1988). Psychotherapy in the Third World: Some Impressions from Pakistan. *International Psychologist, 29*, 3, 20–22.

Name Index

Subject Index

═══